D1163931

BIRTH CONTROL IN NINETEENTH-CENTURY ENGLAND

BIRTH CONTROL IN NINETEENTH-CENTURY ENGLAND

ANGUS McLAREN

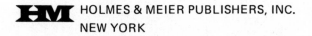 HOLMES & MEIER PUBLISHERS, INC.
NEW YORK

First published in the United States of America 1978 by
Holmes & Meier Publishers, Inc.
101 Fifth Avenue
New York, NY 10003

Library of Congress Cataloging in Publication Data

McLaren, Angus.
    Birth control in nineteenth-century England.

    1. Birth control – Great Britain – History.
2. Great Britain – Social conditions – 19th
century. I. Title.
HQ766.5.G7M3   301   77-16654
ISBN 0-8419-0349-2

Printed in Great Britain

CONTENTS

Preface 9

Introduction 11

Part One: Background to the Birth Control Debate
1. Quackery and Control of Fertility in Eighteenth-Century England 19

Part Two: Contraception and the Class Struggle
2. The Beginning of the Birth Control Debate 43
3. Contraception and Working-Class Movements 61
4. Birth Control and Medical Self-help 78
5. Birth Control and the Morality of Married Life 90

Part Three: Neo-Malthusianism and its Late Nineteenth-Century Critics
6. The Malthusian League 107
7. Birth Control and the British Medical Profession, 1850-1914 116
8. Birth Control and Eugenics 141
9. Socialists and Birth Control: the Case of the Social Democratic Federation 157
10. Socialists and Birth Control: Freedom or Efficiency 174
11. Feminism and Fertility Control 197

Part Four: Theory and Practice
12. Birth Control and the Working Classes 215
13. Abortion in England, 1890-1914 231

Conclusion 254
Index 257

TO ARLENE

PREFACE

I would like to thank the following for their comments and suggestions: Arlene Tigar McLaren, Sally Alexander, Diana Leonard Barker, Rodney Barker, Anna Davin, Brian Dippie, Michael Fellman, Diana Gittins, Deborah Gorham, Marlene Legates, Jean L'Esperance, James Mohr, James Reed, Charles Rosenberg, Sheila Rowbotham, Madeleine Simms, David Stafford, Barb Taylor, Martha Vicinus, Daniel Walkowitz, Judith Walkowitz, Adrian Wilson, the members of the Society for the Social History of Medicine, and the members of the London Women's Research and Resources Centre.

I was able to spend two summers in England working on this book because of Faculty Research Grants from the University of Victoria for which I am greatly appreciative.

Sections of this book have appeared in *Victorian Studies, Comparative Studies in Society and History,* and John Woodward and David Richards, eds., *Health Care and Popular Medicine in Nineteenth Century England* (London, 1977), and I wish to thank the editors and publishers for permission to reprint material which first appeared in those volumes.

INTRODUCTION

In 1906 the *Nineteenth Century* published an angry article by
John W. Taylor, president of the British Gynaecological Society.
Taylor had rushed into print to declare that he and other doctors
viewed the simultaneous declines of the birth and death rates as a
source of 'supreme dissatisfaction and disgust.' Why should figures
which suggested an improvement in public health have occasioned
such hostility? Because, as Taylor petulantly explained, selfish couples,
in employing contraceptives, countered the efforts of patriotic
physicians building up the population by the saving of lives: '. . .all
this work is swept away as though it had never been, by the vicious
and unnatural habits of the present generation. . .'[1] Taylor's outburst
represented one response, and by no means the most bizarre, to the
subject of this study — the emergence in the nineteenth century of
the idea and practice of birth control.

The decline of the birth rate was arguably the most important social
change to occur in Victorian England, but historians have shown
remarkably little interest in the phenomenon. Sociologists and
demographers have led the way. They have informed us that marriages
of the late 1860s, when they lasted twenty years or more, produced
an average of 6.16 births; the marriages of the 1870s, 5.8; those of
the 1880s, 5.3; those of the 1890s, 4.13 and those of 1915, 2.43.
Professor Matras, using statistical analyses to demonstrate the spread
of control of fertility, estimated that of those women born between
1831 and 1845, 19.5 per cent controlled or attempted to control their
fertility, 42.7 per cent of those born between 1861 and 1870, and over
72 per cent of those born between 1902 and 1906.[2] How was fertility
controlled? There was a decline in the marriage rate in the last decades
of the nineteenth century which must have had some effect but there
was little change either in the sex ratio or in the proportion of women
of child-bearing age. The crucial factor appears to have been 'volitional
limitation'. Lewis-Faning, in his account to the Royal Commission on
Population, reported that in his sample 15 per cent of the women
married before 1910 used birth control, 40 per cent of those married
between 1910 and 1919, and 58 per cent of those married between
1920 and 1924.[3]

These quantitative studies are illuminating but they do have their limitations. The reliability of the data diminishes as one moves back in time and with the twentieth century material in the area of sexual practices there is always the problem of 'reportage'. More important, even if we accept that the demographic studies do tell us when people restricted fertility, they rarely tell us why and how. Demographers and sociologists can record and calculate the rise and fall of fertility but such studies often leave unanswered the most interesting questions. They tell us little about abortions and miscarriages which were not recorded, of the recourse to contraceptives that did not work, of the attempts not to control family size *per se* but simply to space births; they say nothing about the relationship of the sexes, attitudes towards sexuality, and the woman's right to control her own body; they show little interest in whether a couple had recourse to traditional means of contraception or relied on quack potions, sought medical aid or patronised the surgical shop; most important of all they do not broach the vital question of the social, moral, and political forces which made birth control ' thinkable' or 'unthinkable'.

The existing histories of birth control have not broached these questions. Basing themselves on what appears to be an obvious reading of the demographic data – namely, that family size was restricted first by the upper classes, next by the middle classes, and finally by the working classes – they have focused on fleshing out a unilinear model of the progressive adoption of contraception. This 'modernisation' thesis has as one of its conclusions that, when working-class fertility fell, it was due to an aping of middle-class behaviour. In short the assumption is made that the fall of family size has been the most dramatic example of the 'embourgeoisement' of the working classes.[4] This book argues against this interpretation. It is my contention that the great interest of the nineteenth century birth control debate is that it reveals that there was not a growing consensus of opinion on the question of family planning but that there were two important cultural confrontations. These were the struggle of middle-class propagandists, both of the right and the left, seeking to manipulate working-class attitudes towards procreation for political purposes, and on a deeper level the clash of the differing attitudes of men and women towards the possibility of fertility control. The very fact that these two issues are central to the whole subject undercuts the usefulness of providing yet another history of 'advances' in birth control. Therefore our main concern will not be the contribution of medical science to contraception or the activities of the Malthusian League or the family patterns of the upper classes. The purpose of this study is to place the idea and practice of birth control in its social and political context and so contribute to a better understanding of nineteenth century society.

At the heart of the nineteenth century discussion of birth control lay the problem of the reproductive behaviour of the working classes in general and women in particular. What I will attempt to do is provide a social history of this issue both from above and below. I begin by establishing the availability of means of fertility control in the eighteenth century and then I mesh this with the intellectual and social responses of middle-class writers to the perceived population problem of the nineteenth century. I conclude by linking the contraceptive attitudes and practices of late nineteenth-century workers and women, setting both in the context of shifts in the economy.

Four themes run through this book; the first is that there was never to be any pure ideology in favour of or in opposition to birth control. The issue was too intimately related to questions of power, property, and moral symbolism to be dealt with simply. Contraception had a dual potential: it could have been an instrument for greater freedom or it could have permitted greater social control. Malthusians, neo-Malthusians, eugenists and socialists all interpreted it to suit their own concerns. The Malthusians launched the debate by attributing all social problems to simple population pressures. They opposed birth control for the reason that it seemed to violate the very self-control and discipline which they were seeking to force upon a nascent industrial work force. Although neither they nor their ideological opponents could claim with any certainty to have either advanced or retarded the adoption of family planning, the way in which they each responded to the issue brings to light many of these movements' basic characteristics which have been overlooked.

The second theme of this book is that, because means of contraception were available by 1800, the spread of family limitation has to be seen as not so much the result of the diffusion of an innovative technique as an adjustment of the working class family to new economic and social conditions. In the century and a half to be examined England moved from the stages of early to full industrialisation. Economic forces in the first period created a demand for child labour that induced workers to adopt a high fertility strategy; the late nineteenth century mature economy rejected the unskilled and uneducated and led to the imposition of fertility control. What has to be kept in mind, however, is that even in the last decades of the eighteenth century and the first of the nineteenth when boom conditions pushed early marriage and large families, the English birth rate never reached its biologically-possible maximum and was never to be as high as that of the developing countries of the twentieth century. Some forms of fertility control were being employed right through the entire period. Moreover when the working class began to bring down its birth rate in dramatic fashion it was by relying on traditional, 'pre-industrial' means of fertility control.

The notion that women's attitudes towards fertility control would differ from those of men is my third theme. The role women would play in the restriction of family size has been strangely played down. It has been assumed that the male would make the decision on the employment of contraceptives and the female passively acquiesce. It is forgotten that it was the woman whose health was endangered, standard of living most jeopardised, and margin of liberty restricted by unwanted pregnancies. What I will seek to show, by an analysis of feminist views of birth control and an examination of the practice of abortion, is that men and women belonged to different sexual cultures and necessarily responded in differing ways to the possibility of fertility control.

The fourth theme which will crop up repeatedly in this study is that birth control was a form of medical 'self-help' which doctors would, for professional reasons, oppose. An analysis of the issue reveals that in this area of medical science the advances were made by 'patients' in face of the opposition of medical practitioners. Doctors were to be as concerned by the threat posed to their power and status by quacks and midwives as they were by the presumed dangers of contraception to health and morality.

The attraction of the history of birth control is that it offers insights into the most private practices of previous generations. By the same token its great challenge is that as a tabooed subject it cannot be completely explored in the traditional sources. For example, when beginning this book I assumed that, because the limitation of family size posed moral problems, a perusal of religious records would prove useful. I discovered that the churches were remarkably cautious and apart from making the usual pronouncements on the ends of marriage and the virtues of the 'fruitful vine' avoided any action which could arouse the ingrained hostility of the masses against clerical meddling in domestic affairs.[5] I have thus had to cast my net wider and, in what follows, the accounts of Holywell Street pornographers and Grub Street journalists, university dons and back street abortionists, midwives and members of the Royal College of Physicians rub cheek and jowl. The purpose of assembling the evidence of such a motley crowd of observers is to place birth control in its nineteenth-century context as a crucial social issue and in so doing reappraise the relationship of the classes and the relationship of the sexes.[6]

Notes

1. J.W. Taylor, 'The Bishop of London on the Declining Birth Rate,' *Nineteenth Century and After*, 59 (1906), p.226.
2. H.J. Habakkuk, *Population Growth and Economic Development Since 1750* (Leicester, 1971), pp.54-73; J. Matras, 'Social Strategies of Family Formation: Data for British Female Cohorts born 1831-1906,' *Population Studies*, 19 (1965), pp.167-181.
3. Royal Commission on Population, *Papers*, 1949, *Report on an Enquiry into Family Limitation During the Past Fifty Years*, pp.6-11; and see Griselda Rowntree and Rachel M. Pierce, 'Birth Control in Britain,' *Population Studies*, 15 (1961), pp.3-31, 121-160; B.R. Mitchell and P. Deane, *Abstract of British Historical Statistics* (Cambridge, 1962), pp.6, 45-6.
4. See Norman E. Himes, *Medical History of Contraception* (London, 1936); R. and K. Titmuss, *Parent's Revolt: A Study of the Declining Birth Rate in Acquisitive Societies* (London, 1942); J.A. Banks, *Prosperity and Parenthood* (London, 1956); Peter Fryer, *The Birth Controllers* (New York, 1965); Peter Willmott and Michael Young, *The Symmetrical Family* (London, 1973); Patricia Branca, *Silent Sisterhood: Middle-Class Women in the Victorian Home* (London, 1975). For a new approach see Diana Gittins, 'Married Life and Birth Control Between the Wars,' *Oral History*, 3 (1975), pp.53-64.
5. On the special hostility to supposed Catholic-style penetration of the home see J.A. and O. Banks, 'The Bradlaugh-Besant Trial and the English Newspapers,' *Population Studies*, 9 (1954-1955), pp.22-3; H.J. Hanham, *Elections and Party Management* (London, 1959), pp.305-6. For the churches' late entry into the birth control debate see Hugh McLeod, *Class and Religion in the Late Victorian City* (London, 1974), pp.242-6.
6. The term 'birth control' was not to be coined until the twentieth century by the American, Margaret Sanger, but it will be used throughout this study to designate the use of appliances or techniques to prevent conception. For an introduction to French work done in this area see J.L. Flandrin, *Familles, parenté, maison, sexualité dans l'ancienne société* (Paris, 1976) and Edward Shorter, *The Making of the Modern Family* (London, 1975).

PART ONE

BACKGROUND TO THE BIRTH CONTROL DEBATE

1 QUACKERY AND CONTROL OF FERTILITY IN EIGHTEENTH-CENTURY ENGLAND

Historians of birth control have persisted in focusing their attention on the nineteenth century when the most dramatic fall in marital fertility occurred and literature defending contraception appeared. Although they inevitably acknowledge the fact that there were some primitive forms of family limitation available before 1800, the basic tenet of their argument is that the crucial factor in the spread of contraceptive practices was the diffusion of some new knowledge or technique which trickled, seeped or percolated down the class structure to the working classes. The counter-argument — that the acceptance of the strategy of restriction of family size would be a consequence of old practices being called into play by new social and economic conditions — needs to establish the fact that adequate methods of fertility control were available in the eighteenth century. The problem is that little work has yet been done in determining just what means of contraception were employed in pre-industrial Europe; it has been generally assumed that, given the nature of the subject, there is little chance of documenting such practices. There was, however, one group of eighteenth-century writers who provided a good deal of information on 'deviant' sexual practices — indeed this group had a monetary interest in such practices — namely the quacks. In this chapter I intend to show how the literature produced by empirics and popular practitioners which appears to address itself only to venereal complaints can be used to gain an insight into the forms of fertility control employed in Hanoverian England.

* * *

On a May evening in 1763 James Boswell, a twenty-three year old Scot who was to win fame as the chronicler of the life of Samuel Johnson, wandered the streets of London in search of female companionship.

> At the bottom of tne Haymarket [he tells us in his diary] I picked up a strong, jolly young damsel, and taking her under the arm conducted her to Westminster Bridge, and then in armour complete did I engage her upon this noble edifice. The whim of doing it there

with the Thames rolling below us amused me very much.[1]

From this anecdote one gathers that the bridges of the metropolis
were neither much frequented nor well lit in the eighteenth century;
the most curious reference made by Boswell, however, is to his 'armour'.
From this and other entries in his diary we learn that prophylactic
devices were in use over two hundred years ago. This information is of
importance because instruments which were initially used to protect
men from disease were eventually to be employed to protect women
from pregnancy.

What the eighteenth-century man feared the most, what he was
most ignorant about and what quacks accordingly claimed they could,
at a price, cure, was the pox. Even reputable physicians could not deal
in any meaningful way with the ravages of venereal disease until the
twentieth century, but the reader of the eighteenth-century press finds
countless claims made for the efficacy of some new balm. Boswell, for
example, was a purchaser of Keyser's Pills which were puffed in the
Public Advertiser, 4 February 1768, as a mild cure for '. . .a certain
disorder, without the least trouble or confinement' which had been
found efficacious by 'ambassadors, ministers of state, and other
noblemen of the first rank.'[2] The same publication also carried
announcements for 'The Lisbon Diet Drink' for those '. . .who had
been injured by a certain disorder, and brought almost to a total
weakness. . .This solution is more pleasant to the taste, will keep
longer, and may be sent to any part of the kingdom put up in pint
bottles, with printed directions, at half a guinea each. To be had at
Mr Woodcock's, perfumer, in Orange Street, Red Lion Square, and
nowhere else.'[3] This nostrum was claimed by one John Leake to be
his monopoly and in a pamphlet he warned customers against
purchasing the wares of Walter Leake, a scoundrel seeking to pass off
useless medicines on the strength of the same surname.[4]

William Hickey, a contemporary of Boswell, sought relief for his
complaints in 'Velnos' Vegetable Syrup'.[5] This was, wrote its English
distributor Isaac Swainson, a French concoction which in addition to
the pox would cure leprosy, gout, scrophula, dropsy, small pox,
consumption, tape worms, cancer, scurvy, and diaorrhea. Such a
marvellous drug should have driven out all competitors but Swainson
was soon complaining that charlatans were selling ineffectual
imitations.[6] He specifically cited John Hodson who in 1790 published
*Nature's Assistant to the Restoration of Health, to Which is Added a
Short Treatise on the Venereal Disease. . .and the Destructive Habit of*

Self-Pollution in which he lauded the benefits of his 'Parisian Vegetable
Syrup' and his 'Persian Restorative Drops' priced at half a guinea a
bottle. J. Burrows produced a similar treatise, *A Dissertation on the
Nature and Effects of a Vegetable Remedy* (1784), lauding the powers
of a similar drink. These men all stressed the mild nature of their
vegetable cures; they were playing on the well-known fact that the
traditional treatment by mercury could be worse than the disease. The
same claims were made by T. Seymour for his *'Poudre Unique'* which
for five shillings six pence vanquished the pox, gout, sciatica, asthma,
and swellings of the joint; by J. Spinke for his 'Anti-Venereal Pills: For
Pox or the French Disease'; and finally by Doctor Trigg for his 'Golden
Anti-Vatican Pills' which presumably cured, not Catholicism, but the
clap.[7]

The fact that quacks appeared to find the sale of cures for venereal
complaints increasingly lucrative was taken by some as evidence that
sexual attitudes were changing. John Corry in *The Detector of Quackery*
(1802) argued that the belief that sexual over-indulgence did not have
to be paid for had led to a breakdown in traditional restraints.
'Dissolute young men are induced to continue in the practice of their
pernicious habits of wantonness and excess, from their mistaken idea
that a nostrum will operate as an effective restorative.'[8] William Buchan
in *Observations Concerning the Prevention and Cure of the Venereal
Disease* (1796) stated that no segment of society was immune to these
changes. 'What was formerly called the gentleman's disease [wrote
Buchan referring to the pox] is now equally common among the lowest
classes of society.'[9] Buchan, an eminent medical man, provided one of
the few objective accounts in the eighteenth century of the question.
He decried the fact that physicians and surgeons, because of their
prudishness, had allowed quacks to monopolise this area of medicine.
He recognised that, aside from simple washing, there were no effective
means medical men could advise as protection. What Buchan failed to
mention, however, even when asserting that prevention was better than
cure, was the device which Boswell referred to as his 'armour'.

It was the quacks who sold the cures for venereal disease who also
sold the instrument described by Boswell. The sheath was originally
designed, not to prevent pregnancy, but to protect the male from the
pox. The first known printed description appeared in a passage dealing
with syphilis in Gabriello Fallopio's posthumously published *De morbo
gallico* (1564).[10] The earliest English reference seems to have been in
John Marten's *A Treatise of all the Degrees and Symptoms of the
Venereal Disease in Both Sexes* (1704). Marten cited Fallopio and the

instrument Marten described was, like the earlier writer's, made of 'Lint or Linnen Rags' which were to be soaked in a special wash before engagement.[11] Marten refused to give details because of his avowed concern that if they became common knowledge sin would abound; his real intent, of course, was to draw customers to purchase his special anti-venereal solution.

Marten was not allowed to sell his instruments in peace. In 1711 a rival quack to whom we have already referred, J. Spinke, attacked him in a publication entitled *Venus's Botcher or, the Seventh Edition of Mr. Martin's [sic] (comical) Treatise, of the Venereal Disease.*[12] It was Spinke's complaint that Marten by both advertising and disparaging the work of other practitioners was attempting to monopolise the market. Spinke stated that he had been singled out by Marten for special censure because he (Spinke) had done the greatest good with what he called the 'blue Apron' — presumably some rival form of prophylactic.

The sheaths were advertised in the same sorts of publications in which quacks paraded the benefits of their pills and potions. That papers should carry such announcements raised the particular ire of Joseph Cam. In *A Rational and Useful Account of the Venereal Disease* (1737) he upbraided one promoter as being as guilty as the inventor. 'Surely, Sir, you advise all Mankind, which is prompt enough of itself to offend, to use *Machinery,* and to fight in *Armour.* If so, you are not the Inventor, but the *Propagator* of Wickedness: But we see how some Persons aim to deceive the world.'[13] In the eyes of Cam and respectable physicians the danger of 'preventives' was that they permitted the promiscuous to indulge their passions without fear of punishment. Indeed there were a number of eighteenth-century medical men who believed that even cures for venereal disease should, for the same reason, not be sought. For this reason it was assumed by many that doctors were chiefly opposed to the use of 'armour' because they feared the loss of much of their clientèle. As early as 1709 this view was expressed in the *Tatler* which inaccurately reported that the philanthropic inventor of the sheath was a patron of Will's Coffee House: 'Such a Benefactor is a Gentleman of this House, who is observ'd by the Surgeons with much Envy; for he has invented an Engine for the Prevention of Harms by Love-Adventures, and has, by great Care and Application made it an immodesty to name his name.'[14]

For some reason, which historians have not yet resolved, the name of this invention was associated in Englishmen's minds, not with John Marten, but with the apparently mythical Mr Condum. In John Grose's

Dictionary of the Vulgar Tongue there appeared the citation:
'CUNDUM. The dried gut of a sheep, worn by men in the act of
coition, to prevent venereal infection; said to have been invented by
one colonel Cundum.' Interestingly enough the French also attributed
the invention to the English. Jean Astruc, in his *Treatise of the Venereal
Disease* translated by William Barrowby in 1737, wrote,

> I am informed, that of late years the Debauchees in *England*, that
> set no bounds to their meretricious amours, make use of a little bag,
> made of a thin bladder, which they call a *condum*, with this they
> arm the *penis*, that they may be preserved safe from the dangers of
> an engagement whose consequences are always doubtful. For they
> imagine, that being arm'd thus *cap-a-pé*, they may with great safety
> face the dangers of promiscuous venery.[15]

Astruc assured his readers that there was no way of avoiding the pox
if it was not by leading a pure, chaste life. For the promiscuous to seek
safety in a slim sheath he found laughable; in his opinion '. . .they
ought to arm their penis with oak, guarded with a triple plate of brass,
instead of trusting to a thin bladder, who are fond of committing a part
so capable of receiving infection to the filthy gulph of a Harlot.'[16]

The sort of covering which Astruc envisaged clearly required a
sacrifice of comfort in favour of security. Even the mid-eighteenth-
century sheath which was made of an animal bladder or fine covering,
tied at the open end with a ribbon, was not entirely satisfactory. They
were too expensive to be used except by the wealthy and, because of
the material of which they were made, required moistening before use;
'. . .dipped my machine in the Canal and performed most manfully'
wrote Boswell of one out-of-doors encounter.[17] Some found such
inconveniences too much to bear. Daniel Turner in *Syphilis: A Practical
Dissertation on the Venereal Disease* (1717) stated: 'The *Condum* being
the best, if not the only Preservative our Libertines have found out at
present; and yet, by reason of its blunting the Sensation, I have heard
some of them acknowledge, that they had often to choose to risk a
Clap, rather than engage *cum Hastis sic clypeatis* [with spears thus
sheathed].'[18] Boswell was a case in point. He prided himself on
engaging only when 'safely sheathed' or in 'armourial guise' but
admitted that at times '. . .I found but a dull satisfaction'. On occasion
he would chance an unencumbered encounter. He wrote of the night
of May 17, 1763: '. . .I picked up a fresh, agreable young girl called
Alice Gibbs. We went down a lane to a snug place, and I took out my

armour, but she begged that I might not put it on, as the sport was much pleasanter without it, and as she was quite safe.'[19]

As the passage from Boswell indicates women were not uninterested in the advantages and disadvantages of 'armour.' On occasion the prostitute provided her customer with the instrument. In his entry for November 25, 1762 Boswell wrote, 'I picked up a girl in the Strand; went into a court with intention to enjoy her in armour. But she had none.'[20] Indeed the two most famous retailers of these devices in the eighteenth century were women — Mrs Philips and Mrs Perkins. Grose cited an advertisement from the *St James Chronicle* in which Mrs Philips boasted of thirty-five years of experience '. . .in the business of making and selling machines, commonly called implements of safety, which serve the health of her customers.' The advertisement ended with the doggerel rhyme:

> To guard yourself from shame or fear
> Votaries to Venus, hasten here;
> None in my wares e'er found a flaw
> Self preservation's nature's law.

Mrs Perkins contented herself with informing the public in simple prose that at the Green Canister in Half-Moon Street opposite the New Exchange in the Strand she made and sold '. . .all sorts of fine machines, otherwise called C–MS.'[21]

Almost all the eighteenth-century references to sheaths concern their use by a man when consorting with a prostitute. The association of this instrument with vice would be a major reason why the respectable would long refuse to acknowledge its efficacy in controlling fertility Yet even in the eighteenth century one can find the argument expressed that honourable women could use it to guard themselves from 'shame or fear.' Such seems to be the message of Joseph Gay's *The Petticoat: An Heroi–Comical Poem* published in 1716.

> This NEW MACHINE a sure Defence shall prove,
> And guard the Sex against the Harms of Love.

> So might the Fair, thus arm'd remain secure
> And brave the Dangers which they shun'd before,
> Safe in their Ramparts all Assaults defie
> And dare the Efforts of the Enemy.

Should now Good natur'd Nymphs (which Heav'n forfend!)
To Grant too early favours condescend;
See here, the happy means propos'd to shun,
The fatal Danger, when the fault is done.[22]

The same argument was made more forcibly still in yet another poem,
White Kennett's *The Machine or, Love's Preservative* (1724).

Hear and attend: In CUNDUM's praise
I sing and thou, O Venus! aid my Lays

By this Machine secure, the willing Maid
Can taste Love's Joys, nor is she more afraid
Her Swelling Belly should, or squalling Brat,
Betray the luscious Pastime she has been at.[23]

* * *

The sheath was, as noted, expensive and could prove uncomfortable
so that even those who did not find it morally objectionable might not
employ it should they seek to limit their fertility. A simpler strategy
was recourse to coitus interruptus or the withdrawal method of birth
control. It is in the quack literature on venereal disease that we learn
about the use of 'armour'; similarly it is in the quack pamphlets on the
evils of masturbation that we learn about the practice of coitus
interruptus. The latter two acts were known in the eighteenth century
as forms of onanism. Onan, according to the book of Genesis, had
defied God's command to have children by his dead brother's wife
and cast his seed upon the ground for which he was punished by death.
Whether God slew Onan simply because of his defiance or because of
the specific form it took was never made clear. Eighteenth-century
quacks were quick to realise the possibilities of exploiting this confusion
in the borderline between morals and medicine.[24] The importance of
the literature on onanism, for the purposes of this chapter, is that it
indicates that in the eighteenth century couples were employing the
withdrawal method in order to limit the number of pregnancies. Those
who had not discovered the practice by themselves or by a perusal of
the Old Testament had their attention sharply drawn to it by the
quacks. It was not the goal of the quacks to popularise the idea; what
they were seeking to do was capitalise on the fear that the spilling of
seed — be it by masturbation or coitus interruptus — led to physical

debilitation.

Having terrified the reader with a long list of illnesses that could be caused by onanism — debility, consumption, loss of hearing, memory, and eyesight — quacks sought to lure the frightened into a purchase of some restorative. For example in the early editions of *Onania* Thomas Crouch advertised his 'Strengthening Tincture' and 'Prolific Powder'. In the 1730 edition it was announced that Crouch had died and that J. Isted would now supply the necessary cordials and draughts. As the century wore on more and more remarkable remedies appeared. W. Farrer brought out a 'Restorative Nervous Elixir', W. Brodum sold a 'nervous Cordial and Botanical Syrup', E. Senate advertised 'Steel Lozenges', James Graham lauded the benefits of an 'Elixir of Life', and Samuel Solomon boasted of the vast sale of his 'Cordial Balm of Gilead'.[25]

It is striking that the first texts on the evils of onanism should have appeared in England in the same years when the sheath was being publicised. The original impetus appears to have been given by a pastor of Neufchatel, J.F. Osterwald, who published in Amsterdam *Traité des sources de la corruption qui regne aujourd'hui parmi les Chrestiens* (1700) and *Traité contre l'impureté* (1707). These works were not particularly innovative; they condemned luxury and sensuality and praised chastity and sobriety. There were only veiled hints that the types of sensuality being attacked were forms of sexual indulgence.[26] The first English work on the subject approached the problem in a much more direct fashion. This anonymous text was entitled *Of the Crime of Onan. . .or the Heinous Vice of Self-Defilement* and from the first page set out to terrify and titillate the reader. The first edition, which appeared sometime before 1717, confined itself primarily to describing the horrible fate that awaited those given to masturbation or what was called the 'school -wickedness'. The author conceded that some would find his work shocking but declared that it was far better that youth be warned than face the eventual judgement of God.

> The great Account Book then shall lie
> Open to every Offender's Eye,
> To try his Self-Defilements by.

> Then sits the Judge upon his Throne,
> And makes all Self-Defilements known,
> When each Onanian knows HIS OWN.[27]

But the warnings were not restricted to the private vices of youth; passing reference was also made to 'The Use, Abuse of, and Frustrating the Marriage Bed' which implied that more than mere masturbation was being condemned. This line of argument was followed up in a work of 1724 entitled *Eronia: On the Use and Abuse of the Marriage Bed by Er and Onan.* Here the reader was reminded that Er had sinned because, out of a desire to maintain his wife's beauty, he had sought to free her from the burden of child-bearing. The author then went on to censure those married persons who indulged in '. . .Embraces that may be thought *Frustraneous,* because Procreation may not be at that Time attainable'.

> There are some Married Persons in the World who think *Children* come too fast, and distrusting the Capacity of maintaining them, frustrate what is appointed for the *Continuance of our Species.* This is a Frustraneous Abuse of the Marriage-Bed, and a very great Crime, which every one ought to avoid, and submit to *Providence* for the Maintenance of what determinate *Number of Children* it has allotted for them.[28]

It is of interest to note that the author assumed that only members of the upper classes engaged in such vices because he called on his audience to remember that 'Working and Labouring People' though only living from hand to mouth made no attempt to limit their fertility.

The fourth edition of *Onania* contained a letter from a woman who declared that the sole purpose of marriage was procreation and that therefore any sexual activity that did not result in offspring was sinful. The author gave the impression that he agreed with her judgement and directly attacked husbands who adopted a strategy which he dubbed the 'retreat'. 'Thousands there are in the married State who provoke and gratify their Lust, as far as is consistent with their destructive Purpose, and no farther, which being as I have said before a Sin of a deep Die, it is hoped, by what is here said of it they will in Time take warning and Repent of.'[29]

In the seventh edition of *Onania* dated 1723 the author changed tack and in reply to the woman's letter cited above declared that marriage was not simply established for procreation; conjugal amity was as important. But having said this he returned to the attack on the use of coitus interruptus as a means of birth control.

. . .there are Married persons, who commit a heinous Sin to God, by frustrating what he has appointed for the Multiplication of our Species, and are commonly such, as think Children come too fast, and distrust Providence for their Maintenance and Education. They indulge themselves in all the Pleasures of the Sense, and yet would avoid the Charges they might occasion; in order to which they do what they can to hinder Conception. What I mean, is, when the Man, by a criminal untimely Retreat, disappoints his Wife's as well as his own fertility. This is what may be call'd a frustraneous Abuse of their bodies and must be an abominable Sin. Yet it is certain, that Thousands there are in the Married State, who provoke and gratify their Lust, as far as is consistent with their destructive Purpose, and no further.[30]

What is remarkable about the fifth and seventh editions of *Onania* is that in addition to the condemnations of onanism they also included a letter which appears to be the earliest defence of the withdrawal method of birth control. The writer identified himself as a poor man with three children who, because of poverty, had to agree with his wife to limit the size of their family.

. . .Now Sir, this melancholy View, which might be much more aggravated, drove us by consent upon this expedient you generally and justly condemn in your Answer to the Ladies [sic] Letter: My conscience seems to Clear me of ONAN's crime, for what he did was out of spite and ill will, and contrary to an express Command of raising up Seed to his Brother, in Contradiction to the Method of our Redemption: Whereas mine is pure necessity in respect both of Body and Soul. . .[31]

The author printed this plea but did not agree with the sentiments expressed. He charged the writer with lack of faith and failure to recognise the physical dangers of his deed. Now it is possible, indeed probable, that the letter was manufactured by the author as an expository device but even if this were the case it still follows that the argument it contains — namely that coitus interruptus was morally justifiable — was presumed by him to be held by many of his prospective readers.

The suggestion that couples were seeking to control fertility by assuming various coital positions was also made in the oldest and most widely read sex manual of the time, *Aristotle's Works*.[32] This compendium of sexual folklore first appeared in 1684 and was frequently re-edited in the course of the eighteenth century. It contained long sections on subjects such as the determination of the sex of offspring, the effect of the mother's imagination on the foetus (for example an adulteress could, by thinking of her husband, make her child resemble her spouse), the birth of monsters, and the causes of barrenness. In the 1772 edition there was in addition a reference made to couples who did not want children: '. . .there are some that desire not to have children and yet are very fond of nocturnal Embraces'[33] What tactics these couples might adopt is suggested by what the manual condemns. Thus the anonymous author warns husbands not to withdraw too quickly for to do so permits cold air to strike the womb and cause illness. Women are cautioned to lie still after coition and in particular to refrain from sneezing. Sneezing at the crucial moment was to enjoy a long reputation as an effective defensive tactic.

The eighteenth-century reader could find similarly helpful information by perusing *Conjugal Love Reveal'd; in the Nightly Pleasure of the Marriage BED and the Advantages of that Happy STATE in an Essay Concerning Human Generation Done from the French of Monsieur Venette*. Here, as in *Aristotle's Works* one would read, 'Nature has taught both Sexes such Positions as are allowable, and that contribute to Generation; and Experience has shown those that are forbidden and contrary to Health.' Couples were warned that to take up such non-prolific positions led to the harming of any possible offspring. 'The Children become Dwarfs, Cripples, Hunchback'd, Squint-ey'd, and Stupid Blockheads, and by their Imperfections fully evidence the irregular Life of their Parents, without putting us to the trouble to search the Cause of such Defects any Farther.'[34] Much the same argument was made by John Armstrong who, in the *Oeconomy of Love: A Poetical Essay,* called on his countrymen to refrain from embraces which because of their unnatural nature had to be of foreign origin.

> But in these vicious Days great *Nature's* Laws
> Are spurned; eternal Virtue, which nor Time,
> Nor Place can change, nor Custom changing all,
> Is mocked to scorn; and *lewd Abuse* instead,
> Daughter of the Night, her shameless Revels holds
> O'er half the Globe, which the chaste face of Day
> Eclipses at her Rites. For Man with Man,
> And Man with Woman (monstrous to relate!)

Leaving the natural Road, themselves debase
Witn Deeds unseemly, and Dishonour foul.
Britons, for shame! Be Male and Female still.
Banish this foreign Vice; it grows not here,
It dies neglected; and in Clime so chaste
Cannot but by forc'd Cultivation thrive.[35]

It is worth noting, that in the literature dealing with coital positions
the idea of the 'woman on top' was invariably condemned. On the
one hand this reflected the traditional male view that the woman had
to be both literally and figuratively 'under' men.[36] On the other hand
there is evidence to suggest that the fear of the woman being on top
was also motivated by the belief that in assuming such a position she
could avoid pregnancy. In the popular poem *Kick Him Jenny* appeared
the lines:

Thus in a Chair the cautious Dame,
Who loves a little of that Same,
Will take it on her Lover's Lap,
Sure to prevent, this way, Misshap:
Subtle Lechers! Knowing that,
They cannot so be got with Brat.[37]

The information that can be gleaned from the eighteenth-century texts
on couples' adoption of coitus interruptus or positions which were
believed to be inapt for conception is important for three reasons.
First, the references usually concern married people and thus the
practice was distinct from those associated with prostitutes and their
clients. Secondly, it is clear that the purpose of the adoption of such
tactics was not to avoid disease as was the case when the sheath was
employed, but to prevent pregnancy. Thirdly, such practices required
the active participation of both partners; the woman was not passive —
indeed some have suggested that increased reliance on coitus interruptus
signified the success of females in domesticating males.[38]

The third form of fertility control to which attention is drawn by
quack literature is abortion. The anonymous author of *Low Life* (1752)
described Sunday evening as the time when both sexes sought medical
aid.

As it is now twilight, reputable young fellows, as students in the law, merchants' clerks, non-commissioned officers, dependent nephews and grandsons, coasting commanders, and mechanics' sons, who have been unhappily scarred in the wars of Venus, are repairing to their several quack doctors and surgeon's pupils, to get safe, easy, and speedy cure for their several disorders. About the same time, young women, whose unhappy minute has been taken advantage of by pretended lovers, rakes of quality, lewd masters, lecherous fornicators, and drinking spiritous liqiors, are repairing to persons of their own sex who live about Ludgate-hill and St. Martin's Lane and put out hand-bills for the cure of all disorders incident to women.[39]

The men were looking for relief of their venereal diseases; the women were seeking aid in the induction of a miscarriage. The handbills which the author refers to would include those for potions such as 'Farrer's Catholic Pills', the *'Poudre Unique',* and 'Velnos' Vegetable Syrup' all of which were supposed to cure 'suppression of the menses' and those for the services rendered by women practitioners such as Ann Laverenst, Mrs Mary Green, and Agnodice, 'The Woman Physician, Dwelling at the Hand and Urinal next Door to the Blue Ball in Hayden-yard in the Minories, near Aldgate.'[40]

Abortion was in some ways a more 'thinkable' option in the eighteenth century than it would be in the nineteenth if only because it was not made a statutory offence until 1803. Throughout the 1700s the view was still held that foetal life was not present until animation or 'quickening'. Women who took drugs before that time would describe their actions as 'restoring the menses' or 'bringing on a period'. These women found their position supported by legal interpretation. Blackstone, in his *Commentaries on the Laws of England* (1765) wrote: 'Life. . .begins in contemplation of the law as soon as an infant is able to stir in the mother's womb.'[41] Abortion, in the legal sense could only take place fourteen weeks after conception; even the few cases so defined which were tried in the eighteenth century were considered as either simple common law misdemeanours or referred to the ecclesiastical courts.

But having said that abortion was not a crime, should not be taken to mean that the practice was looked on with indifference. Indeed the century witnessed a rising tide of hostile comments aimed at such actions. This reflected the assumption increasingly made by male observers — both doctors and laymen — of their right to interfere in women's child-bearing. In Daniel Defoe's *Conjugal Lewdness: or, Matrimonial Whoredom – A Treatise concerning the Use and Abuse of the Marriage Bed* (1727) the topic was broached in a chapter entitled 'The Diabolical Practice of Attempting to Prevent Child-Bearing by Physical Preparations.' A young woman is described as taking 'physick'. For two years she has no children and her spouse becomes suspicious. 'Her Apprehensions now were, that her Husband should suppose either that she still used Art with her self to prevent her being with Child, or to destroy a Conception after it had taken place. . .' Afraid that her husband would try to have the marriage dissolved she begs forgiveness and, '. . .assured him of her being fully satisfied that it was unlawful, and that she had committed a great Crime in what she had done before; that it was a Sin against her Husband; that she had injured him in it, dishonoured her self, and offended against the Laws both of God and Man'.[42]

Defoe portrayed married women seeking to induce their own miscarriage; most commentators assumed that only single women would resort to such stratagems. They reasoned that, since it was so dangerous, the risk would deter all but the most desparate. Thomas Short, for example, referred to it as a form of 'suicide'. 'If Whoredom be a fault, Suicide is a far greater Crime: By Suicide is meaned, not only the Destruction of real Beings in the Womb, Birth, or immediately after; but all nefarious Practices used by wicked Wretches to prevent Conception from their carnal Gratification.'[43] Alexander Hamilton in speaking of the unmarried occasionally attempting abortion stated that it '. . .commonly proves fatal to the mother'.[44] Similar warnings were sounded by the anonymous author of *Thoughts on the Means of Alleviating the Miseries Attendant Upon Common Prostitution* (1799).

> It is not possible to calculate the numbers who, thus circumstanced in mind and body [pregnant], greedily accept and swallow the medicines in vulgar repute for procuring abortion. The ignorant administrators of these baleful drugs destroy the mother, perhaps, not less frequently than the embryo. This hazard, though often foreseen, is willingly encountered.[45]

The theme of the seduced young girl forced to take an abortifacient by the man responsible for her condition not surprisingly attracted the attention of women writers preoccupied by the iniquities of the double standard. In *The Wrongs of Woman, or Maria; a Fragment* (1798) Mary Wollstonecraft presented the classic story of the servant girl whose seduction is followed, on the insistence of her master, by an abortion.

> After some weeks of deliberation had elapsed, I in continual fear
> that my altered shape would be noticed, my master gave me a
> medicine in a phial, which he desired me to take, telling me,
> without any circumlocution, for what purpose it was designed.[46]

Wollstonecraft's heroine survived her ordeal with remarkably little
discomfort. A more lurid tale was told by the religious enthusiast,
Joanna Southcott in her *Letters and Communications. . .lately written
to Jane Towley* (1804); here the seducer provides an abortifacient
which kills both mother and child.

> And now the Truth thou must declare,
> And tell the Woman's doom –
> Now she with child, by him beguil'd,
> And then the shame to Miss;
> He brought the poison then for her,
> But I shall answer this –
> Savine you know is an herb doth grow
> And there the poison laid;
> He said the Child's life it would take
> And there she was betray'd;
> Because her own, he told her then,
> Her life't could never hurt;
> 'Twas but the Child that would be slain,
> Her honour to support.[47]

The vast majority of abortions were no doubt self-induced but there
were in the eighteenth century professional abortionists whose services
could be called on. In *Moll Flanders* Defoe described a woman who had
a vast clientèle: 'Tis scarce credible what practice she had, as well abroad
as at home, and yet all upon the private account, or, in plain English,
the whoring account.'[48] Grose reprinted an advertisement placed by
such an abortionist in the *Morning Post* of April 18, 1780.

> Any Lady whose situation may require a temporary retirement, may
> be accommodated agreeable to her wishes in the house of a
> gentleman of eminence in the profession, where honour and secrecy
> may be depended on, and where every vestige of pregnancy is
> obliterated; or any Lady who wishes to become pregnant may have

the causes of sterility removed in the safest manner.[49]

William Buchan's suspicions were such that he would write in *Domestic Medicine or the Family Physician,* 'I have never heard without shuddering any advertisement of temporary retreats, or pretended accommodations for pregnant ladies. . .'[50]

Whether abortion was as dangerous as its opponents suggested is difficult to determine. Because the public would only be made aware of the unsuccessful − in particular those which resulted in the death of the mother − it is likely that the risks were exaggerated. The very fact that certain drugs were recommended by midwives and older women generation after generation implies that some were found to be relatively effective. Books on cooking and herbal remedies frequently carried recipes for concoctions which would 'bring on a period'. For example in Culpepper's *The English Physician* there were references to 'Eringo, or Sea Holly' which 'procureth women's courses', 'Black Hellebore' which 'used as a pessary, provokes the terms exceedingly', 'Pennyroyal' which 'provoketh women's courses, and expelleth the dead child and after-birth', 'Garden Rue' which 'provoketh urine and women's courses', and 'The Common White Saxifrage' which 'provoketh also women's courses, and freeth and cleanseth the stomach'.[51] Most of these herbs were fairly common and as a result the women of pre-industrial England had ready access to the medications they required.

How did women view abortion? The evidence all seems to support the notion that, though they appreciated the dangers of the practice, many regarded it as their right − should the situation demand − to have recourse to abortion. This point of view was given its clearest expression in a passage in Defoe's *Conjugal Lewdness.* Defoe, in order to make his condemnation of abortion all the more convincing, first provided what he took to be the essence of women's argument in favour of the act.

> . . .that all the while the *Foetus* is forming, and the Embrio or Conception is proceeding, even to the Moment that the Soul is infused, so long it is absolutely not in her Power only, but in her right, to kill or keep alive, save or destroy the Thing she goes with, she won't call it Child; and that therefore till then she resolves to use all manner of Art, to the help of Drugs and Physicians, whether Astringents, Diureticks, Emeticks, or of whatever kind, nay even to Purgations, Potions, Poisons, or any thing that Apothecaries or

Druggists can supply: But she goes farther. . .If Drugs and Medicine
fail her she will call to the Devil for help, and if Spells, Filtres,
Charms, Witchcraft, or all the Powers of Hell would bring it
about for her, she would not scruple to make use of them for her
resolved Purpose . . . Let the cure be wrought, though the *Devil*
be the doctor.[52]

Defoe, a man who described as murderers 'those people. . .who
talk of Physick to prevent their being with child', was not the sort
one would turn to when looking for arguments in favour of abortion.
For this reason the account he gave does ring true. Men's attitudes
towards procreation might have changed but women still retained
the traditional view that life was not present until the foetus quickened.
Until that time they considered it their right to conduct themselves in
any way they saw fit. Moreover, until animation, they perceived
themselves not as pregnant, but as 'irregular'; they took drugs, not to
abort, but to restore the menses.

Historians who use the texts of respected literary and medical writers
are unlikely to have great success in ascertaining popular attitudes
towards birth control. Even the demographic literature of the
eighteenth century contains few references to the practice. Those
writers who discussed population tended to share the belief that the
nation's prosperity depended on a growing citizenry. Their concern
was not how to limit family size but how best to increase it. If like
Thomas Short they referred to means of contraception, it was only to
denounce them.[53] It is the Grub Street literature of the quacks and
popular practitioners which provides the greatest amount of
information on sexual practices. Their works reveal the fact that, in
addition to simple abstention, three of the major means by which
fertility was to be controlled in the nineteenth and twentieth centuries —
abortion, coitus interruptus, and use of the condom — were all tactics
known and written about in the eighteenth century.[54] Moreover
references to all the tactics, save for use of the sheath, indicated that
interest in avoidance of unwanted pregnancies was found in the
working as well as in the upper classes. H.W. Tytler cited Buchan to
the effect that if the population was to be sustained the poor would
have to be rewarded for bearing their children:

'This would make the poor esteem fertility a blessing, whereas many

of them think it is the greatest curse that can befall them.' To this
Dr. Underwood [Michael Underwood, author of *A Treatise on the
Diseases of Children* (1784)] adds, that 'he has known them express
great thankfulness when their children are dead'. The reason of
which in some measure may be, that it is frequently mentioned as
a matter of reproach to a man in low circumstances, that he has a
large family. And in this country, it is usual with such persons to
consult apothecaries, quacks, and old women, for medicines to make
their wives barren.[55]

The availability of birth control does not mean that it will be necessarily
employed to bring down the birth rate. Indeed the population of
England and Wales which increased from 5.8 to 6.5 million in the first
half of the eighteenth century leapt from 6.5 to 9.2 in the second half.
This dramatic acceleration was due first, to a reduction in the virulence
of diseases, a rise in the resistance to them, and an accompanying drop
in the death rate. Secondly there was an increase of fertility because of
earlier marriages and a demand for child labour due to industrialisation.
Preoccupied by the task of explaining this 'demographic revolution'
commentators have overlooked the fact that such growth could occur
in the presence of a knowledge of rudimentary forms of fertility
control.[56]

The social and economic situation of late eighteenth-century England
did not call these birth control tactics into play on a massive scale.
Controls might be employed to space births or protect a mother's
health but a high fertility norm was rational for working people when
children could be put out to work at an early age. Decline of family
size, when it occurred in the nineteenth century, would likewise result,
not from some innovation in contraception, but from changing
economic and social conditions. The irony of the birth control debate
which was to take place in the 1800s was that the propagandists who
first raised the question of the necessity of population control should
have sought to suppress that knowledge of contraception which already
existed. To understand why this should have been the case it will be
necessary to turn in the next chapter to the subject of Malthusian
economics.

Notes

1. F.A. Pottle (ed.), *Boswell's London Journal 1762-1763* (London, 1966), pp.278-9.
2. Frank Brady (ed.), *Boswell in Search of a Wife 1761-1769* (New York, 1956), p.270. See also 'Tracts on the Venereal Disease,' British Museum 1172 b12 and 1175 k7.
3. Brady, *Boswell,* pp.286-7.
4. John Leake, *Dissertation on the Properties and Efficiency of the Lisbon Diet Drink* (London, 1780).
5. Peter Quennel, (ed.), *Memoirs of William Hickey* (London, 1975), p.197.
6. *An Account of Cures by Velnos' Vegetable Syrup* (London, 1792) and see J.J. de Velnos, *Dissertation sur un nouveau remède anti-végétal* (Paris, 1768).
7. See G.H., M.D., *Little Venus Unmask'd Being a Discourse on the French Pox* (London, 1700); T. Seymour, M.D., *A Concise Account of the Properties and Effects of the Poudre Unique* (London, 1774); Job Hallet, *De Venereo Morbo, or a Practical Treatise on the Venereal Disease* (Manchester, n.d.); John Lignum, *A Treatise on Venereal and Syphilic Diseases* (Manchester, 1819).
8. *The Detector of Quackery* (London, 1802), p.58.
9. *Observations* (London, 1796), p.13.
10. Norman E. Himes, *Medical History of Contraception* (Baltimore, 1936), pp.188-201; E.J. Dingwall, 'Early Contraceptive Sheaths,' *British Medical Journal* (3 January, 1953), pp.40-1; Peter Fryer, *The Birth Controllers* (New York, 1965), pp.23-31.
11. *A Treatise* (London, 1708), pp.63-4. Marten cited, in addition to Fallopio, Hercules Saxonica, *Luis venereoe perfectissimus* (1597). See also Casimir Freschot, *Histoire amoureuse et badine du congrès de la ville d'Utrecht* (Liège, 1714), p.166; on Marten see Ralph Strauss, *The Unspeakable Curll* (New York, 1927), pp.26, 206.
12. *Venus's Botcher* (London, 1711), p.11.
13. *A Rational and Useful Account* (London, 1737, 8th edn.), p.46.
14. The *Tatler,* no.15 (12-14 May, 1709).
15. *A Treatise* (London, 1737), I, p.299. See also Giacomo Casanova, *History of My Life,* tr. W.R. Trask (New York, 1967), IV, pp.68-9; and E. Lennard Bernstein, 'Who was Condom?' *Human Fertility,* 5 (1940), pp.172-5, 186.
16. *A Treatise,* I, p.300. For similar warnings see Edme Claude Bourru, *L'art de se traiter soi-même dans les maladies vénériennes* (Paris, 1770), p.238; James Thorn, *An Attempt to Simplify the Treatment of Sexual Diseases* (London, 1831), p.11.
17. Pottle, *Boswell,* p.298.
18. *Syphilis* (London, 1717), p.74.
19. Pottle, *Boswell,* p.287.
20. Ibid., p.76.
21. F. Grose, *Guide to Health, Beauty, Riches and Honour* (London, 1783), pp.11, 12.
22. Joseph Gay [Francis Chute], *The Petticoat* (London, 1716), pp.30, 31, 35.
23. *The Machine* (London, 1744), pp.2-3.
24. Robert H. MacDonald, 'The Frightful Consequences of Onanism, Notes on the History of a Delusion,' *Journal of the History of Ideas,* 28 (1967), pp.423-31.
25. W. Brodum, MD, *A Guide to Old Age or a Cure for the Indiscretions of Youth* (London, 1795) and *To the Nervous, Consumptive and Those of Debilitated Constitutions* (London, n.d.); Samuel Solomon, *A Guide to Health* (West Derby, n.d.); Dr James Graham, *A Lecture on the Generation, Increase and*

Improvement of the Human Species (London, n.d.); E. Senate, *The Medical Monitor, Containing Observations on the Effects of Early Dissipation* (London, n.d.); W. Farrer, *A Short Treatise on Onanism, or the Detestable Vice of Self Pollution* (London, 1767).

26. *The Nature of Uncleanness consider'd* (London, 1708); and see Angus McLaren 'Some Secular Attitudes Towards Sexual Behavior in France: 1760-1860,' *French Historical Studies*, 8 (1974), pp.604-25.

27. *Of the Crime of Onan* (London, 1717), p.30.

28. *Eronia* (London, 1724), p.21. There are earlier references to such practices. Dr Layton, writing to Thomas Cromwell of the debauchery of the abbey of St. Mary at York, stated that the priests were involved, '. . .in kyndes of knaverie, as, *retrahere membrum virile in ipso punctu seminis emittendi, ne inde fieret prolis generatio,* and nunnes to take potations *ad prolem conceptum opprimendum.*' Thomas Wright, (ed.), *Three Chapters of Letters Relating to the Suppression of Monasteries* (London, 1843), p.97; and see P.J.C. Field, 'Chaucer's Merchant and the Sin Against Nature,' *Notes and Queries*, 215 (1970), pp.85-6.

29. *Onania* (London, n.d., 4th edn.), pp.66, 83.

30. *Onania* (London, 1723, 7th edn.), p.99. The shifting of the ends of marriage from procreation to companionship was a product of seventeenth-century Puritan thought. See James T. Johnson, 'English Puritan Thought on the Ends of Marriage,' *Church History*, 38 (1969), pp.429-36; John Halkett, *Milton and the Idea of Matrimony* (New Haven, 1970).

31. *Onania*, p.101. See also *A Supplement to the Onania, or the Heinous Sin of Self-Pollution* (London, n.d.); 'Philo-Castitatis,' *Onania Examin'd and Detected* (London, n.d.); *Letters of Advice from Two Reverend Divines to a Young Gentleman, about a Weighty Case of Conscience* (London, 1724).

32. Ortho Beall,'Aristotle's Masterpiece in America: A Landmark in the Folklore of Medicine,' *William and Mary Quarterly*, 20 (1963), pp.207-22; Janet Blackburn, 'Popular Theories of Generation,' in John Woodward and David Richards, (eds.), *Health Care and Popular Medicine in Nineteenth Century England* (London, 1977).

33. *The Works of Aristotle. His Complete Masterpiece* (London, 1972), p.37.

34. *Conjugal Love* (London, 1720), pp.125, 128. Venette was first translated in 1703; he relied heavily on J.B. Sinibaldus, *Geneathropeiae* (Rome, 1642) which was translated in 1658 as *Rare Verities, or the Cabinet of Venus Unlocked.* See D.F. Foxon, 'Libertine Literature in England, 1660-1745,' *The Book Collector,* 12 (1963), pp.26-36.

35. *Oeconomy of Love* (London, 1739, 3rd edn.).

36. See Natalie Z. Davis, *Society and Culture in Early Modern France* (Stanford 1975), chapter five; and the warning of John of Gaddesden (1280-1336) against women 'jumping backward or too sudden a motion after coitus' in J.T. Noonan, *Contraception: A History of its Treatment by Catholic Theologians and Canonists* (Cambridge, Mass., 1965), p.208.

37. *Kick Him Jenny* (London, 1737, 11th edn.).

38. See Jean-Louis Flandrin, *Famille, parenté, maison, sexualité dans l'ancienne société* (Paris, 1976), 212 ff.

39. *Low Life* (London, 1764 edn.), pp.88-9.

40. On the sale of 'purging pills,' 'opening powders,' and various electuaries see A Physician, *A Rational Account of the Natural Weakness of Women* (London, n.d.); A Physician, *The Ladies' Physical Directory* (London, 1727); 'A Collection of Medical Advertisements,' British Museum 551 a32 and C112 f9.

41. Cited in Bernard M. Dickens, *Abortion and the Law* (London, 1966), p.21.

42. Defoe, *Conjugal Lewdness* (London, 1727), pp.144, 145.
43. Short, *New Observations* (London, 1750), p.74. Although infanticide was at times confused with abortion it is unlikely that the former served as a form of marital fertility control. Given the naturally high rate of infant mortality the actual killing of children would, as eighteenth-century juries recognised, only result from exceptional circumstances, usually the mental instability of the unwed mother. See J.M. Beattie, 'The Criminality of Women in Eighteenth-Century England,' *Journal of Social History,* 8 (1974-1975), pp.84-5; Keith Wrightson, 'Infanticide in Seventeenth-Century England,' *Local Population Studies* (1975), pp.10-22.
44. Hamilton, *A Treatise on the Management of Female Complaints* (Edinburgh, 1824 [1st edn. 1780]), p.115.
45. *Thoughts* (London, 1799), pp.6-7.
46. *The Wrongs of Women* (London, 1798), pp.92-3.
47. *Letters* (Stourbridge, 1804), p.55. See also the letter of 13 December, 1807 in E. Hall, (ed.), *Miss Weeton's Journal as a Governess* (London, 1969, 2nd edn.).
48. Cited in Peter Earle, *The World of Defoe* (London, 1976), p.267.
49. Grose, *Guide,* p.12.
50. *Domestic Medicine* (London, 1827 edn.), p.xiii.
51. Culpepper, *The English Physician* (Gainsborough, 1813). On abortifacients see B.D.H. Miller, 'She Who Hath Drunk Any Potion. . .,'*Medium Aevum,* 31 (1962), pp.188-93; R.V. Schnucker, 'Elizabethan Birth Control and Puritan Attitudes,' *Journal of Interdisciplinary History,* 5 (1975), pp.655-668; Lawrence Stone, 'Marriage Among the English Nobility in the Sixteenth and Seventeenth Centuries,' *Comparative Studies in Society and History,* 3 (1961), pp.182-206; A.D.J. Macfarlane, 'The Regulation of Marital and Sexual Relationships in Seventeenth Century England, with Special References to the County of Essex,' M.Phil. Thesis, London School of Economics (1968), p.154.
52. Defoe, *Conjugal Lewdness,* p.152.
53. R.R. Kuczynski, 'British Demographers' Opinions on Fertility 1660-1760,' in Lancelot Hogben, *Political Arithmetic: A Symposium of Popular Studies* (London, 1938), pp.283-330.
54. On evidence of family limitation see E.A. Wrigley, 'Family Limitation in Pre-Industrial England,' *Economic History Review,* 19 (1966), pp.82-109; Alan Macfarlane, *The Life of Ralph Josselin, a Seventeenth Century Clergyman* (Cambridge, 1970), p.83; David Levine, 'The Demographic Implications of Rural Industrialization; a Family Reconstitution Study of Shepshed, Leicestershire, 1600-1851,' *Social History,* 2 (1976), p.188.
55. H.W. Tytler, (ed. and trans.), Scevole de St. Marthe, *Paedotrophia; or the Art of Nursing and Rearing Children* (London, 1797), p.104.
56. N.L. Trantner, *Population Since the Industrial Revolution* (London, 1973), 41 ff.

PART TWO

CONTRACEPTION AND THE CLASS STRUGGLE

2 THE BEGINNING OF THE BIRTH CONTROL DEBATE

The rapid industrialisation of British manufacture and the accompanying unprecedented growth in population of the late eighteenth and nineteenth centuries led to massive social dislocations. In response to the challenges posed by mechanisation to traditional living and labouring patterns working people were to turn slowly from older forms of defensive action to the new political and social reform programmes of the Chartists and Owenites. But the underlying tenet of such movements, namely that rational men could create a more egalitarian and humane society, had already been met by T.R. Malthus in *Essay on Population* (1798). Attributing misery and poverty, not to the rise of manufacture, but to the bogey of 'over-population' Malthus was to see his name become inextricably associated in English men's minds with the advocacy of any form of fertility control. As a consequence the private practices of family limitation of the eighteenth century were to become the subject of public debate in the nineteenth.

The Malthusian ideology has been the subject of countless studies but the manner in which contraception figured in the discussion has been given short shrift. In this chapter the argument will be made that Malthusianism was not simply a demographic doctrine; its fundamental importance was as a new moral economy. Beginning with an overview of the familiar conservative, political dimensions of Malthusianism I intend to show how they necessarily led to a rejection of contraception which, it was feared, could undermine the premise that population pressures doomed in advance any hopes of major social changes. Once the Malthusians' position is understood the originality of the early birth control propagandists can be appreciated. The utilitarians, though they adopted Malthus' concern for population, jettisoned his moral conservatism and moved on to declare not only the morality but the social necessity of contraception.[1]

Malthus undertook his demographic investigations with the purpose of destroying Godwin's argument as advanced in *An Enquiry Concerning Political Justice* (1793) in favour of a sharing out of property. The result of such an utopian scheme, declared Malthus, would be that the

43

population would soon overshoot the food supply and be overwhelmed by vice and misery. For his contemporaries his most striking revelation, however, was not that food supplies were increasing in arithmetic and population in geometric progressions, but that the major cause of existing poverty was the 'reckless over-breeding of the poor'. Here was a modern, scientific justification for the maintenance of privilege in a society in which power was shifting from rural landowners to urban capitalists. Malthus had proved that despite the dreams occasioned by the French revolution reform was futile.

> A man is born into a world already possessed if he cannot get subsistence from his parents on whom he has a just demand, and if society do not want his labour, has no claim of right to the smallest portion of food, and, in fact, has no business to be where he is. At Nature's mighty feast there is no vacant cover for him. She tells him to be gone, and will quickly execute her orders.[2]

The crux of the Malthusian doctrine was that population growth was such that if not kept down by vice, misery or self-restraint, it would soon outstrip the means of feeding it. From this it followed that, first, the poor were responsible for their own misery and indeed endangered society as a whole by their over-breeding; secondly, the charity of the better-off simply aggravated the situation by providing a reward for improvidence; thirdly, the efforts of labour to force up wages were doomed because the wage fund (the ratio of capital to labour) could only respond to the iron law of supply and demand; and finally, the sole remedy was to educate the worker in the science of political economy so that on the one hand he could rationally understand his situation and the necessity of deferring marriage and on the other spurn the blandishments of radicals who suggested that there was any alternative.

The power of the Malthusian doctrine lay in its claims to be an objective, scientifically-proven analysis of reality. In the name of political economy the Malthusians guiltlessly advanced an argument that freed the wealthy from their traditional responsibility to the poor while burdening the latter with the moral onus of their plight. Even when handing down such a pitiless judgement on the lower classes economists were secure in the knowledge that they were not acting hypocritically; some would even claim that their message could be considered optimistic inasmuch as it held out the prospect of improvement to those who practised the virtues of thrift and foresight.

It was the use of Malthusian doctrines by opponents of the Poor Law that most dramatically focused attention on the population question. Shrugging off the charge that they were 'stoney-hearted and cold-blooded' the Poor Law reformers attacked charity – be it public or private – on the grounds that provisions for the poor were but bounties held out to the thriftless. Lord Brougham in his role as Lord Chancellor informed the House of Lords in 1834 that,

> Anything more mischievous, anything more fatal to the country, anything more calculated to multiply indefinitely the numbers of the poor, cannot be conceived than the applying to them of any regular and fixed provision. . .Those who framed the statute of Elizabeth were not adepts in political science – they were not acquainted with the true principles of population – they could not foresee that a Malthus would arise to enlighten mankind. . . – they knew not the true principles upon to which to frame a preventive check, or favour the prudential check to the unlimited increase of the people.[3]

This same message was voiced by a host of Malthusians. The Reverend George Glover declared that charity, by stripping the poor of the incentive to work, degraded and depraved them. The social investigator J.P. Kay claimed that in fact the source of poverty was the 'injurious legislation' which rewarded indigence. Pauperism, in the words of W.H. Bulwer, had become a profession.[4]

Working-class women were a favourite target of such writers, frequently caricatured as luxuriating in poverty. Save for a few years before and after marriage they would, stated Glover, spend their whole lives on relief. Charity available for the care of their children was, declared Kay, simply a bonus offered to the promiscuous: 'The most destitute and immoral marry to increase their claim on the stipend appointed for them by the law, which thus acts as a bounty on the increase of a squalid and debilitated race, who inherit from their parents disease, sometimes deformity, often vice, and always beggary.'[5] Similar tales of women seeking illegitimate births in order to have a better claim on the parish formed a standard part of the attack on the Old Poor Law. The New Poor Law with its stringent administration based on the policy of 'less eligibility' was a victory of sorts for Malthus' disciples though there were some who opposed public relief of any kind. Misery was the 'positive check' which held population at a reasonable level; it would have to remain so until the masses were educated to accept the necessity of the 'preventive check' of deferred marriage.

If the preventive or moral check were to be popularised it was necessary, so political economists recognised, to break the working classes to restraint and postponement of gratification. The only feasible way in which to implement such a policy was to win the minds of labour. John Wade, for example, toyed with the notion of some sort of legal restriction on marriage but came round to the idea of indoctrinating the masses with an ideology of temperance and foresight. The task was, as he admitted, a daunting one: 'The "immorality of marrying without the means of supporting a family" is a doctrine of recent promulgation, and can hardly yet be considered generally impressed on the understandings and feelings of the community.'[6] Yet as Richard Whately, Archbishop of Dublin, warned, if the poor were left uninformed of the truths of political economy there was the danger they would fall prey to Owenite agitators.

> There are some very simple but important truths belonging to the science we are now engaged in, which might with the utmost facility be brought down to the capacity of a child, and which, it is not too much to say, the Lower Orders cannot even safely be left ignorant of. . .Can the labouring classes, (and that too in a country where they have a legal right to express practically their political opinions,) can they safely be left to suppose, as many a demagogue is ready, when it suits his purpose, to tell them, that inequality of condition is inexpedient, and ought to be abolished — that the wealth of a man whose income is equal to that of a hundred labouring families, is so much deducted from the common stock, and causes a hundred poor families the less to be maintained; — and that a general spoiliation of the rich, and equal division of property, would put an end to poverty for ever?[7]

Whately answered that they could not and led the Malthusians in swamping the country with didactic tracts that spelled out in simple terms the laws of population. The model for this sort of literature had been already established by Mrs Jane Marcet's *Conversations on Political Economy* (1816) which was re-published in 1817, 1819, 1821, 1824, 1827 and 1839. A typical passage read:

> Caroline: No amelioration of the condition of the poor can than be permanent unless to industry they add prudence and foresight.
> Mrs. B: Certainly, were all men as considerate as your gardener,

Thomas, and did not marry till they had secured a provision for a family, or could earn a sufficiency to maintain it; in short, were children not brought into the world until there was bread to feed them, the distress which you have just been describing would be unknown, excepting in cases of unforeseen misfortunes, or unless produced by idleness or vice.[8]

Harriet Martineau produced similar tales aimed at a working-class audience in the *Illustrations of Political Economy*. With the avowed purpose of converting the masses to the dogmas of her friend, Malthus, she put into the mouths of Scottish crofters these words:

'And all this time,' continued Angus, 'these very quarrelers [farmers and fishermen] go on marrying early, and raising large families — that is, they bring offspring into the world while they are providing as fast as possible for their future starvation.' 'There is no reason to do here as the Romans did,' said Mr. Mackenzie, 'and as many other nations have done — no need to offer bounties for the increase of population.'
'I think not indeed,' said Ella, 'it seems a thing to be checked, rather than encouraged.'[9]

It was appropriate that women writers should have played such an important role in the popularising of population theories. It signified on one level the implicit middle-class belief that the moral instruction of workers — like that of children — could best be accomplished by females. More importantly, the role of women in determining family size was recognised by all writers who interested themselves in the subject of fertility control. Nicoll, for example, suggested that a way of holding down population was to improve employment opportunities for females: 'Increased employment for females would often tend to prevent imprudent marriages. A young woman who can obtain a very scanty subsistence — perhaps nothing beyond an allowance from the parish, will often marry for a home — this at least procures a present relief to her misfortunes and she has learned to think little of the future.' The result was, declared Nicoll, over-population but it could be avoided if women assumed the positions held by men in the service sector. The results would be doubly beneficial for '. . .in many shops the service by males is always unnecessary, and not seldom offensive' and a woman who worked would lay in a store for her future family.[10]
Half a century later Henry Fawcett, husband of the suffragist Millicent

Garrett, made similar attacks upon the laws that restricted women from certain trades.[11] The Malthusians included in their ranks a number of such 'feminists'; they wished to improve women's employment opportunities in order that marriage could be deferred and the population thus restricted.

Apart from the popular tracts there were other means which the Malthusians recognised could be utilised in providing correct 'moral instruction.' Wade spoke of '. . .institutions among ourselves of the nature of Temperate Societies which might be useful.' Kay lauded the potential of the Mechanics' Institutes and a popular press freed from restrictive taxes. And finally the upper classes were asked by these writers to participate in this education of the poor by setting an example and so give some credence to the notion that economic and moral advances did go together.[12]

The extent of the popularising activities of the Malthusians was impressive but more impressive still was the repeated complaint that the message had not yet been adequately presented. As late as 1862 Mrs Grote could, after the campaigns of Martineau and Marcet, still bewail the fact that, 'We have in vain listened for some one to tell the working classes that the secret of ameliorating their condition is to limit their numbers. Nobody will "bell the cat".'[13] For several generations the workers had apparently withstood the message that only by raising their moral standards could they escape poverty. Such obstinance was taken by the Malthusians to mean that the poor were listening to other theorists. Who were they? The Malthusians singled out for particular attention the anti-corn law leaders and supporters of emigration schemes, the Owenites, and finally the proponents of birth control.

The emigrationists and free traders provided short-term answers to the Malthusians' concerns in advocating either the export of surplus population or the importation of cheap food stuffs. Neither of these measures necessarily ran counter to Malthus' teachings; many of their advocates were sympathetic to his views. Nevertheless the more rigid Malthusians expressed the fear that both policies, in offering an apparent 'safety-valve' for population pressures, would be used by the masses as an excuse for sidestepping the vital issue of self-control. Thus Morrison and Fawcett would attack emigration as both an ineffective and expensive stop-gap measure.[14] Fawcett was similarly aroused by reports that some members of the working class were deluded into believing that the coming of free trade and cheap bread would somehow resolve the population issue. It was an obligation, he wrote, to inform them that the condition of the poor was not appreciably altered by the abolition of the corn laws.[15] Some might find such ruminations unduly gloomy; the Malthusians replied that the point was that no lasting economic benefits could accrue from any economic system if the prudence of the poor were not maintained.

Emigration schemes and anti-corn law agitation did not overly preoccupy the Malthusians; their main political concern was, of course, caused by those who sought by social reforms to redistribute the wealth of the nation and so provide the poor with unearned assistance. Malthus had originally launched his tract to answer the egalitarian propositions of Godwin and Condorcet. His disciples remained true to the course he had set. Nicoll stated that Robert Owen's plans for reform were simply 'amusing' but offered no answer to Malthus. Morrison, basing his pronouncements on the wage fund theory, declared that if the poor were to be assured of assistance and spared the 'physical check' of misery, all of Europe would be reduced to poverty in a generation. The same theory was wielded by Kay to prove that unions were their own worst enemies; by artificially forcing up wages they drove employers to introduce machinery that replaced skilled labour. Wade insisted that labour held the key to its own prosperity in self-restraint; the government was impotent when faced with the iron laws of economics. Symons concluded that even short-term advantages won by the worker could only be damaging: '. . .the highest paid artisans are usually the least virtuous'.[16]

The fact that the Malthusians were violently opposed to the social reformers and in particular the Owenite socialists was natural enough and has been noted by a number of commentators. What has escaped attention is the concern expressed by Malthus and his followers at the appearance of birth control propaganda which informed the public that the answer to population pressures lay, not in the deferment of marriage, but in the artificial control of fertility. Malthus' famous plea for 'moral restraint' consisted of asking the poor to postpone marriage for as long as possible. Some of his disciples went a step further and called on the poor to show as much foresight *after* marriage as before by practising abstinence. The main point is that Malthus was completely opposed to birth control in the sense of any means taken to prevent conception during intercourse. In the first edition of *An Essay on the Principle of Population* he specifically attacked Condorcet for alluding to such stratagems: 'To remove the difficulty in this way, will, surely, in the opinion of most men, be, to destroy that virtue and purity of manners, which the advocates of equality, and of the perfectibility of man, profess to be the end and object of their views.'[17] In the same spirit John Wade, when noting the activities of Francis Place and Richard Carlile in the 1820s, stated:

> To meet this dilemma [of population pressure] a class of philosophers has appeared, who have sought to divest marriage of its impoverishing consequences. I am venturing on delicate ground I am aware, but I do not see how I can discharge my duty to our present subject without some notice of a matter that has excited considerable attention. The speculations to which I am alluding have certainly given a shock to the public mind. . .

Wade would go no further in the discussion; he expressed the belief that to recommend, '. . .any artifice to frustrate conception might be positively mischievous, since, by the disgust it would excite, like an indecent attack on established religion, it would prevent the temperate investigation of a subject of national importance.'[18] A writer of like mind wrote to *The Times* that the Malthusians could in no way be legitimately associated with doctrines, '. . .at which enlightened and benevolent posterity will blush'. An anonymous pamphleteer agreed and censured the evils which resulted from '. . .the obstructive principle and anti-nuptial practice'.[19]

The economist J.R. McCulloch made it abundantly clear why, in the Malthusian's eyes, birth control was both economically and morally wrong.

> Could we subject the rate of increase to any easily applied physical control, few, comparatively, among the poorer classes, would be inclined to burden themselves with the task of providing for a family; [McCulloch adds in a footnote: The readiness with which the lower classes send their children to foundling hospitals seems sufficient proof of this.] and the most effective stimulus to exertion being destroyed, society would gradually sink into apathy and languor.[20]

The possibility of effective birth control thus posed a real threat to Malthusian doctrines for it permitted one to accept the demographic premises of the political economists while holding out a means by which they could be circumvented. The Malthusians' squeamishness on the subject of birth control was not occasioned by simple prudery; the same writers showed no hesitation when it came to discussing acts reputedly endemic to working-class areas such as infanticide or illegitimacy. Their concern was that the preaching of birth control could completely undermine both the economic and moral foundation of their argument. They saw in it a new optimistic ideology that ran counter to their own which held that civilisation was based on self-denial and progress on competition resulting from pressure of numbers. The Malthusians did not seek to abolish population pressures. At the very heart of their doctrine lay the belief that such a force was necessary to drive man — at least working-class man — from his naturally lethargic state. It was only an 'apprehended deficiency' of what N.W. Senior, author of the Poor Law Report of 1834, referred to as 'Necessaries, Decencies, and Luxuries' and Richard Jones, Malthus' successor at Haileybury, as 'Primary and Secondary wants' that inspired prudence and foresight.[21]

The inherent pessimism of the strict Malthusians in both morals and economics meant that they had to oppose contraception. If we turn to the utilitarians we find a different structure of thought displayed. They adopted much of Malthus' demographic data but were not prevented by either religious qualms or by any faith in the capability of the married poor to control family size by 'natural' means from accepting the logical necessity of contraception.[22] Thus in the utilitarian writings appeared the first formal statements arguing for the social necessity of birth control. Such apologies for the practice were first restricted to allusive asides. Jeremy Bentham referred in 'Situation and Relief of the Poor' (1797) to the use of 'sponges' to keep down the poor rate. James Mill, writing on the topic 'Colony' in the *Supplement to the Encyclopaedia Britannica* (1824) hinted that other means than emigration could be found to maintain a balanced population if '. . .the superstitions of the nursery were discarded'.[23] Middle-class radicals were not prepared to sacrifice their reputations by speaking more openly. Had they done so it is still unlikely that they would have won over many members of the working class, suspicious as they were of the utilitarians' motives. In the person of Francis Place, the 'radical tailor of Charing Cross', the Benthamites did have, however, a go-between who could carry out a campaign of propaganda in favour of contraception designed to win the attention of the artisan.[24]

In 1823 Place had unsigned handbills distributed in working-class districts in London and the midlands which explained in detail the use of the sponge and the withdrawal methods of contraception.[25] At the same time he sought the support of the well-known champion of the 'pauper press', Richard Carlile. Carlile, once won over, became the first man in England to put his name to a work devoted to the subject of birth control: *Every Woman's Book; or What is Love? Containing Most Important Instructions for the Prudent Regulation of the Principle of Love and the Number of the Family* (1826).[26] Carlile described three methods of prevention: the woman's use of the sponge as a crude diaphragm, the man's use of the *baudruche* or 'glove', and partial or complete withdrawal. The cautious approval of Carlile's book that was voiced by Robert Dale Owen in the American paper *New Harmony Gazette* brought down on him the charge of aiding in the propagation of immoral doctrines.[27] Dale Owen was in fact distressed by the style if not the content of Carlile's work and his unfounded assertion that his father, Robert Owen, had introduced French birth control techniques to Britain. To make his own position clear the younger Owen published *Moral Physiology: or a Brief and Plain Treatise on the Population Question* (New York, 1830; London, 1832). After devoting sixty-five of the pamphlet's seventy-two pages to a justification of the morality of contraception, Owen gave an account of the three methods recommended by Carlile but warned against the dangers of incomplete withdrawal. The work of the American physician Charles Knowlton, *Fruits of Philosophy or, the Private Companion of Young Married People,* which appeared in New York in 1832 and was reprinted in London in 1834 was the last of the early nineteenth-century birth control tracts and approached the queston in a more clinical fashion than the earlier ones. Knowlton's main contribution to the discussion was to cast doubts on the effectiveness of the sponge if it were not accompanied with a saline douching solution.[28]

Having noted the utilitarian heritage of the birth control movement the question inevitably posed is, was it, as its detractors in the popular press were to contend, simply a refined version of Malthusianism? Was it yet another means of forcing the poor to sacrifice themselves for the maintenancce of the rich? What was the general social ideology propounded by the birth controllers and how was it received by the spokesmen of the working-class movement?

The first impression one receives on reading the early literature on birth control is that all its disseminators were very much aware of the need to reply to the challenge that they were not the true friends of the working class; that by seeking to limit the labouring population they were serving the interests of the propertied. They saw as their first task the necessity of disassociating themselves from Malthus. Their arguments on population growth were, they admitted, based on his calculations but they held that their opinion of the working class' ability to improve its situation was diametrically opposed to Malthus' pessimistic prophecies. He had no understanding, stated Place, of the workers' ceaseless attempts at self-improvement: 'He can know but little of the shifts continually made to preserve a decent appearance. Of the privations endured, of the pains and sorrows which the working people suffer in private, of the truly wonderful efforts long continued, even in the most hopeless circumstances, which vast numbers of them make "to keep their heads above water".'[29] Malthus had sentenced the poor to a life, at best of abstinence, at worst of vice and misery. His call for late marriages, argued the birth controllers would, if acted upon, result in increased prostitution and immorality.[30] His plea for the ill-fed and uneducated to practice a moral restraint not demonstrated by their 'betters' was strangely hypocritical.

The birth controllers asserted that they were responding to a situation which Malthus had ignored. The working class was already using injurious means to attempt to regulate births and was thereby making known its desire for reliable methods. To supply the required knowledge would result in the elimination of abortion and infanticide.[31] It would spare women repeated unwanted pregnancies, attendant illnesses, and the dangers of miscarriage. The married would be more faithful and youth more chaste. Women would no longer be viewed as simple propagators of the species, but as men's helpmates. The plight of orphans, bastards, and women dying in labour or during induced abortions could, claimed the birth controllers, all be avoided.[32]

The birth controllers thus offered the lower classes a means of avoiding Malthus' options of either abstinence or misery. But did their propagation of a new solution to the population problem mean that they were nevertheless agreed with liberal economists that the poor were the authors of their own distress? The birth controllers were obviously sensitive to the charge that they offered only short-term palliatives. They responded by asserting that, in favouring immediate improvements, they were not seeking to postpone more fundamental forms of social change but providing for its advancement. 'Let us do the good we can do', wrote Carlile, 'and still pursue, and thus strengthen ourselves in the pursuit of that which is remote'.[33] A contributor to the *Newgate Monthly Magazine,* published by Carlile's shopmen, declared, 'That man cannot be a friend of the working classes who knowing an evil which affects them fails to point it out. . .'[34] It was over-population, contended the birth controllers, that led to extremes of wealth and poverty, of social and political inequality. If the working-class family was of moderate size it could win not only a more respectable standard of living but more time for self-improvement: '. . .all might be comfortably circumstanced and leisure and means for acquiring knowledge brought within reach'.[35] The healthy, educated worker would prove more successful in struggling for social reforms. No debased or ignorant people, wrote Place in reference to Ireland, had ever overthrown a tyranny.[36] The birth controllers were, in short, sketching out a theory that the rising expectations of the lower classes would be a force for, not against, social and political change. This was a remarkably modern view of politics, but one that owed its elaboration chiefly to the need to respond to the discrediting assertion that the birth controllers were defenders of the *status quo*.

The birth controllers presented themselves as social reformers. The limited nature of their radicalism was made clear, however, by the fact that after having declared at length their dissatisfaction with existing society, they tended to fall back on some variant of the wage fund theory. Accepting the premise that the amount of money available for wages was limited, they argued that workers could only avoid exploitation by limiting the supply of labour. Robert Dale Owen was the most cautious in spelling out the economic benefits of birth control; he described it as an 'alleviation', not a 'cure'.

It is true, and ought to be remembered, that the check I propose, by diminishing the number of labourers, will render labour more scarce and consequently of higher value in the market; and in this view, its political importance is considerable: but it may also be doubted whether our present overgrown system of commercial competition be not hurrying the labourer towards the lowest rate of wages, capable of sustaining life, too rapidly to be overtaken, except in individual cases, even by a prudential check to population.[37]

Place and Carlile were more sanguine. The effectiveness of unions, they contended, was restricted to opposing repressive legislation that interfered with the free movement of labour; they could not drive wages up beyond a level determined by the forces of supply and demand.[38] If the lower classes restricted the numbers entering the labour pool, however, they could command higher compensation. Working men would win sufficient wages for the support and comfort of their families; no longer would their women be driven into prostitution and their children into factory work.

Contraception was of course, not to be forced on the worker, but the knowledge of such an option had to be available. No truth was dangerous, declared Dale Owen; one was free to act only after having been informed of the choice.[39] Moreover it was frequently stated that only a small degree of family limitation was necessary to attain the economic advantages posited by the birth controllers. William Longson, a correspondent of Place, estimated that the prevention of only one or two births per hundred would make all the difference in the living standards of the poor.[40] A letter by 'Amicus' in Carlile's *Republican* included the assurance that he did not seek to have the population 'unnecessarily' restricted.[41] Knowlton even suggested that contraception would be used, not so much to restrict population growth *per se* as to permit it to take place in an orderly fashion: 'In my opinion, the effect would be a good many more families (and on the whole as many births), but not so many overgrown and poverty-stricken ones.'[42]

To appease the suspicions of those artisans who persisted in regarding any discussion of the population question as a ploy of the propertied classes, several of the birth controllers claimed the socialist Robert Owen as a comrade-in-arms. Place stated in a letter to the *Labourer's Friend* of 5 August, 1823 that the older Owen was preoccupied by the danger over-population could pose to his experimental communities and had visited France for the purpose of informing himself on methods of contraception.[43] The claim that Robert Owen had brought back such information to England was repeated by Carlile. The *Newgate Monthly Magazine* went so far as to assert that Owen's 'Society of Harmonists' in America was utilising certain contraceptive techniques.[44] Robert Owen was to deny these claims, but the fact that his son Robert Dale Owen produced *Moral Physiology* helped to buttress the argument that there was no necessary contradiction between defending contraception and struggling for a reformed society. The birth controllers, of course, insisted that the former should enjoy top priority. Robert Dale Owen stated that even the most perfect society could not function if over-populated. The *Newgate Monthly Magazine* followed the same line in declaring the knowledge of birth control as essential as good government: 'With this knowledge the co-operative communities may be prosperous, but without it they will not only devour themselves but augment an evil the consequences of which are even now grievous and lamentable.'[45]

The birth controllers concluded their argument that their activities were not part of a veiled attack upon the working class by pointing to

the hostility with which their pronouncements were met by the
wealthy. Though the birth controllers emphasised that an immediate
improvement in the living conditions of the poor depended more on
self-help than class struggle, they did suggest that the knowledge of
contraception had been kept secret by some sort of class conspiracy.
The theme that the lower classes should take advantage of methods
hitherto monopolised by the rich was repeatedly sounded. 'The
remedy has long been known in this country', wrote Carlile 'and to
the aristocracy in particular, who are always in search of benefits
which they can particularly hold, and be distinct from the body of
the labouring people.'[46] 'Do as other people do, [wrote Place] to
avoid having more children than they wish to have and cannot easily
maintain. What is done is this. . .'[47] Similarly, it is not unlikely that
Place's handbill 'To the Married of Both Sexes in the Genteel Life'
was so entitled to attract the curious artisan's eye.

The birth controllers were appealing to a suspicion of one's
'betters', not to class solidarity, but many of their pronouncements,
though lacking in political sophistication, were obviously gauged to
play on traditional hostilities. When Knowlton's publications led to
legal entanglements a defender attributed his persecution to the upper
classes' fear of an enlightened work force: 'He has made the knowledge
too cheap and that is not the worst of it, he has permitted common
people, people who can be benefitted by the knowledge to have access
to it.'[48] Carlile in response to attacks on his work retorted: 'The only
natural enemies that my book should find, are among the Royal
families, the Aristocracy, and the Priests, and that only because it is
calculated to elevate mankind above the injuries of their political and
religious machinations.'[49] Even their opposition was mere cant; they
already used the methods revealed to the poor in *Every Woman's Book:*
'. . .they would hold it as a luxury too good for the poor and too
dangerous to themselves politically in its enlightenment.'[50]

In parading his animosity towards the 'priests' Carlile was touching
on one aspect of the birth controllers' ideology that has been often
ignored — the natural interest free thinkers would have had in
contraception. Birth control would be for them the most dramatic way
in which freedom for the artisan from the moral dictates of christianity
could be demonstrated. The birth controllers not only adopted a
utilitarian, materialistic approach to morality, they waged an active
campaign against the forces of revealed religion. Robert Dale Owen
was relatively cautious in his dealings with the clergy. Carlile and
Knowlton went out of their way to attack the Church, the former

interspersing his examination of contraceptive practices with suggestive asides on the sexual proclivities of nuns and the phallic symbolism of the cross. The birth controllers were in turn lumped together as propagators of, '. . .a system combining blasphemy, atheism, infidelity, adultery, lewdness, removing all moral and religious and legal checks upon human depravity, and leading to a community of property and striking directly at tne foundation of civil society'.[51] Carlile's main preoccupation in the 1820s was in fact his crusade against priestcraft. He was attracted to birth control at least in part because it was the most direct way of attacking the moral hegemony of the Church.[52] In dedicating volume eleven of the *Republican* 'To Women' Carlile wrote,

> . . .you cannot be dutiful wives and mothers while you are religious. . .the religious mind must be in a certain ratio destitute of social and domestic affections, destitute of a degree of useful knowledge that might have been otherwise acquired, destitute of health that might have otherwise been studied and acquired, and estranged from all that is really good and solid in human happiness.[53]

Evil, he declared in the *Lion* of 10 October, 1828, was caused by '. . .the foul pretence of future-life-pleasures' which permitted sorrows such as unwanted children to be stoically accepted as part of God's plan.[54] Knowlton was of a similar opinion and insisted that it was his infidelity, which provided the basis for his birth control arguments, that was the real reason for his persecution.[55]

It would be the radical freethinkers James Watson (one of Carlile's shopmen), Henry Hetherington, John Cleave, Edward Truelove, and Austin Holyoake who distributed birth control tracts as part of their anti-clerical campaigns. Advertisements for these works were occasionally even carried in the penny papers which were ostensibly opposed to the doctrine of family limitation. For example publicity for Owen's *Moral Physiology* appeared in the *Examiner,* the *Crisis,* the *Poor Man's Guardian,* the *Destructive,* and the *Working Man's Friend and Political Magazine.* It has been estimated that 700 to a 1,000 copies of Knowlton's pamphlet were sold each year in England from 1834 to 1876 and that by 1877, 75,000 copies of Robert Dale Owen's were in print.[56] Witnesses before the Committee on the Factories Bill of 1832 and Dr Loudon's Medical Committee testified that 'certain books, the disgrace of the age' were circulating in working-class areas. In 1837 Dr Michael Ryan asked his readers, 'Are not the most revolting vices now unblushingly recommended in almost

every bye-street through which we pass?'[57] That the birth controllers
expected to meet opposition was made clear by the defensiveness
with which they advanced so many of their arguments. The question
now posed was how the leaders of the working-class movement would
respond to such overtures.

Notes

1. On the population debate see D.E.C. Eversley, *Social Theories of Fertility
   and the Malthusian Debate* (Oxford, 1959); D.V. Glass (ed.), *Introduction to
   Malthus* (London, 1953); G.T. Griffith, *Population Problems in the Age of
   Malthus* (London, 1967).
2. *An Essay on the Principle of Population* (London, 1803), p.531.
3. *Corrected Report of the Speech of the Lord Chancellor in the House of Lords*
   (London, 1834), pp.8, 29-30 cited in Nicolas C. Edsall, *The Anti-Poor Law
   Movement 1834-1844* (Manchester, 1971), p.20.
4. Glover, *Observations on the Present State of Pauperism in England* (London,
   1817), pp.1-4; Kay, *The Moral and Physical Condition of the Working Classes*
   (London, 1832), p.4; Bulwer, *England and the English* (London, 1833), I,
   p.208.
5. Glover, *Observations*, pp.5-6; Kay, *Working Classes*, p.47.
6. Wade, *History of the Middle and Working Classes* (London, 1833), p.335.
   See also Rev. W.F. Lloyd, *Two Lectures on Checks to Population* (London,
   1832), p.3.
7. Whately, *Introductory Lectures on Political Economy* (London, 1832),
   pp.201-2. See also J.M. Goldstrom, 'Richard Whately and Political Economy
   in School Books 1833-1880,' *Irish Historical Studies*, 15 (1966-1967),
   pp.131-46 and *The Social Content of Education 1808-1870. A Study of the
   Working-Class School Reader in England and Ireland* (Shannon, 1972);
   R.K. Webb, *The British Working-Class Reader 1790-1848* (New York, 1971
   2nd edn.).
8. Marcet, *Conversations on Political Economy* (London, 1839), p.135.
9. Martineau, *Illustrations of Political Economy no.6 Weal and Woe in Garveloch*
   (London, 1832), pp.43-4.
10. S.W. Nicoll, *A View of the Principles on Which the Well-Being of the Laboring
    Classes Depends* (London, 1819), pp.22, 23.
11. Fawcett, *Pauperism: Its Cause and Remedies* (London, 1871), p.99.
12. Wade, *History*, p.334; Kay, *Working Classes*, p.92 and see also the article of
    Arthur Houston in the *Working Man* (5 May 1866), p.274. On education see
    William Ellis, *Education as a Means of Preventing Destitution* (London, 1851)
    and Robin Gilmour, 'The Gradgrind School: Political Economy in the
    Classroom,' *Victorian Studies*, 11 (1967), pp.205-24.
13. Grote, *Collected Papers* (London, 1863), p.65.
14. Charles Morrison, *An Essay on the Relations Between Labour and Capital*
    (London, 1854), p.58; Fawcett, *Pauperism*, p.99.
15. Fawcett, *Pauperism*, p.109; see Leslie Stephen, *Life of Henry Fawcett*
    (London, 1886 5th edn.), 150 ff.
16. Nicoll, *A View*, p.3; Morrison, *An Essay*, p.60; Kay, *Working Classes*, p.207;
    Wade, *History*, p.207; Jelinger C. Symons, *Arts and Artisans at Home and
    Abroad* (Edinburgh, 1839), p.101. For the argument that *employers* could
    combine for self-defence see A.H. Moreton, *Civilization or a Brief Analysis*

of the Natural Laws that Regulate the Numbers and Condition of Mankind (London, 1836), pp.70-75.

17. Malthus, *An Essay on the Principles of Population* (London, 1798), p.154.
18. Wade, *History,* pp.327, 337.
19. Anon., *An Appeal to the Editors of The Times Newspaper in Behalf of the Working Class* (London, 1845), p.37; Agrestis, *Thoughts on Population and the Means of Comfortable Assistance* (London, 1863), pp.25-6.
20. McCulloch, *The Principles of Political Economy* (Edinburgh, 1849 4th edn.), p.242. On the need for such stimuli see also R.W. Hamilton, *The Institutions of Popular Education* (London, 1843), p.8.
21. N.W. Senior, *An Outline of the Science of Political Economy* (London, 1849), p.42; W. Whelwell, (ed.), *Literary Remains Consisting of the Lectures and Tracts of the Late Reverend Richard Jones* (London, 1859), pp.245-6.
22. On the early birth control movement see J.A. Field, *Essays on Population* (Chicago, 1931); Norman E. Himes, *Medical History of Contraception* (Baltimore, 1936); J.A. Banks, *Prosperity and Parenthood: A Study of Family Planning Among the Victorian Middle Class* (London, 1954); F.H. Amphlett Micklewright, 'The Rise and Fall of English Neo-Malthusianism,' *Population Studies,* 15 (1961-1962), pp.32-51.
23. Bentham, *Annals of Agriculture and Other Useful Arts,* 29 (1797), p.422; Mill, *Supplement to the Encyclopedia Britannica* (Edinburgh, 1824), III, p.261.
24. On Place's role see the notes and introduction of Norman E. Himes to Francis Place, *Illustrations and Proofs of the Principle of Population* (London, 1930).
25. G.J. Holyoake, *Sixty Years of an Agitator's Life* (London, 1900), I, 126 ff.; Norman E. Himes, 'The Birth Control Handbills of 1823,' *Lancet,* n.s. 3 (6 August, 1927), pp.313-17; and see also the documents conserved at the British Museum in the Place Collection, 68.
26. *What is Love?* first appeared in Carlile's *Republican* (6 May, 1825) and was brought out as a pamphlet in February 1826. Eight editions were produced by 1828. Carlile's imprisoned shopmen supported his argument in the *Newgate Monthly Magazine.* See Carlile to Place (8 August, 1822), Place to Carlile (17 August, 1822; 1 September, 1824), Place Collection 68; Place to Carlile, *Republican,* 10 (12 November, 1824), 581.
27. *Free Enquirer* (7 August, 16 October, 23 October, 1830).
28. Norman E. Himes, 'Charles Knowlton's Revolutionary Influence on the English Birth Rate,' *New England Journal of Medicine,* 199 (1928), pp.461-5.
29. Place, *Illustrations,* p.155.
30. Knowlton, *Fruits of Philosophy* (London, 1841), pp.7-8; Owen, *Moral Physiology* (New York, 1831), p.25.
31. Carlile, *Every Woman's Book* (London, 1838), p.19; Owen, *Moral Physiology,* p.36; Knowlton, *Fruits of Philosophy,* p.40.
32. Carlile, *Every Woman's Book,* pp.23-4; Knowlton, *Fruits,* p.37; Owen, *Moral Physiology,* p.35.
33. *Lion* (3 October, 1828).
34. *Newgate Monthly Magazine* (1 June, 1826).
35. *Newgate Monthly Magazine* (1 January, 1826).
36. Place Collection, 68.
37. Owen, *Moral Physiology* (London, 1832, 8th edn.), p.25. This section on the wage fund was not included in earlier editions.
38. On Place's laissez-faire views see Place to George Rogers (15 January, 1832), Place Collection, 68; W.E.S. Thomas, 'Francis Place and Working-Class History,' *Historical Journal,* 5 (1962), pp.61-70; Brian Harrison, 'Two Roads to Social Reform: Francis Place and the Drunken Committee of 1834,'

Historical Journal, 11 (1968), pp.272-300.

39. Owen, *Moral Physiology,* p.19.
40. William Longson, 'Letter I: On Population and Their Wages; Addressed to the Labouring Classes by an Operative Weaver,' (15 September, 1824), Place Collection, 68.
41. *Republican* (5 May, 1826).
42. Knowlton, *Fruits,* p.40; see also Knowlton to the *Boston Investigator* (11 January, 1833).
43. Place to the *Labourer's Friend* (5 August, 1823).
44. *Newgate Monthly Magazine* (1 January, 1826) and for the continuation of the myth see the *Black Dwarf* (24 September, 1823; 1 October, 1823); Holyoake, *Sixty Years,* I, 126 ff.; J.F.C. Harrison, *Robert Owen and the Owenites in Britain and America: The Quest for the New Moral World* (London, 1969), p.61. Owen denied the charge in a letter to the *Morning Chronicle* (8 October, 1827).
45. *Newgate Monthly Magazine* (1 June, 1826). William Thompson foresaw the possible use of some 'preventive check' in his reformed community but his main interest was in the advantages it held for the health of women. See chapters four and five.
46. Carlile, *Every Woman's Book,* pp.25-6; and see also Owen, *Moral Physiology,* pp.37-8.
47. Place, 'To the Married of Both Sexes of the Working People,' Place Collection, 68
48. *Boston Investigator* (15 February, 1833).
49. *Lion* (3 October, 1828).
50. *The Lion* (3 October, 1828).
51. S.D. Parker, *Report on the Argument of the Attorney of the Commonwealth at the Trial of Abner Kneeland for Blasphemy* (Boston, 1834), p.89.
52. G. Aldred, *Richard Carlile, Agitator: His Life and Times* (London, 1923).
53. *Republican* (1 January, 1825), preface; see also the writings of Eliza Sharples Carlile in the *Isis* of 1832.
54. *The Lion* (10 October, 1828); Place also spoke of the need to overcome the 'squeemishness' induced by religious teachings; Place to *Morning Chronicle* (30 August, 1825).
55. Charles Knowlton, *A History of Recent Excitement in Ashfield* (Boston, 1833); *Two Remarkable Lectures* (Boston, 1833); *Elements of Modern Materialism* (Adams, Mass., 1829); for Knowlton's lectures in Frances Wright's Hall of Science, see the *Correspondent* (11 April, 6 June, 1829) and the *Free Enquirer* (6 May, 10 June, 1 July, 22 July, 1829).
56. On circulation figures see D.V. Glass, *Population Policies and Movements in Europe* (London, 1967), 31 ff; Himes, 'Charles Knowlton,' pp.461-5; F.B. Smith, 'The Atheist Mission, 1840-1900,' in Robert Robson, (ed.), *Ideas and Institutions of Victorian Britain: Essays in Honour of George Kitson Clark* (London, 1967), p.220.
57. Ryan, *Philosophy of Marriage* (London, 1837), p.6.

3 CONTRACEPTION AND WORKING-CLASS MOVEMENTS

Despite the efforts of the birth controllers to disentangle their ideology from that of Malthus' the general public continued to associate any discussion of fertility control with his teachings. To understand the response to the proposals made by the birth controllers it is first necessary to say something of the reaction to Malthusianism. It was, despite the objections of its formulators, popularly perceived as a self-serving doctrine produced by the upper classes for the purpose of controlling the lower classes. It was natural that the defenders of the poor, both radical and traditionalist, would be forced to reply. They countered by damning Malthus' message as immoral; they then offered their own analyses of England's economic woes; finally they advanced hypotheses of how population growth could be curbed without recourse to positive or preventive checks.[1]

The strongest element in the criticism of Malthus lay in the charge that his theory was not scientific but class-biased, not objective but immoral. What was especially striking was the extent to which traditional morality was relied upon, even by radicals, to meet a recognisably powerful and persuasive argument. The labour organiser John Doherty referred to Malthusianism as this 'Infernal Philosophy.' The *National Cooperative Leader* castigated it as this 'dismal and blasphemous creed.' The conservative Michael Sadler accused Malthus of cruelty, corruption and gross impartiality in creating an unchristian system. The economist G.P. Scrope declared that Malthus had the temerity to write, '. . .that human suffering is *not* the consequence of human error, but the necessary result of the law of God and nature; — that no relief offered by legal or spontaneous charity to the miserable *can* mitigate misery. . .'[2] These Scrope condemned as 'anti-social and barbarizing errors' which encouraged the indolence of the rich and the pessimism of the poor. The radical conservative Richard Oastler declared:

> I wish, Sir, that we could obliterate the party names, which serve only to bewilder, and hereafter be known as the followers of *Christ* or of *Malthus*. Then we should know who are the friends, and who the foes of the poor and needy, and those institutions which were

established, to defend their rights, against the gripe of the covetous worshippers of Mammon.[3]

The Tory lawyer Archibald Alison agreed that there was in fact no problem which Christian benevolence could not solve.[4]

The strange twist of logic executed by Malthus so that the miserable were expected to manifest a self-restraint not demonstrated by their social superiors drew the fire of a long line of anti-Malthusians. In addressing the National Association for the Promotion of Social Science the Christian Socialist J.M. Ludlow asked how it was that economists forbade the worker to use unions to restrict the labour pool while they advised him to restrict the size of his family.

> What! you bid the working man, by disciplining his will, by the severest self-restraint, for the sake of rendering his labour scarce, and therefore, of gaining a higher price for it; you bid him, I say, bind down those family instincts which are, in one view, the very safety-valves of society; and you would fain discourage him from endeavouring, by every means which the like discipline and self-restraint can afford, to wring by combination the highest price for his labour without stifling those instincts![5]

Such a plan was not simply unfair, it was, declared Thomas Carlyle, unworkable: 'O wonderful Malthusian prophets! Millenniums are undoubtedly coming, must come one way or the other: but will it be, think you, by twenty millions of working people simultaneously striking work in that department [marriage] ; passing, in universal trades-union, a resolution not to beget any more till the market become satisfactory?'[6] The same sort of ridicule was evident in Scrope's condemnation of the theory of postponed marriages as '. . .the *ne plus ultra* of moonstruck, Laputan, philosophy.'[7]

These attacks on Malthus were not restricted to the writings of economists and moralists. The anti-Malthusians also produced a popular literature designed to meet the propagandising efforts of Marcet and Martineau. Charles Dickens' Scrooge in *A Christmas Carol* was to become the best-known personification of the Malthusian miser; for a similar satirical view one can turn to 'Ode to Malthus' in which the radical poet Thomas Hood has his Malthusian grumbling:

> There is a dreadful surplus to demolish,
>   And yet some Wrongheads,

> With thick not long heads,
> Poor metaphysicians!
>   Sign petitions
>   Capital punishment to abolish;
> And in the face of censuses such vast ones
>   New hospitals contrive
>   For keeping alive,
> Laying first stones, the dolts! instead of last ones![8]

In the Owenite journal, the *New Moral World,* a play entitled 'Community' by the reverend Joseph Marriott answered such fears. Leon, a visitor to the socialist commune, is assured by Eliza that when labour is organised the population problem disappears. And she continues, 'To be candid with you too, I do not like Malthus and I and the other women in the community exerted ourselves so much, that we prevented a statue being erected in this country to his memory. . .If he were here, we would punish him by making him the only old bachelor among us.'[9]

In the popular press there were repeated attacks on the Malthusian contention that unemployment was a 'natural' problem which could only be overcome by a restriction of the labour pool.

> If Messrs Malthus, M'Culloch, Place & Co are to be believed, the working classes have only to consider how they can most effectively restrict their numbers, in order to arrive at a complete solution of all their difficulties. . .Malthus & Co. . .would reduce the whole matter to a queston between Mechanics and their sweethearts and wives rather than a question between the employed and their employers — between the Mechanic and the corn-grower and monopolist — between the tax payer and the tax inflictor.[10]

The *Trades Newspaper* declared that the Malthusians' intention was to make marriage among the poor harmless to the rich. The Brighton *Co-operator* noted that the spectre of over-population had been conjured up by the propertied classes; labourers knew instinctively that no problem would be posed once the 'consuming non-producers' were eliminated. The *Labourer's Friend and Handicraft's Journal* described Malthus' propositions as 'monstrous;' Bronterre O'Brien thundered, '. . .in spite of the devil and Malthus the work people are resolved to live and breed'.[11]

The opponents of Malthus did not say that population pressure would never pose a problem to society but they insisted that one served the forces of reaction in suggesting that it should be dealt with before social reform. Richard Carlile was of this opinion when he first broached the question in 1822: 'I maintain. . .*that bad government and a priesthood constitute the evil which at present degrade* [sic] *the people of this country. . .I will never complain of too many human beings, whilst all these removable evils exist.*'[12] Carlile later abandoned this position but the bulk of the working-class press continued to argue that the discussion of numbers only hindered the advancement of social reform; if there were a problem it could only be resolved in an equitable fashion after the establishment of good government. The *Black Dwarf* declared that one could not talk of lack of food as a sign of population pressure as long as one man expended that which could keep another hundred men alive. The *Northern Star* stated that after the upper classes had eliminated every social inequality the regulation of population could be discussed. Four hundred years would pass, the *London Dispatch* predicted, before it was a serious issue.[13]

Turning to the political ramifications of population control the *Black Dwarf* asked what would be the consequences of a restricted labour pool. The answer was that the workers would still be forced to accept subsistence wages; to contend that they were able to bargain freely and so push up salaries was ludicrous. But would family limitation be a good thing if it only improved the health of the people? The editor of the *Black Dwarf* replied that it would not if the effect of improved conditions was to postpone reform.

> The natural remedy for such a corrupt state of things, is the INCREASE of population, even to the extreme of pressure against the means of subsistence, for it is the nature of the multitude to bear with oppression and want, as long as their animal necessities will permit them; and it is only by reducing them to a state bordering on despair, that they will ever be induced to avenge their wrongs, or to claim their rights.[14]

This idea that the misery that attended population growth in an unreformed society was a harbinger of revolution had been earlier enunciated by Piercy Ravenstone in his attack on Malthus: 'The wretchedness of a people is a sure forerunner of revolt.'[15]

Whereas the working class movement's ethical critique of Malthus drew heavily from Christian teachings on charity it relied for its economic arguments on the new labour theory of value sketched out

by William Thomson, John Gray, and Thomas Hodgkin.[16] Its central
tenet was that as labour was the producer of all value so too it should
gain, not simple subsistence, but the full benefits of its product. Thomas
Hopkins, the early socialist, noted that labour produced ever greater
wealth but was deprived of its fruits. This deprivation was not due to
population pressure; it was the growing citizenry which permitted the
division of labour. It was not due to a 'law of nature' but to '. . .the
unjust and rapacious regulation of society'. Drawing on his studies of
London, Henry Mayhew came to the same conclusion. The population
was increasing but not as fast as profits. The task was to redistribute
wealth, not dissuade the poor from marrying. J.F. Bray, whose work
was a synthesis of Owenism and anti-Ricardian economics, denied the
existence of any 'glut of labour'. Each man produced more than he
consumed; support for each should therefore pose no problem. This
stance was also adopted by Charles Bray, a Coventry ribbon
manufacturer drawn to the Owenites. While acknowledging that some
workers could not find employment, he pointed out that the population
pressure was not the cause. Unemployment was a consequence of the
introduction of machinery from which labour should have benefited but
did not.[17] Machines were similarly regarded by Ludlow who asked what
kind of a society it was in which they were cherished but children
viewed as burdens.

> Of all the hypocrisies which this country has seen go forth under
> high heaven, I know none more insolent than that of modern
> plutonomy, inculcating 'the prudential check' upon working man,
> and advocating the unlimited, unregulated, introduction of
> machinery. . .If there is a morality of the one action, there is also
> of the other; if the one current of production is to go on
> unrestrained at the hands of one class, why not the other too?[18]

The answer was that Malthus had not provided an objective analysis
of reality. His class bias was such, wrote Hopkins, that the upper classes
found in his pages freedom from social responsibility and flattery for
their foresight. The poor, wrote Vincent, found in these same pages
that they were to be punished for their poverty. When one spoke of
abstaining from marriage, declared Livesy of the *Moral Reformer,* one
referred only to restricting the marriage of workers. In the existing
society married life offered the poor the only margin of security in
times of illness and old age but, as Rickards pointed out, Malthus was
now asking them to abandon even this refuge. In Hickson's eyes

marriage was a school for responsibility and temperance; if the working class was prevented from entering it the result would not be greater abstinence but increased prostitution and criminality.[19]

The hub of the anti-Malthusian argument was that population pressure did not cause poverty; poverty caused population pressure. If you wanted to make the poor prudent it would be first necessary to provide a standard of living which it would be prudent to seek to maintain. In short they had to be given a stake in society, an idea which manifested itself in a number of land reform projects which were to surface in the course of the century. In the late eighteenth century Thomas Spence and William Ogilvie had asserted that the establishment of small holdings was the best way in which to increase the numbers and happiness of the population.[20] In the early nineteenth century both Robert Owen and William Cobbett had somewhat similar ideas that land reform would favour population growth. Under the impact of Malthus' pessimistic prognostications, however, those in favour of such policies began to reverse the argument. Alison, Hennell, and Bray, citing French evidence, declared that the provision of small farms helped to *curb* population increases. Samuel Laing junior argued that the worker in being driven off the land lost all constraints previously associated with property holding. He followed his father, Samuel Laing senior, in lauding the small holding as providing an 'economical constraint'. W.T. Thornton in *Over-Population and its Remedy* (1846) and *A Plea for Peasant Proprietors* (1848) brought together the arguments of those in favour of land redistribution so effectively that he won the support of many liberals including John Stuart Mill. Indeed one of the peculiarities of the demand for reform of the existing land settlement at mid-century was the fact that it united Chartists such as Fergus O'Connor, James Bronterre O'Brien and Ernest Jones with liberals such as Thornton and Mill.[21] The idea of giving the poor a stake in society rested on the assumption that misery had social, not natural, causes. It was in Scrope's words, not the product of unchanging laws but of '. . .the force or fraud of the powerful, and the control of unjust or unwise institutions'. If the standard of living was raised the population would be naturally restrained. According to Alison this would occur because the prospect of new wants would instil 'habits of foresight'. Rickards agreed that population was self-regulating and was moderated in its growth as civilisation advanced.[22]

It was symptomatic of an age fascinated by biological discoveries that a number of anti-Malthusians went on to attempt to prove how certain physiological changes occasioned by improvements in standard of living would naturally restrict fertility. In 1816 John Weyland noted the 'number of childless and unmarried among the higher orders' and attributed his finding to a dispensation of Providence that picked them out as the mental leaders of the community and freed them of the burden of children. Their affections were lavished not on offspring but on the nation. Weyland hailed increasing female celibacy as yet another sign of the progress of 'superior delicacy'.[23] Turning from the dispensations of Providence to those of nature Charles Loudon in *Equilibrium of Population and Sustenance Demonstrated* (1836) argued that extended breast-feeding held fertility in check. Loudon was opposed to contraception: 'No excuse can justify the means employed for non-conception and abortion.'[24] Natural control was available as long as women fulfilled their maternal duty of nursing.

Loudon's argument was criticised by a fellow anti-Malthusian, Thomas Doubleday, who, in *The True Law of Population,* declared that diet lay at the root of the population problem. Good eating led to less prolific breeding and vice versa. As evidence he cited the Irish who had the poorest diets and the largest families. The reason was that seminal fluid was alkaline in nature and a poor vegetable diet exacerbated the situation leading to 'an alkalescent state'. To control fertility it was necessary to neutralise the semen by raising the acid level through the consumption of more expensive foods such as wine and white bread. Thus as living standards improved the families of the poor could be expected to diminish in size.[25] William Hickson, a noted educationalist and reformer took up Doubleday's food argument. In *An Essay on the Principle of Population in Refutation of the Theory of the Rev. T.R. Malthus* (1849) Hickson sketched out a cultural theory that the higher the animal the lower the fecundity. In the human race luxury led to small families and poverty to large. The argument pointed toward the necessity of improving the lot of the working class while 'artificial' birth control was, as in the case of Loudon, condemned: 'Any scheme of this kind acted upon by the educated classes (as it is said to be by some portion of them on the Continent), if confined to those classes, must always have the effect of adding to the disproportion, already too great, between the ignorant and the intelligent. . .'[26]

These theories of fertility control might appear bizarre but they obviously filled the need of providing a 'scientific' counter-argument to Malthus' doctrine. The most influential formulation of this sort was Herbert Spencer's 1852 article, 'A Theory of Population, Deduced from the General Law of Animal Fertility.' Spencer presented population as a prime agent for progress, not a scourge. It made man more sociable, more efficient and so played a vital role in evolution. Population would not expand forever, however, because of an inverse ratio of brain size and fertility. The greater the mental activity the less the sperm production.

> Thus, the fact that intense mental application, involving great waste of the nervous tissues, and a corresponding consumption of nervous matter for their repair, is accompanied by a cessation in the production of sperm-cells, gives strong support to the hypothesis that the sperm-cells consist essentially of neurine. And this becomes yet clearer on finding that the converse fact is true — that undue production of sperm-cells involve cerebral inactivity.[27]

Following this schema the more intelligent would be less likely to over-breed and more likely to make better use of their environment. Here was a totally optimistic doctrine that stood Malthus on his head. This 'physiological check' was to figure centrally in several later anti-Malthusian works; in particular W.R. Greg's 'Malthus Notwithstanding' and the anonymous *Malthus: Re-examined by the Light of Physiology* (1868). This faith in a self-regulating mechanism culminated in the works of Walter Bagehot. Slighly refining Spencer's theory Bagehot differentiated between the two sexes' role in diminishing fertility. For women simple mental activity was sufficient to limit births.

> Probably of all the causes which regulate the pace of population, the nervous state of the woman is the most important, and it seems to have a kind of cyclical course as society advances. . .education and the habit of using the mind tend almost certainly to diminish the producing power. There is only a certain quantity of force in the female frame, and if that force is invested, so to say, in one way, it cannot be used in another.

For men it was clearly not quite the same; they had always been using their minds. If they were less fertile in the modern world it had to be due, not just to mental effort but to the *anxiety* engendered by industrial society: 'But anxiety, as has been said, does so tell, and we have seen that there is reason to believe that it much tends to slacken the growth of population; and probably, any of the higher exercises of the mind, which cause as they all do obscure and subtle pain, have a similar effect.'[28]

It was natural that the working class press should have welcomed the writings of theorists who held that the population problem would be resolved by raising the standard of living of labour. But how did it respond to the arguments advanced by Place, Carlile and Owen that in the short run the working class should adopt contraceptive tactics? This suggestion was met in the popular press with unrelieved hostility. The main reason for this animosity was that, protest as they may, the birth controllers were invariably portrayed as Malthus' creatures. Cobbett described Carlile as an '. . .instrument in the hands of others. . . He is a tool, a poor half-mad tool, of *the enemies of reform.* He wants no reform, for the end of his abominable book, is, to show, that the sufferings of the people do not *arise from the want of reform;* but from the *"indiscreet breeding" of the women!'* 'A retailer of the wisdom of Francis Place' and a 'bought tool of the Malthusian party' were the labels used by the *London Mercury* to damn writers sympathetic to birth control.[29]

The argument of the birth control propagandists that the artisan could improve his lot by following the lead of his 'betters' in adopting contraception was ineffective. Indeed it ran counter to both the political analysis of the reformers and the traditional popular portrayals of aristocratic degeneracy. Outraged articles on the debased sexual habits of the wealthy were a familiar feature of the popular press. Indications that contraceptive practices were percolating down the social structure were construed as a spread, not of enlightenment, but of debasement. 'Thus we may trace to our artificial right of property, by neither a long nor a circuitous route, that vanity, — that excessive love of expense, in all classes, which makes prostitutes of our women and fraudulent knaves of our men, and plunges all classes in vices and crimes.'[30]

Underlying the political opposition of the working-class movement to birth control was a hostility born of a traditional morality. It was a reluctance to interfere with the workings of God, providence or nature that made the suggestions of the birth controllers appear even more shocking than those of Malthus. A strong element of anti-clericalism ran through much of the writings of the Owenites and Chartists but this manifested itself primarily in attacks on the Church, not on Christian morality. Indeed it was frequently stated by the popular press that the object of overthrowing the tutelage of the clergy was to permit the artisan to return to the simple teachings of the primitive church. On those infrequent occasions when the working-class press distinguished between the Malthusians and the birth controllers, the message of the latter was always characterised as the more immoral.

> The supply and demand philosphers again divide themselves into two parties; one which is named after its leader, Mr Malthus, and the other, which is without a name, because nobody has as yet been found so regardless of public opinion, as openly to couple his name with its almost nameless doctrines. The Malthusians content themselves with simply expounding the abstract doctrine, that when the working classes cannot subsist by what the employing classes choose to give them for their labour, they are necessarily too numerous, and have themselves to blame for being so. But the nameless take a wide stride beyond this; they do not choose, like the Malthusians, *to leave matters where they found them, and trust to Providence for a remedy;* they think it wise to go a shorter way to work, and try their own hand at mending the order of things; they have no idea of allowing Madame Nature to go on as they say she has been doing, in overpeopling the domains of capital, and are determined to place such checks upon her prolific propensities, that she shall produce just as many labourers, and no more, as are wanted to do the work of those only lords of creation (in the eyes of the Nameless), the holders of a thousand pounds a year and upwards.[31]

This defence of the workings of 'Madame Nature' and attacks on 'unnatural' acts found a place in all the arguments opposing birth control. The *Examiner* declared simply, 'It is unnatural to check the increase of population.' The *Bulldog* likened those who followed such practices to catamites and prostitutes. For the *Trades Newspaper* these acts were a 'damning impiety,' unnatural manoeuvres analogous to, '. . . a mill going constantly, yet grinding nothing, except the tithe boll of the parson; a gardener setting out potatoes but first cutting all the eyes out of them; a hen hatching marbles; what a foil is to a sword, or glove to the hands of a boxer'. The *Black Dwarf* insisted that it was not worried about 'the ordinary cant about violating the laws of nature' but then repeated the argument that contraception was immoral, both in itself and because one would be led inevitably from 'prevention to destruction' of children.[32]

In *On Population* (1820) Godwin was responding to Malthus but his portrayal of a beneficent nature was to be taken over by the opponents of birth control: 'She has not left it to the caprice of the human will, whether the noblest species of beings that She has planted on this earth, shall continue or not. She does not ask our aid to keep down the excess of human population.'[33] As the spokesmen for a movement which they believed was ordained by providence or nature to be the natural development of human society, the writers of the working-class press treated the suggestion that the lower classes utilise 'artificial' means to regulate family size as unacceptable. Such a plan, in their eyes, implied that the birth controllers did not even have the Malthusians' confidence in the poor's prudence and self-control. So ready were the writers of the 'pauper press' to respond to such supposed slurs that they were at times led to argue in favour of what was, in everything but name, Malthus' moral restraint.

> To marry, with no other prospect than want before you is to do a very wicked thing, for the same nature which dictates to you to marry dictates to you the duty of providing for your offspring. But beyond the necessity of making this provision we know of no restriction to which the state of marriage can or ought to be subjected.[34]

Birth control offered and symbolised a new individualism. It is not surprising that it should have been viewed with suspicion by men who stressed the citizen's responsibilities to nature and the community. The contraception controversy revealed the extent to which the spokesmen of the working-class movement shared with traditional moralists the belief that the family was the source of all public morality and the sacrifice of individual pleasures the basis of social cohesion.

> . . .it is one of the clearest duties of a citizen to give birth to his like, and bring offspring to the state. Without this he is hardly a citizen: his children and his wife are pledges he gives to the public for good behaviour; they are his securities, that he will truly enter into the feeling of a common interest, and be desirous of perpetuating and increasing the immunities of his country from generation to generation.[35]

Opponents of birth control concluded that the question was not if the individual had a right to contraception, and in particular if the woman had a right to avoid unwanted pregnancies; the question was if self-interest was to prevail over loyalty to class and community.

What did the average artisan think of the debate? It is difficult to tell but there is evidence that the press was successful in fixing in some working-men's minds the idea that contraception was a highly individualistic act prompted by selfishness, an act unworthy of the artisan who had faith in either God or the forces of reform. A letter addressed to Francis Place provides an indication of the quandary in which some would find themselves.

> Sir having read in the Republican your Advice for Regulating Family according to their Income By Means of Preventing Conception and as I Am situated as a Journeyman Shoe Maker I find it moor than I Can Do to Support My Present Family which Is myself wif & 4 Children under seven years of Age and I'm likely to have as many moor Should Life Remain, So I have taken the liberty of Applying to you in hopes you will Be So Kind as to Inform Me of all the means I Am to Apply to Prevent me from Being Launched further into Poverty By having a Larger Family and I should wish to git through without coming to a Workhouse Though I believe that Need not be the case under a Better system than what we live under. So By Such Information you will much oblige your Humble Servant
>
> Benjamin Base[36]

What of the anti-Malthusian Owenites? More than one historian has suggested that they were both feminists and birth controllers. J.F.C. Harrison wrote of '. . .the Owenites championing of feminism, divorce and birth control'. D.E.C. Eversley has stated, 'The main demands for women's rights and the forecast of a reduction in the birth rate as a consequence, has come from socialist thinkers.' David Martin has recently written, 'Many Owenites saw artificial birth control as necessary to maintain the stability of agrarian communities.'[37] This belief that the early socialists favoured the birth control campaign springs firstly from the idea that, because Robert Dale Owen wrote tracts in favour of it, his father Robert Owen must have been similarly inclined. Secondly, it arises from an acceptance of the contemporary reports that the Owenites were using some means to control fertility in their communities. As early as 1819 Hutches Trowser wrote to David Ricardo, 'It is a pity your friend Malthus had not been a Physician, instead of a Member of the Church, as probably he might have been more successful than Mr. Owen in discovering a check for population.'[38]

The claim that the Owenites were carrying out sexual experiments formed part of the anti-socialist propaganda; the cry was repeatedly raised that reformers were seeking to destroy the family. Ralph Wardlaw in *Lectures on Female Prostitution* (1842) described, '. . .a class of persons, that has recently risen up among us, and whose members have given themselves "a local habitation and a name", whose system of principles disowns the word *illicit* altogether. In regard to the intercourse of the sexes, they deny the legitimate authority of any restriction, admit no rule but that of natural impulse, and would reduce us to the *socialisme* of the brutes.' Wardlaw declared himself most concerned, not by Owen's economic theories but by his desire for, '. . .the abrogation of the connubial bond, and the substitution for it of the indiscriminate intercommunion of the sexes, according to all the irregularities of temporary libidinous inclination'.[39] An equally colourful description of socialism was drawn by G. Simmons in *The Working Classes; Their Moral, Social, and Intellectual Condition* (1849): 'One of the worse effects of Socialism is the weakening of the family tie; to them there is nothing sacred, nothing which seems to inspire them with more respect for their own kindred than for others.'[40]

But, upon close examination, the writings of the early communitarians such as Robert Owen, Goodwyn Barmby, and James Morrison who were known for their 'feminist' leanings and criticism of existing family life appear far less radical than their enemies suggested. Robert Owen did attack the 'single-family-arrangement' and the 'selfishness' of contemporary child-rearing.[41] Barmby did call for women's political liberty: 'We must have unsexual chartism! How can the stream of freedom flow clearly when slavery is at its fountains! How can we allow the political subalternity of women when we advocate her social equality. If woman is not free, man must ever be a slave.'[42] Given these men's sympathy for women it might have been expected that they would have accepted the importance of birth control. It appears, however, that these reformers who in theory broke down the old laws of matrimony, attempted in practice to establish a higher morality in which contraception had no place. They envisaged a better future for women in which they would enjoy social and political equality. But this led them to discuss the state of motherhood primarily as it would be after the ultimate social transformation. It often made them blind to the very real problems posed by child-bearing to nineteenth-century women. Owen applauded the prolific family and castigated '. . .Mr. Malthus and his ardent, but inexperienced disciples.' Goodwyn Barmby insisted, 'We. . .know of all the gabble about moral physiology and preventive sexualism, but we have no fear, no aspen-leaved doubt but that the world can maintain all its population, present and future, without check or limit.'[43] Without underestimating the seriousness with which these men broached the issue of motherhood it has to be recognised that they overlooked the question of whether or not the individual woman had the right to contraception. If a woman's marriage was based on love, not on material considerations; if the community protected her children from want, what possible reasons could she have for not raising a large family? The assumption was easily made that if society provided the necessary means of support women could be expected to accept pregnancy after pregnancy uncomplainingly. Owen even suggested that the community had a right to supervise in some way such breeding with the eugenist goal in mind of '. . .the improvements of the organisation of man'.[44]

To the charge that they were undermining the family the Owenites replied that on the contrary they were seeking to set it on a firmer foundation. Charles Southwell in *An Essay on Marriage Addressed to the Lord Bishop of Exeter* (1840) maintained that Owen was only attempting to reform marriage by the establishment of divorce; 'promiscuous intercourse' had no place in his plans. Similarly the Saint-Simonians in England declared their opposition to 'licentious and scortatory love' and their support for the reforms of married life suggested by Milton.[45] The early socialists obviously played an important role in advancing a critique of the existing family structure. But, with the exception of Robert Dale Owen and William Thompson (whose special contribution to the debate will be analysed in the following two chapters), most ignored the role birth control might play in their restructured society.

The defenders of the poor denied Malthus' gloomy predictions and embraced the optimistic doctrines of Doubleday and Spencer. They would not accept, however, the birth controllers' arguments that contraception should be adopted. In the main their response was triggered by the view that such practices were immoral and unnatural. In an allusion to John Stuart Mill, Rickards wrote that insulting propositions had been made to the working class. 'Writers of considerable ability have not scrupled to propose, and to explain in unequivocal language, means whereby the passions might be gratified, and the natural consequence of the intercourse of the sexes prevented from taking place.' Samuel Laing noted that in France such ideas received a degree of official support, but the *National Cooperative Leader* stated that in England 'vices' of this nature were only ever met with in the upper orders: 'In thousands of instances we see celibacy and preventive intercourse resorted to by certain grades of society, not from fear of poverty, but with an intention of augmenting their possessions, or keeping them to a certain line of descent.' The message was clear. These practices, individualistic and anti-social, were foreign to the working-class movement.[46]

Notes

1. For overview see Harold A. Boner, *Hungry Generations: The Nineteenth Century Case Against Malthusianism* (New York, 1954); John Peel, 'Birth Control and the Working Class Movement,' *Society for the Study of Labour History Bulletin*, 7 (1963), pp.16-22.
2. R.G. Kirby and A.E. Musson, *The Voice of the People: John Doherty, 1798-1854. Trade Unionist, Radical and Factory Reformer* (Manchester, 1975), pp.283, 286; *National Cooperative Leader* (29 March, 1861), p.229; G. Poulett Scrope, *Principles of Political Economy* (London, 1837), pp.282-3. See also Michael Thomas Sadler, *The Law of Population* (London, 1830), 389 ff.
3. *The Fleet Papers Being Letters to Thomas Thornhill from Richard Oastler* (30 January, 1841), I, p.40.
4. Alison, *The Principles of Population* (London, 1840).
5. Ludlow, 'Trade Societies and the Social Science Association,' *MacMillan's Magazine*, 3 (1860-1861), p.323.
6. Carlyle, *Chartism* (London, 1840 2nd edn.), pp.109-110.
7. Scrope, *Principles*, p.276.
8. John Clubbe, (ed.), *Selected Poems of Thomas Hood* (Cambridge, Mass., 1970), p.275.
9. *New Moral World* (16 September, 1837), p.1.
10. *Trades Newspaper* (31 July, 1825) cited in E.P. Thompson, *The Making of the English Working Class* (London, 1966), p.777.
11. *Trades Newspaper* (11 September, 1825); the *Cooperator* (1 September, 1 October, 1829); *The Labourer's Friend and Handicrafts Chronicle* (1 January, 1821); *London Mercury* (2, 9 April, 1837). See also the *Pioneer* (25 January, 1 February, 1834); the *London Cooperative Magazine* (1 April, 1 May, 1827). As early as 1805 Charles Hall had warned of plans to use 'the preventive method' to restrict the poor — like cattle — to the numbers needed by the rich; *Effects of Civilization* (London, 1850 2nd edn.), pp.246-7.
12. *Republican* (12 November, 1824).
13. The *Black Dwarf* (3 December, 1823); the *Northern Star* (31 March, 1838); the *London Dispatch* (29 January, 1838).
14. The *Black Dwarf* (17 September, 1823). The debate over birth control that appeared in the columns of the *Black Dwarf* from November 1823 to January 1824 was between its editor, Wooler, Francis Place writing as 'A.Z.' and the young John Stuart Mill writing as 'A.M.'
15. Ravenstone, *A Few Doubts as to the Correctness of Some Opinions Generally Entertained on the Subject of Population and Political Economy* (London, 1821), p.428.

16. William Thompson, *An Inquiry Into the Principles of the Distribution of Wealth Most Conducive to Human Happiness* (London, 1824); John Gray, *A Lecture on Human Happiness* (London, 1825); Thomas Hodgkin, *Labour Defended Against the Claims of Capital* (London, 1825).

17. Hopkins, *Great Britain for the Last Forty Years* (London, 1834), p.301. Mayhew, *London Labour and the Labouring Poor* (London, 1967 reprint), II, 319 ff.; J.F. Bray, *Labour's Wrongs and Labour's Remedies* (Leeds, 1839), p.104; Charles Bray, *The Philosophy of Necessity* (London, 1841), II, p.394.

18. Ludlow, 'Trade Societies,' p.323. See also the *Northern Star* (31 March, 26 May, 1838); James Leach, *Stubborn Facts from the Factory* (London, 1844).

19. Hopkins, *Great Britain*, p.55; G.G. Vincent, *A Letter to the Editor of The Times in Cause of the Poor* (London, 1844), p.25; J. Livesy, *Moral Reformer* (1 February, 1831), pp.39-41; Rickards, *Population and Capital* (London, 1854), p.256; W.E. Hickson, *An Essay on the Population in Refutation of the Theory of the Rev. T.R. Malthus* (London, 1849), p.75. See also Robert Dick, MD, *Marriage and Population; Their Natural Laws* (London, 1848), p.11.

20. Arthur W. Waters, *Trial of Thomas Spence* (Leamington Spa, 1917); Olive R. Rudkin, *Spence and His Connections* (London, 1927); William Ogilvie, *The Right of Property in Land* (1781) in M. Beer, *The Pioneers of Land Reform* (London, 1920).

21. Alison, *Principles*, I, 86 ff.; Mary Hennell, *An Outline of the Various Social Systems and Communities Which Have Been Founded on the Principle of Cooperation* (London, 1844), xxiv, lxxiii; Samuel Laing jr. *Atlas Prize Essay. National Distress; Its Cause and Remedies* (London, 1844), pp.68-71; Samuel Laing sr., *Notes of a Traveller* (London, 1842), pp.336-48; C. Kingsley, *Alton Locke, Tailor and Poet* (London, 1850), II, p.231 and *Yeast: A Problem* (London, 1851), p.228; Thornton, *Over-Population and its Remedy* (London, 1846), pp.329-85, and see also David Martin, 'Land Reform,' in Patricia Hollis, (ed.), *Pressure from Without in Early Victorian England* (London, 1974), 131 ff.

22. Scrope, *Principles*, p.279; Alison, *Principles*, I, pp.86-93; Rickards, *Population*, p.256.

23. Weyland, *The Principles of Population and Production* (London, 1816), p.427.

24. London, *Equilibrium of Population and Sustenance Demonstrated* (London, 1836); Charles Loudon, *Solution du problème de la population et de la subsistence* (Paris, 1842), p.121. See pages 301, 311 for refutation of Doubleday.

25. Doubleday, *The True Law of Population* (London, 1842). See the 1853 edition for attacks on Loudon and Spencer. Doubleday, a radical Newcastle soap manufacturer was invited to speak to the Northern Political Union. See *Northern Star* (19 October, 1839).

26. Hickson, *An Essay*, pp.62, 74.

27. Spencer, *A New Theory of Population* (New York, 1853 reprinted from the *Westminster Review* 1852), p.33. See also Spencer, *The Principles of Biology* (London, 1899), II, pp.509-12; Spencer, *Principle of Ethics* (London, 1899), I, pp.550-3; J.D.Y. Peel, *Herbert Spencer; The Evolution of a Sociologist* (London, 1971), pp.138-9. The claim that hard physical labour was 'anti-propagational' was also made by Samuel Laing sr., *Notes*, p.348.

28. Bagehot, *Economic Studies* (London, 1888), pp.141, 142.

29. *Weekly Register* (15 April, 1826) and see also the issues of 22 April and 30 September, 1826 and 3 November, 1827. Carlile replied that he had not even read Malthus; *Republican* (21 August, 1826). See also 'Marriages and No Mothers; or the Stage Coach Battle of Cobbett and Carlile,' *Paul Pry* (6 May,

1826), Place Collection, British Museum, 61; *London Mercury* (2 April, 28 May, 1837); Dr Robert Black and Henry Hetherington were the men under attack.

30 Thomas Hodgkin, *The Natural and Artificial Rights of Property Contrasted* (London, 1832), pp.154-5.

31. *Trades Newspaper* (11 September, 1825); see also the *Bolton Express* (27 October, 1827).

32. The *Examiner* (21 August, 1825); the *Bulldog* (9 September, 1826); the *Trades Newspaper* (11 September, 1825); the *Black Dwarf* (3 December, 1823).

33. Godwin, *On Population* (London, 1820), p.219.

34. *Trades Newspaper* (17 July, 1825).

35. Godwin, *On Population,* pp.585-6.

36. Base to Place (21 June, 1825), Place Collection, British Museum, 68; and see also 'P.H.G.' to the *Poor Man's Guardian* (9 March, 1833).

37. Harrison in S. Pollard and J. Salt, (eds.), *Robert Owen: Prophet of the Poor* (London, 1971), p.9; Eversley, *Social Theories of Fertility and the Malthusian Debate* (Oxford, 1959), p.156; Martin, 'Land Reform.' p.140.

38. Piero Straffa and M.H. Dobb, (eds.), *The Works and Correspondence of David Ricardo* (Cambridge, 1962), Trowser to Ricardo (19 September, 1819), VIII, p.71; see also Ricardo to Malthus (10 September, 1821), IX, p.62.

39. Wardlaw, *Lectures,* pp.10, 11.

40. Simmons, *The Working Classes,* p.73.

41. Owen, *Lectures on the Marriages of the Priesthood of the Old Immoral World* (London, 1840, 4th edn.), p.11.

42. *The Promethean or Communitarian Apostle* (January 1842), p.14; and see also the *Educational Circular and Communist Apostle* (November 1841), p.4; and see also Dorothy Thompson, 'Women and Nineteenth Century Radical Politics: A Lost Dimension,' in J. Mitchell and A. Oakley, *The Rights and Wrongs of Women* (London, 1976), pp.112-38.

43. Owen, *Lectures,* p.31; the *Promethean* (25 January, 1834), p.163 and see also on the communitarians James Morrison's the *Pioneer* (25 January, 1834); Frances Morrison, *The Influence of the Present Marriage System* (Manchester, 1838), p.14; J.E. Duncan's the *Sun Beam* (1840?), p.6; William Hodson's the *Working Bee and Herald of the Hodsonian Community Society,* Mania Fen, Cambridgeshire (10, 17, 24, 31 October, 1840); Alexander Campbell, *Letters and Extracts from the Ms. Writings of James Pierrepont Greaves* (Ham Common, 1843-1845), I, pp.1-76; J.E. Smith's the *Shepherd* (11 November, 30 December, 1837).

44. Owen, *Lectures,* p.32.

45. Southwell, *An Essay,* p.21; M. Fontana and Joachim de Prati, *St. Simonianism in London* (London, 1833), p.26.

46. Rickards, *Population,* p.194; Laing sr., *Notes,* pp.341, 345; the *National Cooperative Leader* (26 April, 1861).

4 BIRTH CONTROL AND MEDICAL SELF-HELP

In the previous chapter it was shown that the leaders of the working-class movement of the first half of the nineteenth century were generally hostile to the discussion of birth control. It is difficult to determine what the average artisan's views were. The evidence of popular knowledge of forms of fertility control in the eighteenth century prevents one from making the simple assumption that the working class was passively awaiting enlightenment. Indeed to understand fully the ideology propounded by the early birth control propagandists contraception has to be viewed as a form of working-class medical self-help. A glance at the advertisements for the birth control tracts that appeared in the popular press serves to put the movement in context. These appeared on the same pages along with those for a variety of quack medicines: Dr Henry's French Meroine Pills, Dr Lambert's Cordial Balm of Life, Dr H.'s Golden Anti-Venereal Pills. In neighbouring columns were announcements of the meetings of phrenological and temperance societies. From the 1820s onwards greater publishing opportunities allowed any practitioner a hearing; new advertisement schemes popularised revolutionary medicaments.. The desire for a common man's medicine, preferably with a monistic message, resulted in an early nineteenth century upsurge of health movements combating alcoholism, gluttony, 'folly in dress', and a host of other ills.[1] The campaign for birth control was in many ways just one more medical self-help movement. Like the others its motto was 'Know thyself'. The fact that the literature it produced provided the artisan with a better understanding of his body's function and an accompanying sense of independence and self control was as important as the actual practice of contraception.

In this chapter I will attempt to cast a fresh light on the early birth control movement by setting to one side the economic and moral arguments of its advocates and focus attention on their belief that illness was caused by ignorance — in particular that the illnesses associated with repeated unwanted pregnancies and unnecessarily large families were a consequence of an ignorance of contraception. I will first deal with those men who had a professional interest in maintaining and exploiting the sexual fears and confusions of the public — the purveyors of handbooks of sexual folklore and quack medications.

78

Secondly, I will sketch out the response of the medical profession to the issue of birth control prior to 1850. Finally, I will present the birth controllers' arguments in favour of contraception and show how they formed part of a more general belief in medical self-help.

The birth controllers were, of course, not the first to provide the public with information on the question of sexuality. There already existed a large popular literature dealing with reproduction. In the first place there was the folklore of sexual knowledge led by *Aristotle's Works*[2] which continued to enjoy a wide circulation in the nineteenth century. A London doctor lamented the fact that in the 1830s it was '. . .in great circulation, though replete with error and obscenity from beginning to end.'[3] In the second place there was the unremitting deluge of pamphlets and tracts produced by quacks and charlatans to advertise their wares. A contributor to the *Medical Times* complained in 1839, 'Handbills of the most disgusting character are thrust into the hands of all who venture into public thoroughfares, — and thus the eyes of female delicacy and innocence is insulted, and the mind of youth defiled, by a detail of the filthy pretensions of these public nuisances.'[4] Such was the concern of the medical profession at the circulation of 'scandalous' quack information in the popular press that it sought to curb such announcements through the establishment of the 'Union for the Discouragement of Vicious Advertisements'.[5]

Much of the quack literature of early Victorian England has been lost but the more substantial of the tracts and pamphlets give a clear idea of the message conveyed. There was, for example, Gross and Company, *The Aegis of Life* (1830) and *Hygaeiana, a Non-Medical Analysis of the Complaints Incidental to Females* (1830), J.L. Curtis and Company, *Manhood* (1840), J. Jordan and Company, *Human Frailty; Embracing Remarks. . .on the Disease Caused by the Abuse of the Reproductive Functions* (1842), R. and L. Perry and Company, *The Secret Friend* (1845), R. and J. Brody and Company, *The Secret Companion* (1845), Dr Ricord, *Essence of Life* (1860), and Dr Paris, *Treatise on Nervous Debility* (1861). Almost all these works followed the same plan. They provided first, a terrifying account of the innumerable diseases which were a consequence of 'evil habits' and 'sexual excesses', secondly a description of the miraculous effects obtained in combating such complaints by the consumption of the quack's potion, finally a number of letters purportedly from satisfied customers testifying to the amazing qualities of the product in question. The publications of Gross and Company were typical of this literature, promising to cure debility caused by 'excessive indulgence in venereal engagements', abstinence, nocturnal emission' venereal disease, constitutional imbecility, peculiar formation, intensive study, long residence in tropical climates, and masturbation.

The increasing number of pseudo-scientific handbills and pamphlets produced by quacks was an indication of the expansion of publishing facilities and the appearance of new advertising schemes. In the eighteenth century quacks limited their propaganda to the well-to-do; in the nineteenth they shifted their attention to the new urban work force. Dr Andrew Ure declared, 'Nothing strikes the eye of a stranger more in Manchester than the swarms of empirical practitioners of medicine. Nearly a dozen of them may be found clustered together in the main streets; all prepared with drastic pills and alternative potions to prey upon credulous spinners.'[6] The circulation of the quacks' literature was in addition an indication of the public's continuing desire for some type of instruction on procreation. Only the briefest mention of generation was contained in the respectable popular medical texts such as John Wesley's *Primitive Physick* (1747) or William Buchan's *Domestic Medicine* (1769). This would be true as well for serious nineteenth-century works such as Andrew Combe's *The Principles of Physiology* (1835) and John Elliotson's *Human Physiology* (1835) and vulgarised publications such as *The Book of Health* (1829), *The Express, or Every Man his own Doctor* (1823), *The Physiology of Health* (1841), and *The Poor Man's Medical Guide in Emergency* (1823). The reason for such omissions was spelled out by Henry Bickersteth in *Medical Hints* (1829). It was not the doctor's duty, he declared, to instruct laymen on the details of procreation for such information might be then used to escape the punishment ordained by God for sexual misdemeanours. 'In female complaints some other questions are necessary; but it is not intended to extend these directions to them, nor to the disease which the Almighty has been pleased to inflict as a bitter scourge on the unlawful indulgence between the sexes.'[7]

The attitude of the quacks towards sexuality was quite different. They did provide some crude analysis of the functioning of the reproductive system, but their main purpose was, of course, not to give an accurate account of human physiology. Their aim in the nineteenth century as it had been in the eighteenth was to terrorise the male public with tales of the horrible consequences of sexual excesses into the purchase of restorative cordials and medications. Rather than assure the reader that there was knowledge available which could permit him to avoid illness, quacks claimed that only their *secret* remedies could cure the 'nervous debility' into which all would eventually plunge. In a similar fashion quacks attributed a whole range of female diseases to disruption of the menstrual cycle. A wide variety of 'French' or 'female pills' were guaranteed to cure a 'suppression of the menses'. The distributors of such medications, though they paraded a concern that their products be used in an attempt to terminate a pregnancy, implied that they were abortifacients and no doubt many women purchased them for this reason. Indeed as England became more urbanised and the traditional herbal remedies of the countryside were lost it is likely that women relied increasingly on prepared potions.

What was the response of the medical profession to the public's interest in reproduction and in particular to the possibility of controlling births? It is impossible to know what individual doctors told their patients in the privacy of their consulting rooms; here we can only deal with prescriptive literature.[8] Even this is scarce for the first half of the nineteenth century. Only a few medical men made allusions to actual birth control practices or 'precautions'. In *Observations on the Mortality and Physical Management of Children* (1827) Dr John Robertson simply acknowledged that, 'Since the publication of Malthus' profound work on population many absurd, and some criminel, notions have been promulgated on the subject of CHECKS to the increase of mankind, most of them originating in a misapprehension of the opinion of this writer.'[9] But doctors could not ignore the public's attempt to regulate births. The common occurrence of abortion was frequently noted in the medical press. 'In some of the manufacturing districts', wrote a contributor to the *Cottage Physician,* 'the use of large doses of Epsom or Glauber's salts to procure abortion, is understood to be very common.'[10] The low illegitimacy rate of the factory towns of Lancashire was frequently attributed to working women's recourse to abortifacients. 'The deduction we draw', wrote W.R. Greg, 'is also materially confirmed by the practice, which it is painful to state, is far from uncommon among the abandoned females of these districts of destroying prematurely the fruit and evidence of their guilt.'[11] Dr Robert Venables was so concerned that even those references to therapeutic abortions contained in erudite medical texts would '. . .circulate among the vulgar and less-informed classes of society. . .' via the popular press that he refrained from dealing with the topic in print.[12]

Moreover the factory reports of 1831 and 1833 revealed that doctors were aware of the circulation of birth control tracts in working-class districts. Dr James Blundell declared that, '. . .where individuals are congregated as in factories, I conceive that means preventive of impregnation are more likely to be generally known and practised by young persons.'[13] Dr Hunter complained, '. . .books or pamphlets, which are a disgrace to any age or country have been offered for sale. . .' in Leeds.[14] The doctors disagreed on the question whether such knowledge of contraception was actually put into practice, but they were as one in expressing their disgust at the publication of this information.

A complete condemnation of birth control was finally provided in *The Philosophy of Marriage* (1837) by Dr Michael Ryan. Ryan began by upbraiding his colleagues for their reticence on the subject and then proceeded to condemn such 'checks' on medical grounds because the 'various abominable means' proposed to regulate births were not only immoral but '. . .were contrary to the dictates of nature'. In closing he said what other medical commentators would only allude to in their censure of birth control, namely that the availability of safe contraception would undermine the existing family structure.

> None can deny that, if young women in general were absolved from the fear of the consequences, the great majority of them, unless the comparatively few who are strictly moral and highly educated, would rarely preserve their chastity; illicit amours would be common and seldom detected — seduction would be facilitated, and prostitution become almost universel, unless among the virtuous and small class, already accepted.[15]

In short the doctor saw his main duty in maintaining the existing moral code — not in supplying medical information desired by a segment of the population.

It would be misleading to give the impression that the medical profession was actively debating the pros and cons of birth control in the first half of the nineteenth century. Its main response to the issue of artificial means of fertility control was almost total silence. Dr Ryan's *Philosophy of Marriage* which condemned contraception was itself condemned by the *British and Foreign Medical Review* for even dealing with such an objectionable subject.[16] The writings of the birth control advocates were completely ignored by the British professional journals while in America the *Boston Medical Journal* felt obliged to apologise for even noting the appearance of Knowlton's *Fruits of Philosophy:* 'We think, however, that the less known about it by the public at large, the better it will be for the morals of the community; and it is only as a production of a medical man, and in a work read by medical men that we have thought it expedient to notice it.'[17] The official silence of the profession would be maintained for the better half of the century.

The silence of doctors was the most eloquent expression of their hostility to the whole issue of birth control. Such hostility reflected, of course, the contemporary attitudes of respectable society. Moreover it has to be recalled that the social standing of the profession was in the very process of being established; its members were accordingly sensitive to the dangers of associating with disreputable doctrines.[18]

Gynaecologists and obstetricians who were seeking to convince the public that, '. . .one sex only is qualified by education and powers of mind to investigate what the other sex has alone to suffer'[19] were, not surprisingly, the most cautious. Since the nature of their specialisation left them open to the charge of violating public decency, they were all the more adamant in their defence of conservative moral norms.[20]

> I shall remind the reader, [wrote Dr E.J. Tilt] that a profession which has the confidence of women holds in its hands the fate of society. . .it has the power, not only for the curing of disease and the maintenance of individual health, but also for imparting a healthy tone to society, and for the healing of its wounds.[21]

If the doctor had defended contraception he would have risked his reputation; by defending traditional morality with new scientific arguments he assumed the position previously monopolised by the priest — that of the defender of public virtue. The medical profession was to take a jaundiced view of all health reforms and home cures; its disavowal of birth control was all the more understandable inasmuch as it irritated both its moral and professional susceptibilities.

The activities of the advocates of birth control take on more meaning when placed in this context. On the one hand quacks were exploiting the public's ignorance in sexual matters; on the other the medical profession was refusing to acknowledge that birth control was an issue with which it should concern itself. The medical arguments that the birth controllers advanced in defence of contraception were quite straight forward. They asserted that they were only responding to a situation to which doctors had turned a blind eye: 'All states of pain are evil: all states of pleasure are good. The greater amount of animal life is a state of pain, and the duty of humanity, virtue or what is called morality, is to lessen the amount of pain; and the principle of preventing painful conceptions is a positive good to society.'[22] The working class was already using injurious means in an attempt to regulate births and was thereby making known its need for reliable methods. To supply such knowledge would result in the decrease of abortion and infanticide. It would spare women unwanted pregnancies, attendant illnesses, and the dangers of miscarriage. Marriages would no longer have to be postponed for financial reasons and as a result masturbation, prostitution, and similarly unhealthy substitutes for legitimate intercourse would disappear. The plight of orphans, bastards, and women dying in labour or during induced abortions could, claimed the birth controllers, all be avoided.[23]

With the appearance of the birth control tracts the artisan interested in the queston of reproduction finally had something to refer to besides *Aristotle's Works* and the quacks' sensational handbills. The nineteenth-century doctors might condemn the charlatan's treatises on sexuality but they were loth to provide an alternative. It was left to the birth controllers both to supply the public with accurate information and to combat popular misconceptions as best they could. Thus, by the 1830s, one could find in the penny press alongside advertisements for Solomon's Cordial Balm of Gilead and Dr Hallet's Pills Napolitaines announcements of the sale of Owen's *Moral Physiology* and Knowlton's *Fruits of Philosophy*. Yet the birth control literature was condemned by the medical profession while in the words of Knowlton, '. . .other works of like purpose, as well as that dirty useless thing called *Aristotle* are publicly sold with impunity'.[24]

The relationship of the birth controllers to the medical profession was a complex one. On the one hand they sought to give the impression that their efforts received medical support. Francis Place claimed in his handbills that the methods he described were recommended by 'eminent physicians' and 'first rate accoucheurs'. According to Robert Dale Owen English and French doctors were agreed that contraception could be practised '. . .without any injury to health.'[25] Richard Carlile stated that, '. . .where a state of health will not justify a pregnancy, it is common, in London for the physician to recommend the means of prevention, for it is well understood, that abstinence and domestic happiness cannot coexist.'[26] On the other hand the birth controllers maintained that doctors had no intention of spreading contraceptive information. They implied that physicians had access to knowledge which they were limiting to an elite.[27] Here again the birth controllers appealed to the artisans' suspicion of their 'betters' and in particular the suspicion that the medical profession was drawing benefits from the ignorance of the people.[28]

The extent to which the birth controllers themselves viewed the profession with mistrust was indicative of their attitudes toward social reform. A believer in *laissez-faire* such as Place made it clear in his own life that he had more confidence in his own bleeding techniques and cold water treatments than in medical prescriptions, but he made few public criticisms of doctors.[29] Charles Knowlton, a medical man himself, attacked the profession's failure to deal with the crucial question of procreation. 'In books, pamphlets, journals, etc., they have laid much before the public representing eating, drinking, bathing, lacing, air, exercises, etc., but have passed by this still more important subject now before us, giving only here and there some faint allusion to it.'[30] Knowlton sought to take information to the people, not only through his writings, but in 'A Course of Physiological Lectures as Connected with Moral Philosophy' at Frances Wright's Hall of Science in New York.[31] For Carlile, a crusader for political reform, the medical profession's attempt to monopolise certain types of knowledge represented yet another aspect of 'Old Corruption' and he accordingly labelled doctors '. . .as wicked a set of imposters as priests.'[32] It was in the writings of the two men who combined an interest in birth control and communitarian experiments — William Thompson and Robert Dale Owen — that the most thorough denunciation of organised medicine was found. For Thompson most diseases were the simple consequence of '. . .imprudence, intemperance, and distraction of other vices.'[33] In the existing competitive society the doctor benefited from the spread of disease and had no interest in the sort of preventive medicine which birth control represented.

> Competition calls into being a set of men who necessarily trade in the curing of wounds and diseases. The more wounds and diseases, if accompanied with the ability of paying for the cure, the better for this trade, as the greater the demand for cottons and silks the better for the manufacturers of these articles. . .It is moreover no part of their [the doctors'] profession, as it has been no part of their study, to preserve health to the healthy: it is on the contrary their vulgar interest, as forming one of the trades of competition, that the healthy should become diseased.[34]

Only in a society of Mutual Cooperation would the citizen find his good health the subject of the interest of his fellows.[35] In the reformed community each would be taught '. . .what every human being ought to know, the physiology. . .of the human frame and the laws of health'.[36] The sexual passions would at last be understood by all and be permitted to '. . .find their level of gentle and healthful gratification and contentment: and when all possible consequential evils, such as an injurious increase in numbers or abstraction of time from useful employments, are by appropriate regulations, guarded against, all the evils now arising from the misdirection of the passions would be avoided.'[37]

Robert Dale Owen followed very much the same line of reasoning as Thompson.

But, however desirable for the masses of mankind that they should be taught how to retain the first of blessings, health; and that they should further be taught how to regain it, when lost — it is *not* the interest of the physician. It is not his interest that his neighbours should know anything about their own bodies; it is not his interest that they should be taught how to retain their health, nor how to arrest an incipient malady by some simple remedy. Other men's ignorance is his gain. Their follies fill his purse. If they were educated as common sense dictates, he would be a poorer man. . .However beneficial, therefore, it might be, that we should know our own diseases and learn to prevent and cure them, we must not expect that physicians, as a class, will take much pains to destroy their own avocation. . .We must not expect that physicians will risk at once their reputations and their fortunes, in order to tell us, that if we are but rational and practical physiologists, we should regret the morality which now prevails, as unnatural, and productive of suffering and disease; nor can we require that physicians should labour zealously to promote temperance and thus to prevent diseases. All this it were unreasonable to expect, because men do not like to ruin themselves, nor even to diminish their own earnings.[38]

Turning specifically to the question of sexuality Owen declared that if one found an 'honest and enlightened physician' he would tell, '. . .of the prudish severity with which society dooms one sex to unnatural restraints, and of the temporarizing injustice with which she winks at the scarcely-veiled libertinism of the other. . .Ask him what *he* thinks of orthodox morality in itself and he will tell you, that *as a physiologist,* he disapproves and condemns it. But as a physician he profits by it. . .'[39]

The birth controllers thus differed on the extent to which they believed social reforms had to be pushed if disease were to be eradicated. Radicals such as Carlile and Place whose political programmes were restricted to attacks on privilege simply called for 'free trade' in medical knowledge. Owen and Thompson who were outlining plans for cooperative societies seemed to be suggesting that in the future each man would be his own physician and the medical profession wither away.[40] But all were agreed on the basic point that illness was largely a consequence of ignorance that could be overcome by medical self-help. In particular the unnecessary sufferings of women in undesired pregnancies and the maladies of children of over-large families were declared to be the result of a lack of contraceptive knowledge.

If the early birth control movement is looked at as a self-help medical campaign it becomes obvious why its advocates should have been hostile to the medical profession and why, in turn, physicians should have opposed contraception on professional as well as moral grounds. Doctors were trying to educate the nineteenth-century layman so as to instil in him a 'faith' in medicine. Their line of argument was well presented by Dr John Conolly who began *The Physician* with the promise, 'Unlike the common books of popular medicine, so eagerly purchased by the poorer as well as the richer classes of readers, this publication is not meant to supersede an application of the sick to persons competent to cure them, but to show that it is only such persons that they can safely trust.'[41] The sponsors of the birth control movement were approaching the problem from the opposite angle; they were responding to the artisan's faith in himself and his concern to control his own life. They recognised his desire for independence; they presented contraception as the one form of self-help medicine which could best assure it.

Notes

1. Richard Shryock, *The Development of Modern Medicine* (London, 1948), 205 ff.; Brian Harrison, *Drink and the Victorians* (London, 1971), p.185.
2. See chapter one.
3. Michael Ryan, *Philosophy of Marriage* (London, 1837), p.6.
4. *Medical Times* (28 September, 1839), p.6. See also John Corry, *The Detector of Quackery* (London, 1802); James Parkinson, *The Villager's Friend and Physician* (London, 1800), pp.79-80; J.C. Feldman, *Quacks and Quackery Unmasked* (London, 1842); *Monthly Gazette of Health*, 7 (1822), p.786; *Lancet*, 2 (1842), p.781; *Quarterly Review*, 141 (1842), pp.83-105.
5. *Lancet*, 1 (1851), p.72-3.
6. Andrew Ure, *The Philosophy of Manufactures* (London, 1835), p.386; and see also James Philip Kay, *The Moral and Physical Condition of the Working Classes* (London, 1832), 65 ff.; Joseph Adshead, *Distress in Manchester: Evidence of the State of the Labouring Classes in 1840-1842* (London, 1842), p.50; Friedrich Engels, *The Condition of the Working Class in England in 1844* (London, 1950), p.104.
7. Henry Bickersteth, *Medical Hints* (London, 1829); and for doctors jealousy of

the quacks' success in exploiting the concern with venereal complaints see Robert John Thornton, *The Medical Guardian of Youth* (London, 1816), pp.71-2, 86-7; James Thorn, *An Attempt to Simplify the Treatment of Sexual Diseases* (London, 1831), p.11; Michael Ryan, *A Manual of Midwifery* (London, 1831, 3rd edn.), p.377.

8. For an overview see John Peel, 'Contraception and the Medical Profession,' *Population Studies,* 18 (1964), pp.133-46.

9. *Observations on the Mortality and Physical Management of Children* (London, 1827), p.5.

10. *Cottage Physician* (London, 1825), p.59.

11. W.R. Greg, *An Inquiry into the State of the Manufacturing Population* (London, 1831), p.25; and see also Edward Bulwer Lytton, *England and the English* (London, 1833), I, p.204; P. Gaskell, *The Manufacturing Population of England* (London, 1833), p.85; William Dodd, *The Factory System Illustrated* (London, 1842), p.26; Lord Ashley, *Hansard,* 7 Victoria, 73 (1844), p.1093. On the claim that infanticide was being practised in working-class districts see Dr Lyon Playfair, *Report on the State of Large Towns in Lancashire* (London, 1845), 128 ff.; George Greaves, 'Observations on Some of the Causes of Infanticide,' *Transactions of the Manchester Statistical Society* (1862-1863), pp.2-13.

12. *London Medical Gazette,* 8 (10 September, 1831), pp.777-8.

13. 'Committee on the Factories' Bill,' *Parliamentary Papers,* 15 (1831-1832), pp.10887.

14. 'Dr Loudon's Medical Report,' *Parliamentary Papers,* 21 (1833), p.18.

15. Ryan, *Philosophy,* p.10.

16. *British and Foreign Medical Review,* 5 (1838), pp.443-6.

17. *Boston Medical Journal,* 27 (1843), p.256.

18. On the reluctance of doctors to say anything about sex see S. Mason, *The Philosophy of Female Health* (London, 1845), 1 ff.; and John Pocock Holmes, *Popular Observations on Diseases Incident to Females* (London, 1831), vi.

19. Edward J. Tilt, *On Diseases of Women and Ovarian Inflammation* (London, 1853), p.9. For advice to women on how they should discuss their problems with the physician see 'A Lady,' [E.W. Farrar], *The Young Lady's Friend* (London, 1837), p.53 and Holmes, *Popular Observations,* p.24.

20. On the old suspicion of the obstetrician see P. Thicknesse, *Man-Midwifery Analyzed and the Tendency of that Practice Detected and Exposed* (London, 1764) and *The Danger and Immodesty of the Present Custom of Unnecessarily Employing Men-Midwives* (London, 1772); J. Blunt, *Man-Midwifery Dissected* (London, 1793); M. Adams, *Man-Midwifery Exposed* (London, 1830); Jean Donnison, *Midwives and Medical Men: A History of Inter-Professional Rivalries and Women's Rights* (London, 1977).

21. E.J. Tilt, *On the Preservation of the Health of Women at the Critical Periods of Life* (London, 1851), p.41.

22. Carlile, *Every Woman's Book* (London, 1838), p.37. It should be recalled that some doctors even considered the administering of anaesthetics to women in labour as a violation of the biblical injunction 'In sorrow shall she bring forth.' See J.Y. Simpson, *Answer to Religious Objections Advanced Against the Employment of Anaesthetic Agents in Midwifery and Surgery* (Edinburgh, 1847).

23. Carlile, *Every Woman's Book,* 19, pp.23-24; Owen, *Moral Physiology* (New York, 1831), pp.35-36; Knowlton, *Fruits of Philosophy* (London, 1841), pp.37, 40.

24. *Boston Investigator* (11 January, 1833).

25. See also Place, *Illustrations,* p.324; Owen, *Moral Physiology,* p.60.

26. Carlile, *The Lion* (3 October, 1828).
27. Ibid.
28. On the extent of the working class' suspicion of surgeons which manifested itself at the time of the 1832 cholera epidemic see *Poor Man's Guardian* (25 February and 8 September, 1832); *Cosmopolite* (8 September, 1832); Henry Gaulter, *The Origins and Progress of the Malignant Cholera in Manchester* (London, 1833), pp.137-8; James Simpson, *Necessity of Education as National Object* (Boston, 1834), p.23.
29. Mary Thale, ed., *The Autobiography of Francis Place, 1771-1854* (London, 1972), *passim*.
30. Knowlton, *Fruits,* p.37.
31. See chapter two, ft. 55.
32. *Republican* (11 March, 1825) and see also the attack on doctors made by Carlile's wife, Eliza Sharples, in *Isis* (2 June, 1832).
33. William Thompson, *Appeal of One Half of the Human Race, Women, Against the Pretensions of the Other Half, Men* (London, 1825), p.142.
34. Thompson, *Practical Directions for the Speedy and Economical Establishment of Communities* (London, 1830), p.195.
35. Thompson, *Labour Rewarded: The Claims of Labour and Capital Conciliated* (London, 1827), p.67.
36. Thompson, *An Inquiry into the Principles of the Distribution of Wealth* (London, 1824), p.339.
37. Thompson, *Practical Directions,* pp.200-201.
38. *Free Enquirer* (18 February, 1829).
39. Ibid.; and see also Robert Dale Owen, *Situations: Lawyers-Clergy-Physicians-Men and Women* (London, 1840); Joel Pinny, *An Exposure of the Present Deteriorated Condition of Health* (London, 1830), p.165.
40. Owen and Thompson were the only well-known communitarians to defend contraception, but most utopian socialists were sympathetic to the less controversial forms of fringe medicine such as vegetarianism, teetotalism, and fresh air and cold water baths. See J.F.C. Harrison, *Robert Owen and the Owenites in Britain and America* (London, 1969), p.179.
41. John Conolly, *The Physician* (London, 1832), p.9.

5 BIRTH CONTROL AND THE MORALITY OF MARRIED LIFE

The traditional view is that there was little discussion of birth control
from the time of Richard Carlile and Robert Dale Owen's activities in
the early 1830s to the Bradlaugh-Besant trial of 1877. Peter Fryer has
described it as a period of quiet infiltration.[1] As has been seen in the
analysis of the Malthusian and anti-Malthusian doctrines, however,
birth control continued to attract attention from commentators on
both sides of the population issue; both recognised that it threatened
to bring into the debate a number of issues such as the role of the
family and the rights of women which had heretofore been quietly left
to one side. This chapter, after having provided a necessary overview
of the discussion of contraception at mid-century, will examine these
new dimensions of the controversy.

The most serious challenge the birth controllers had to face in the late
1830s was the charge that they would go so far as to defend infanticide.
This claim was foisted on them by an anonymous writer signing himself
'Marcus' who in 1838 produced a pamphlet entitled *On the Possibility
of Limiting Populousness*. In it the author skillfully attributed to both
Malthusians and birth controllers the acceptance of 'The Theory of
Painless Extinction.'[2] The pamphlet created an immediate uproar.
Edwin Chadwick wrote to *The Times* on 10 January, 1839 to report
that the anti-Poor Law leader, the reverend Mr Stephens, had charged
the Poor Law Commissioners with writing the tract in which it was
recommended that all children in excess of three per family be killed.
Mr Johnson Gedge, editor of the Bury *Post*, corroborated Chadwick's
account and declared that the rumour had to be replied to. 'Marcus'
came to symbolise the birth controller-cum-euthanasiast and was
accordingly castigated in radical publicatons such as G.R. Wythen
Baxter's *The Book of Bastiles or, the History of the Working of the
New Poor Law* and Stephen W. Fullham's *Poor Law Rhymes; or
Anti-Marcus*. Both Carlyle and Doubleday referred to 'Marcus' in their
anti-Malthusian works as the logically evil consequence of any attempt
to limit population artificially.[3]

Richard Carlile responded to these charges in his *Political Register* of 2 November, 1839: 'I do not, with the horrid Marcus, say, destroy them [children] ; but I do say avoid the production where destruction, such as that now of the cotton mill, the workhouse, and other places is inevitable; for to produce under such circumstances, is the voluntary and preliminary step to the final murder or inevitable destruction.'[4] This was followed up in 1841 by the appearance of an anonymous answering tract *Notes on the Population Question* signed 'Anti-Marcus', which was put out by the radical publisher Watson.

The task set for the birth controller by the 'Marcus' controversy was the old one of convincing the workers that he had their best interests at heart. As early as 1825 a handbill had appeared, no doubt due to the machinations of Francis Place, entitled *Dialogue Between a Parson and a Mechanic.* The latter confounds the churchman's pessimism by arguing that there is another way aside from either abstinence or infanticide by which to control births. In the middle decades of the century the birth controllers continued to produce propaganda with the same purpose of showing that fertility control was not harmful; that indeed it did not have to be considered antagonistic to reformist programmes. James Linton in reviewing Robert Dale Owen's pamphlet asserted, 'The name of Owen is sufficient guarantee that this is no Poor-Law scheme for sacrificing the industrious at the shrine of the indolent and selfish "respectability".'[5] Linton went on to state that even when equality was attained birth control would still be needed to avoid individual pain, distress, and disease.

John Stuart Mill was, as indicated by Rickards' earlier allusion, popularly viewed though never publicly acknowledged as a defender of birth control. In his *Political Economy* he attempted to show that socialism and population control were not necessarily antagonistic doctrines. Indeed he suggested that in the communist state community pressures would be applied to prevent 'culpable self-indulgence'. 'The communistic state, instead of being particularly open to the objection drawn from the danger of over-population, has the recommendation of ending in an especial degree to the prevention of that evil.'[6] In a somewhat similar vein the anonymous author of a pamphlet, *Morality,* presented birth control as part of a reformist package. In his projected society, inspired by the 'Co-adjutive Principle' the 'proletaires' would be better fed and housed, the 'feudal governing class' overthrown, and breeding given the attention it deserved.[7] A full synthesis of birth control and socialist ideas was striven for by George Miles in *The Economy of Life* (1868). Miles accepted both the labour theory of value and the wage fund theory. He accused capitalists of seeking to

prevent tne spread of contraceptive information out of fear that
reduced births would force up wages. It was the ruling class' desire to
monopolise both wealth and sexual love: 'Those individuals who have
the command of most food and repose, have also the command of
most sexual love; the former kind of wealth being always exchangeable
for the latter kind of wealth.'[8] In this confused but daring work which
is in some ways reminiscent of Fourier, Miles argued that the poor were
impoverished sexually as well as materially; birth control offered an
answer to both problems.

But when all was said and done the leading advocates of birth
control could only go so far with social reformers. The latter implied
that poverty and population problems were a consequence of evil
institutions and would disappear once social reforms were implemented.
The birth controllers did not, like the orthodox Malthusians, attribute
poverty solely to the failings of the individual but they did argue that
he could, by adopting family planning methods, improve his condition.
Moreover James Linton, John Stuart Mill, and George Miles in placing
contraception in the context of redistributive social reforms represented
what was to become a minority opinion in neo-Malthusian thought.
Carlile and Place became increasingly conservative in their old age.
Carlile in one of his last papers, the *Political Register* created in 1839,
mingled his pleas for birth control with attacks on Chartism, universal
suffrage, and trade unionism. In seeking in 1840 to win the working-
class leader William Lovett to the cause Place made the same claim that,
'. . .neither Universal Suffrage, nor Owenism, nor any other ism' could
answer the threat posed by population pressures.[9] The general decline
of radicalism which occurred at mid-century with the exhausting of the
forces of Chartism and Owenism was thus mirrored in the mainstream
birth control propaganda which from the 1850s onward was increasingly
dominated by social conservatives such as George Drysdale and Charles
Bradlaugh. Drysdale made his sentiments abundantly clear by entitling
one of the chapters in his *Physical, Sexual and Natural Religion,*
'Poverty: Its Only Cause and Only Cure'. The 'only cause' was, as
Malthus himself would have had it, 'over-population'; the 'only cure',
was 'preventive sexual intercourse'; no changes were to be made in
existing social institutions. The same principle was advocated by
Drysdale in the *Political Economist and Journal of Social Science;* he
ridiculed the land reform schemes of Jones and Carlyle and tossed aside
as baseless the optimistic population theories of Spencer and
Doubleday.[10] Drysdale also contributed to the *National Reformer*
which, under the editorship of Charles Bradlaugh, carried the discussion

of neo-Malthusianism into the 1860s. Bradlaugh, although he enjoyed the admiration and respect of vast numbers of workers because of the courage with which he defended his free-thinking convictions, accepted completely the notion of the wage-fund theory and opposed with enormous energy the emergence of the modern socialist movement. For him combinations were futile; strikes, simply destructive; the struggle of class against class, pointless. Cooperative movements he was willing to accept as serving an educational and partly remedial function. It was education which the worker most needed if he was to appreciate the importance of control of family size.[11] Conservative notions of a similar cast were contained in the spate of birth control pamphlets which appeared in the early 1870s: 'M.G.H.,' *Poverty: Its Cause and Cure* (1870), Austin Holyoake, *Large or Small Families? On Which Side Lies the Balance of Comfort?* (1870), Jno. Hy. Palmer, *Individual, Family and National Policy* (1875).[12]

Yet the fact that much of the birth control literature was increasingly tinged by social conservatism did not make it any more respectable as reading matter. Prior to 1877 the belief that the birth control propagandists were seeking to undermine the existing family structure was sufficiently potent a charge that few members of society dared defend the practice publicly. It was symptomatic of the situation that only radicals of relatively modest backgrounds such as Carlile, Holyoake and Bradlaugh — men who had little to lose — would risk public censure. The charge that one was sympathetic to such doctrines was used on more than one occasion to blacken an opponent's reputation or destroy a career. The most famous example was the loss of the 1868 South Devon election by Lord Amberley (Bertrand Russell's father) after it became known that he had participated in a discussion of the 'small family system' at the Dialectical Society.[13] Abraham Hayward played a role in two similar cases. In 1845 he attempted to sabotage the election of the radical J.A. Roebuck by publicising the information that he had been present with John Stuart Mill at the London Debating Society in the 1820s when birth control doctrines were examined. In 1873 Hayward repeated his charges against Mill with the intention of so besmirching his memory that his burial at Westminster Abbey would be impossible.[14] Given the venomous attacks to which one could be subjected it was not unnatural that some birth controllers purposely maintained a low profile. Thus George Drysdale's authorship of *Physical, Sexual and Natural Religion* was not to be acknowledged in his own lifetime. And John Stuart Mill would say of this same book in a private letter, 'J'y trouvai d'excellents choses, avec quelques autres qui ne me plaisent pas' but in a public declaration feel compelled to state, 'I have most certainly never on any occasion whatever, in public or private, expressed any approbation of the book. . .'[15]

The advocates of birth control could not make themselves respectable, even by embracing conservative economic tenets, for the reason that their works contained a radical critique of existing sexual relations. Indeed the most original aspect of their activities was the unprecedented seriousness with which they treated the rights of women. Yet the 'feminism' of the birth controllers has been curiously played down. J.A. and O. Banks in their classic study *Feminism and Family Planning* (1964) argued that, '. . .neither feminism as such nor the emancipation of the middle-class woman from her traditional role of home-maker were important causal factors in the decline of family size.'[16] The effect of the Banks' work has been to establish in historians' minds the notion that nineteenth-century feminists and birth controllers were mutually exclusive groups. On the one hand we have feminists seeking political and professional reforms but turning their backs on the issue of birth control; on the other, neo-Malthusians advancing simple economic arguments in favour of fertility control but anticipating no major change in the relationship of the sexes. The Banks do concede that William Thompson and John Stuart Mill did relate the status of women to the population question but the main thrust of their argument is that women acquiesced to the demands of men in the adoption of family planning. Birth control would, according to the Banks, be decided upon by middle-class men alone and would be adopted as a strategy to meet the economic constraints – not the feminist claims – of the 1870s.

The Banks' thesis has been useful in casting light on social currents in the latter decades of the nineteenth century; especially in the way in which it lends support to the argument made by J.A. Banks in his earlier *Prosperity and Parenthood* (1956) that a perceived standard of living influences motivation to control family size. But the thesis is weak in its treatment of ideological issues. Even restricting the focus here to works produced before the Bradlaugh-Besant trial of 1877 it is possible to demonstrate that feminism and family planning were intimately related. It is, of course, an anachronism, but one which will be committed to avoid clumsy circumlocutions, to employ the term 'feminism' in the first half of the nineteenth century when it was not widely used until the 1890s. Nevertheless all the birth controllers could be called feminists to the extent that they took an unprecedented interest in the health of women and in their right to control their own bodies. These advocates were almost all men but we do have evidence that women responded positively to their writings. This suggests that there was a 'domestic feminism' which manifested itself in the desire to avoid needless pregnancies. Traditionally women's means of protecting themselves had been limited. The appearance of the birth control propaganda gave legitimacy to their struggle to control their fertility and offered new strategies that they could pursue. They could not always act freely; the Banks might be quite right that the male still made the final decision and based it on economic considerations. The evidence suggests, however, that it was not all that simple. The fact that the right of the woman to avoid pregnancy was being articulated and that new female contraceptives such as the douche and sponge were being publicised must have made the decision-making process more complex than has been usually assumed.

A cursory examination of the birth control literature makes abundantly clear the feminist concerns of its various authors. It was significant that the one socialist leader to defend birth control was the one who had shown the greatest interest in the rights of women — William Thompson. Inspired by Anna Wheeler, Thompson produced a vehement defence of women in *Appeal of One Half the Human Race, Women, Against the Prejudices of the other Half, Men* (1825). He condemned the existing double standard and in particular the servitude to which women were reduced in child-bearing. Birth control he presented as a 'gentle exercise' which could have the effect of benefiting both the individual couple and the nation: 'A mental effort on the side of refinement, not of grossness is all the price to be paid, and by only one party [alluding to male withdrawal], for early marriages and mutual endearments, and where the circumstances of society permit no increase of population.'[17] Place, Carlile, Knowlton, and Owen all likewise went out of their way to enumerate the particular advantages that control of fertility offered to women. No longer would they have to be subjected to repeated pregnancies, dangerous miscarriages, and attendant illnesses. No longer would they be forced into acts of abortion or infanticide, acts which both degraded women in the eyes of society and undermined their mental and physical health. No longer would women have to postpone marriage and so run the risk of bearing children late in life. At last men and women could marry, not to simply bear children, but to secure their mutual affection.[18]

Owen and Carlile went on to declare that the availability of contraception would destroy the double standard in sexuality. Just how far these men had to move in order to escape the moral conventions of the age that women could not be freed from the threat of pregnancy if social stability were to be maintained was indicated by a letter of Carlile to Place. Before being convinced of the necessity of contraception Carlile had accepted the commonplace belief that women '. . .had an almost constant desire for copulation; the customs of society alone, I think debar them from it. . .'[19] A few years later in their birth control tracts Carlile and Owen set out to lay to rest this myth that a knowledge of contraception would reduce every woman to a state of debauchery. Indeed Owen went so far as to suggest that the wise father would protect his daughter from the consequences of a possible seduction by providing her with an 'innocent preventive'.[20]

The birth controllers could not, of course, totally disentangle themselves from contemporary attitudes towards sexual practices. Thus, one finds them all expressing the familiar nineteenth-century fear of the horrible consequences of masturbation.[21] Similarly they accepted the notion that the sexually unsatisfied female was susceptible to hysteria. Place wrote to Harriet Martineau that he had been assured by physicians that delayed marriages posed a physical danger to women. Drysdale declared celibacy as great an evil as prostitution and poverty.[22] Carlile claimed that it was noticed,

> . . .that women who have never had sexual commerce begin to droop when about twenty-five years of age, that they become pale and languid, that general weakness and irritation, a sort of restlessness, nervous fidgettyness takes possession of them, and an absorbing process goes on, their forms degenerate, their features sink, and the peculiar character of the old maid becomes apparent.[23]

That these men should have accepted such notions is not particularly surprising. What is of interest is that they should have turned popular prejudices to their own purposes. The availability of contraception, they argued, would allow men and women to escape the harmful results of frustrated sexual desires. The old maid and the 'self-polluter' would be creatures of the past once marriage freed from the burden of over-large families was available to all.[24]

The present interpretation, that feminism and birth control were intimately connected, is further supported by the fact that those attacking the birth controllers frequently assumed and imputed such a connection. Thus in *Paul Pry* for 6 May, 1826 appeared a spoof entitled *Marriages and No Mothers: or the Stage Coach Battle of*

Cobbett and Carlile in which the latter is accused of having, '. . .printed a directory for young females to stop the tide of nature with a SPONGE!' Frances Wright, a defender of women's rights and colleague of Robert Dale Owen, was cited in an anonymous tract, *Twelve Letters to Young Men on the Sentiments of Frances Wright and Robert Dale Owen* (1830) for seeking to relieve women of the burden of motherhood.[25] Carlile was the target of an identical attack; Edward Hancock berated him for having defended free love:

> You are the publisher of a certain book, to mention its title is unnecessary here, for such an infamous book has had circulation sufficient to the great injury of many. . .To establish such an abominable system [as free love], you have published instructions, and particularly recommended them to be adopted by females, as a sure method of avoiding the consequences.[26]

Eliza Sharples who assisted Carlile in his propagandising efforts was in turn slandered by Hancock as Carlile's 'new moral mistress.' At mid-century the reverend Brewin Grant assumed the role of champion of respectability and charged James Linton and George Jacob Holyoake with purveying immoral doctrines. In the *National* Linton had analysed the inequities of the existing property and divorce laws, defended Robert Dale Owen and questioned the morality of a society that executed the murderer but left unpunished the man who killed a woman by forcing her to bear large numbers of children. In the *Reasoner* Holyoake advertised the birth control tracts.[27] In the same journal in 1848 it was reported that Emma Martin, a popular social lecturer, was now seeking to extend the knowledge of midwifery '. . .and to diffuse a knowledge of the human organisation among those who, as wives, mothers, and nurses, so much need it'. She proposed to offer a course of private physiological lectures to ladies and a text, *Young Mother's Guide.*[28] The evidence strongly suggests that these contained birth control information.

In the works of John Stuart Mill, the most famous feminist of the nineteenth century, the relationship between the status of women and the population question was most fully analysed. In *Principles of Political Economy* (1848) he stated that, as women increased their political rights, so too would they free themselves from the restraints of their physical functions.

It is seldom by the choice of the wife that families are too numerous;

on her devolves (along with all the physical suffering and at least a full share of the privations) the whole of the intolerable domestic drudgery resulting from the excess. To be relieved from it would be hailed as a blessing by multitudes of women who now never venture to urge such a claim, but who would urge it, if supported by the moral feelings of the community. Among the barbarisms which law and morals have not yet ceased to sanction, the most disgusting surely is, that any human being should be permitted to consider himself as having a *right* to the person of another.[29]

In *The Subjection of Women* (1869) Mill continued his critique of marriage which empowered the husband to '. . .enforce the lowest degradation of a human being, that of being made the instrument of an animal function contrary to her [the wife's] inclinations'.[30]

As Mill pointed out women were still restrained from publicly supporting birth control. His statement lends strength to our contention that the mere absence of explicit female writings in defence of contraception does not in itself prove a lack of interest in the subject. Victorian pressures of respectability prevented women from writing about what a later generation would consider the most innocent of areas. That they would not be found penning contraceptive tracts could hardly occasion surprise. There are, however, several instances in which it can be inferred that women were effectively using men as their mouthpieces. William Thompson's attention was drawn to the problems of the existing relationship of the sexes by Anna Wheeler; Richard Carlile was enlightened by Eliza Sharples, Robert Dale Owen by Frances Wright and John Stuart Mill by Harriet Taylor. The exact contributions which these women made to men's appreciation of women's attitudes towards fertility control is difficult to determine but in an indirect way they were making themselves heard.

What appears to be the earliest *direct* expressions of female support for birth control came as a consequence of the work of George Drysdale. This Scottish physician was an active campaigner at mid-century for fertility control and a vehement supporter of the woman's movement. His *Physical, Sexual and Natural Religion* (1855), in addition to being a major work on contraception, contained attacks on existing marriage relationships as forms of 'legal prostitution' and defences of prostitutes as the victims of both a double sexual standard and the restriction of women's employment. In 1856 Drysdale established the short-lived *Political Economist and Journal of Social Science;* in its columns appeared letters from women supporting the birth control crusade. One reported that many had read Drysdale's work.

> Numbers of young women have told me that they look upon life in quite a different light now that they learn that nature has not been so cruel to them, as to give them but the choice of a married life, in which probably all the highest aims of life must be sacrificed, and the wife reduced to the level of a breeding animal, or a life of celibacy.[31]

Another wrote to ask for cheap tracts which she could distribute to the poor; she declared that the middle class were already knowledgeable. This woman described her own propaganda activities as those of a 'Missionary'. 'I myself have advocated the doctrine of preventive intercourse for ten years amongst the suffering poor.' She had heard thousands say they did not want children but the idea of prevention was still foreign to them: 'Their argument is "it is murder". Once remove this false notion and the way will be a little clear. I quite agree with you that the women must take the lead in such matters, for the men don't like much trouble but the false delicacy of our women is frightful.'[32] Thanks to Drysdale's publication we know of this woman's actions; how many others were of like minds and involved in similar work can only be determined by further work in the field.

What is clear is that, on the intellectual level at least, the connection between a specific type of feminism and birth control was well established by the 1870s. Richard Harte's *On the Laws and Customs Relating to Marriage* (1870) carried a well-argued thesis that access to divorce and contraception were vital for the emergence of the new middle-class family. Harte asked his readers for the '. . .open recognition that sexual intercourse, which does not take place with the intention of procreation, is justifiable, honourable, and praiseworthy'. Moreover if marriage were to be more than legalised prostitution it would be necessary, wrote Harte, that women enjoy economic independence and so have a choice of whether or not to marry.[33] This point was reiterated by Montagu Cookson in 'The Morality of Married Life' which appeared in the *Fortnightly Review* of 1872. To relegate women simply to the breeding of children reduced them to the level of brutes: 'To suffer for the sake of posterity may, in individual cases, be self-devotion of the highest order; but to inculcate this as a general duty would be to promulgate the revolting doctrine that the scheme of creation is one of progressive misery.'[34] Cookson recognised that there was 'a set of feminine thinkers' who opposed family limitation on moral grounds. His response was that they ignored the physical and psychological damage done the woman: '. . .the concentration of the mother's whole being on the details of the domestic drama grows and must grow with each new birth, until at last her daily life becomes one theatre of trivialities, the curtain of which is never allowed to drop.' The morally responsible would have to accept the fact that the conditions of modern life required, '. . .the limitation of the number of the family. . .and that such limitation is as much the duty of married persons as the observance of chastity is the duty of those that are unmarried.'[35]

We have seen that birth control was not a dead question at mid-century and that it was not considered in isolation from the rights of women. But perhaps the most important problem concerns the response of women to the contraceptive propaganda being diffused. Did they respond to the birth control campaign or were they, as the Banks suggest, passive observers? As has been indicated above there is evidence that some did take a great interest in the discussion. Additional evidence is naturally limited because middle-class women could only speak to their doctor about the subject and the medical profession was publicly opposed to the practice. When it was reported that the Dialectical Society had debated the pros and cons of the 'small family system' the *Medical Press and Circular*, the *Lancet*, the *British Medical Journal*, and the *Medical Times and Gazette* all repudiated the involvement of the medical profession in the affair. 'We cannot find words sufficiently strong to express our utter abhorrence and condemnation of the idea of discussing such a question as a purely medical one. It is not a medical question,' asserted the editor of the *Medical Times and Gazette*, 'and will never become so. . .'[36] Given this hostility it is not strange that there are few instances in which doctors would report that their women patients spoke to them about family planning methods. But that such discussions were taking place was made clear in a letter written by Mary Ann Ayres to Lord Amberley. She reported that she had consulted with Drs Czerny, Ryan, and Mosely in 1846 and adopted a method of contraception as a result.[37] She did not say whether her husband was in agreement. In the testimony of Dr William Acton there are references to the emergence of feminist ideas leading to the sort of women's 'revolt' which the Banks deny:

During the last few years and since the rights of women have been so much insisted upon, and practically carried out 'by the strongest

molds of their sex' numerous husbands have complained to me of
the hardships which they suffer being married to women who
regard themselves as martyrs when called upon to fulfill the duties
of wives. This spirit of insubordination has become more
intolerable — as the husbands assert — since it has been backed by
the opinions of John Stuart Mill, who in his work on 'The Subjection
of Women,' would induce the sex to believe that they are 'but
personal bodyservants of a despot.'[38]

Feminism and family planning were intimately related. Every writer
who dealt with the issue of birth control expressed the belief that it
would directly improve the physical and psychological life of the
woman. Women by 1870 had at their disposal an articulated doctrine
which held that they had a right and an obligation to limit their
pregnancies. Thus when the decision was posed in the middle-class
home whether or not to limit family size the question would not be
resolved simply according to economic considerations; the health and
happiness of the wife had now been raised in the eyes of many to a
place of equal importance. The Banks have suggested that women
played a passive role in such decision-making because the respectable,
publicly identifiable form of 'feminism' did not condone birth control.
We have seen that there was a body of ideas and beliefs which could
be called 'domestic feminism' which accepted such practices and incited
women to play an active part.[39]

Notes

1. Peter Fryer, *The Birth Controllers* (London, 1965), p.107.
2. See also Anon., *An Essay on Populousness* (London, 1838) which makes a
   similar argument and on the affair see Sidney and Beatrice Webb, *English Poor
   Law History* (London, 1963 2nd edn.), pt.2, I, pp.164-5.
3. Thomas Carlyle, *Chartism* (London, 1840), p.110; Thomas Doubleday, *The
   True Law of Population* (London, 1853), xxxix.
4. *Political Register* (2 November, 1839), p.37.
5. Linton, the *National* (29 June, 1839), pp.364-5. See F.B. Smith, *Radical
   Artisan: William James Linton 1812-1897* (Manchester, 1973).
6. Mill, *Principles of Political Economy* (Toronto, 1965 [1st edn. 1848]), p.206.
7. Anon., [By the author of *Adaptability*], *Morality: And its Practical
   Applications to Social Institutions* (London, 1856), pp.12-3.
8. Miles, *Economy of Life, or, Food, Repose, and Love* (London, 1868), pp.116-7.
9. *Political Register* (19 October, 1839), 1; Place to Lovett (19 September, 1840,
   F. Place, *Illustrations. . .of Population* (London, 1930), p.341; Henry Vincent
   was one working-class leader won over. Though he never made his conversion
   public he wrote Place in 1840 that he was '. . .now thoroughly convinced of

the soundness of the doctrines taught by Malthus and yourself.' Joyce M. Bellamy and John Saville, (eds.), *Dictionary of Labour Biography* (London, 1972), I, p.330.

10. *Political Economist* (9 November, 1856), pp.324-5.

11. See John Saville, (ed.), *A Selection of Political Pamphlets of Charles Bradlaugh* (New York, 1970) See especially *Jesus, Shelley and Malthus* (1861), *Poverty* (1863), *Why Do Men Starve?* (1865), *Labour's Prayer* (1865).

12. For an apolitical approach see Anon., *Valuable Hints. . .to Fathers Having Increasing Families but Limited Incomes* (London, 1866).

13. On the Amberley affair see Betrand and Patricia Russell, (eds.), *The Amberley Papers* (London, 1937), II, pp.168-249; F.W. Newman, *Fraser's Magazine* (April, 1871), p.453.

14. T. Falconer, *Note on a Paper Circulated by Abraham Hayward Esq.* (London, 1845); Henry E. Carlisle, (ed.), *A Selection from the Correspondence of Abraham Hayward Q.C.* (London, 1886), 2 vol.; George Jacob Holyoake, *Sixty Years of an Agitator's Life* (London, 1893), I, 129 ff.; Holyoake, *Bygones Worth Remembering* (London, 1905), I, pp.259-9; Holyoake, *John Stuart Mill as Some of the Working Classes Knew Him* (London, 1873), p.22.

15. Mill to Eichthal (30 May, 1869), Mill to Rev. David King (October 1870), Frances E. Mineka, (ed.), *The Later Letters of John Stuart Mill 1849-1873* (Toronto, 1969), IV, pp.1611, 1768.

16. Banks, *Feminism and Family Planning,* p.84.

17. *An Enquiry into the Principles of the Distribution of Wealth* (London, 1824), p.549; See also *Practical Directions for the Speedy and Economical Establishment of Communities* (London, 1830), pp.200-241; *Labour Rewarded: The Claims of Labour and Capital Conciliated* (London, 1827), 70 ff.

18. Carlile, *Every Woman's Book* (London, 1838), pp.19, 13-4; Owen, *Moral Physiology* (New York, 1831), pp.35-6; Charles Knowlton, *Fruits of Philosophy* (London, 1841), pp.37, 40.

19. Carlile to Place (8 August, 1822), Place Collection, British Museum, 68.

20. Owen, *Moral Physiology*, p.46.

21. Knowlton, *Fruits of Philosophy,* p.38; Owen, *Moral Physiology,* p.42.

22. Place to Martineau (8 September, 1832) in Place, *Illustrations,* p.324, George Drysdale, *Physical, Sexual, and Natural Religion* (London, 1855).

23. Carlile, *Every Woman's Book,* p.35.

24. For the view that Carlile 'squelched' the birth control movement by discussing sexual freedom see William J. Langer, 'The Origins of the Birth Control Movement in the Early Nineteenth Century,' *Journal of Interdisciplinary History,* 5 (1975), p.677.

25. 'An Observer,' *Twelve Letters* (Philadelphia, 1830), p.10. See also the reference to Frances Wright as 'that Jezebel beast of a woman' in Albert Cunningham, *Practical Infidelity Portrayed* (New York, 1836), p.51.

26. Edward Hancock, *A Candid Warning to Public Men in a Series of Letters* (New York, 1836), pp.11-12, 15.

27. Linton, the *National* (29 June, 1839), p.365; Brewin Grant, *Report of a Public Discussion Between the Rev. Brewin Grant and George Jacob Holyoake* (London, 1853), 191 ff.; *Discussion Between the Rev. Brewin Grant and Mr George Jacob Holyoake* (Glasgow, 1854), pp.137-53, 192.

28. *Reasoner* (1848), p.177; See also Emma Martin, *The Bible No Revelation* (London, n.d.) and *Religion Superceded* (London, n.d.).

29. Mill, *Principles,* p.372; See Holyoake's review linking Mill to Owen and Anti-Marcus in the *Reasoner* (1848), pp.83-4.

30. *Subjection of Women* (London, 1909), p.59.

31. *Political Economist* (11 January, 1857), p.85.
32. Ibid., p.86.
33. Harte, *On the Laws* (London, 1870), p.33. Harte had been present at the Dialectical Society meetings and indirectly defended Amberley.
34. *Fortnightly Review,* 12 (1872), p.400.
35. Ibid., pp.399, 412.
36. Cited in Russell, *Amberley Papers,* p.174.
37. Ayres to Amberley (16 August, 1868) in Russell, *Amberley Papers,* p.236.
38. Acton, *Functions and Disorders of the Reproductive Organs* (London, 6th edn., n.d. [1st edn. 1857]), p.142, cf.139, pp.214-5.
39. For similar developments in America see Daniel Scott Smith, 'Family Limitation, Sexual Control and Domestic Feminism in Victorian America,' *Feminist Studies,* 1 (1973), pp.40-57.

PART THREE

NEO-MALTHUSIANISM AND ITS
LATE NINETEENTH-CENTURY CRITICS

6 THE MALTHUSIAN LEAGUE

The early birth control ideology was a curious amalgam. Its 'progressive' dimensions were exemplified by its interest in women's rights and medical self-help; its conservatism, by its adherence to neo-Malthusian economics. With the general hardening of party lines which occurred in the latter half of the nineteenth century such a hybrid growth proved increasingly difficult to maintain. The emergence of organised feminist and socialist movements lured away potential radical recruits from the birth control campaign and as a consequence it fell ever more under the sway of the social conservatives. The effect that this would have on the late nineteenth-century discussion of fertility control is the concern of this chapter.

The defence of birth control which had begun to be publicly articulated in the 1820s was finally institutionalised with the appearance in 1877 of the Malthusian League. Its establishment, just at the point in time when the birth rate began its long-term decline (family size as measured by marriage cohorts dropped from 6.16 in 1861-1869 to 2.46 in 1915-1919), has led some to assume that the neo-Malthusians were responsible for this demographic transition.[1] But the fact that the birth rate of other west European countries, even those deprived of neo-Malthusian propagandists,[2] tumbled in the last third of the nineteenth century suggests that the emergence of the League was a symptom, not a cause, of a social situation in which restriction of family size was occurring. Indeed the argument can be made that the League hindered as much as helped the acceptance of contraception by the British masses. Adhering to a rigid Malthusian economic analysis which even academic economists in the 1880s found increasingly out of date, it draped its birth control literature in a reactionary shroud which made much of it unacceptable to labour.

The Malthusian League was an offshoot of the mid-Victorian secularist movement which, between the decline of Chartism and the rise of socialism, served as an outlet for both popular anticlericalism and radical working-class political activity. In its early years it was led by the former Owenite lecturer and cooperator George Jacob Holyoake.[3] It was Holyoake and the freethought publishers James Watson and Charles Watts who continued through the middle decades of the century to produce and sell the tracts of Owen and Knowlton.

The secularists were a heterogeneous group but in the 1860s the dynamic young Charles Bradlaugh sought to bring some order to the movement by establishing the National Secular Society. Though an advanced radical, as we have seen, in questions of religion and birth control, Bradlaugh was an economic conservative. His ascendancy in the movement was thus marked by it becoming increasingly orthodox in its economic pronouncements while it became ever more outspoken in the defence of contraception. This growing social conservatism of secularism was if anything accentuated by the fact that it was being supplanted by the socialists as *the* radical group in English politics.

In the first issue of his *National Reformer* Bradlaugh printed George Drysdale's 'The Population Doctrines' and proceeded in the early 1860s to broach the idea of launching a movement to popularise the tenets contained in *The Elements of Social Science*.[4] Initially the idea was not well received within the secularist camp. Bradlaugh's co-editor, Joseph Barker, took advantage of this suggested shift in policy to resign and establish a competing journal, *Barker's Review*. Even Holyoake, who had applauded the appearance of *The Elements* in 1857, cautioned prudence.[5] Bradlaugh's plan was rejected because of the secularists' concern that such a concentration of effort would weaken their effectiveness in other areas. But they continued to advertise and distribute birth control literature. What catapulted this peaceful propagandising into becoming the basis for an organised crusade was the public response to the prosecution of Bradlaugh, Annie Besant, and Edward Truelove for the sale of such tracts. Their 1877 trial has been described at length elsewhere.[6] Here it is only necessary to note that what began as simply one more attempt by secularists to use the courts to publicise their freethought doctrines became the vehicle by which the public's interest in birth control information was dramatically demonstrated. Thus an issue which was only alluded to by the respectable in the 1860s became a *cause célèbre* in the 1870s. The immediate result of the prosecution was the massive sale of Knowlton's pamphlet; during the three months of the trial 125,000 copies of *Fruits of Philosophy* were sold. Such was the demand that Annie Besant produced her own tract *The Law of Population* which as the title suggests linked contraception to Malthusian economics. Before she withdrew it from circulation in 1890, 175,000 copies were purchased. The second consequence of the discovery of the massive public interest in fertility control was the creation of the Malthusian League with Charles Robert Drysdale, brother of George Drysdale, as president. The League, which began with close to a thousand members, saw itself as playing primarily an educative role.[7] Its duty was not so much to provide practical information on fertility control as to demonstrate the validity of Malthus' arguments which made recourse to such controls necessary.

A history of the Malthusian League has recently appeared; the tedious task of plotting the development of the Drysdale family's campaign does not have to be dealt with in detail.[8] For the purpose of setting the late nineteenth-century birth control debate in context it is necessary, however, to establish the League's attitudes towards the working classes, women, and doctors. The story of its attempts to win these groups to a belief in the social necessity of birth control was one of continual frustration. The columns of its journal, the *Malthusian,* were filled with a constant stream of acticles bewailing the fact that workers spurned Malthus and turned to socialism, feminists preferred suffrage activities to birth control propagandising, and doctors were either reluctant to declare themselves on the question or were drawn to the more scientifically exciting doctrine of eugenics.

The failure of the Malthusian League was born of its monistic message. As its name implied it could only conceive of birth control as a logical extension of Malthus' economic teachings. There were contributors to the *Malthusian* who recognised that the avowed purpose of spreading a knowledge of contraception would be impeded if the League insisted on presenting it as part of a conservative social programme. George Standring protested in 1879 that the very name *Malthusian* was a stumbling block.[9] John M. Robertson who wrote a large number of articles for the journal flaunted a radicalism that appeared very much out of place in contrast to the Drysdales' conservatism. But it was they who set the policy of the League. In an article of 1885 entitled 'Thorough Malthusians and moderate Malthusians' Charles Drysdale declared that only the former position was tenable.[10] The sole cause of poverty was an excess of births. Any attempt at social reform which did not begin by addressing itself to this issue could not be supported by the League. Thus strikes − including the great dock strike of 1889 − were declared by the *Malthusian* to be ineffectual, General Booth's Salvation Army castigated as useless, and Keir Hardie's proposal of an eight hour day declared preposterous.

In the first half of the nineteenth century the advocates of birth control had attempted to argue that their views and those of social reformers were not irreconcilable. The Malthusian League took a much harder line. Its members were resolutely opposed to any form of socialism. The Drysdales claimed that socialism provided a totally erroneous analysis of the economy and that socialist agitators were as a consequence directly responsible for keeping the working class in ignorance of contraceptive information essential for its well-being. Yet the League itself made only sporadic attempts to meet the working class. The *Malthusian* was written by and for members of the middle class; no journal was produced for the poor. The assumption behind this educational policy was that if the respectable were convinced of the validity of the Malthusian doctrine and acted on such beliefs the lower orders would soon follow their example.

The main attempt to meet the workers on their own ground took place in the 1880s when League speakers set out to do battle with representatives of the socialist parties such as Herbert Burrows and J.L. Joynes. These debates in such disparate settings as the Phoenix Temperance Hall, the Zetetical Society, the Lambeth Democratic Federation, the Stratford Radical Club, the Hatchman Liberal Club, and the Goat Tavern, Battersea, began to taper off in the 1890s once both movements realised that neither was going to be annihilated by simple force of argument. The *Malthusian* thereafter contented itself in reiterating that the socialists, by their refusal to accept the necessity of birth control were turning their backs on the iron law of economics.[11]

Socialists, as will be shown in a later chapter, were not all opposed to the discussion of birth control. George Standring who was on the executive of the Malthusian League and published the *Malthusian* was also on the executive of the Fabian Society (1893-1908 and 1909-1911) and published its tracts.[12] Edward Aveling, the translator of Marx, found, like Standring, no great difficulty in defending secularism, neo-Malthusianism, and socialism.[13] What the Malthusian League was referring to when it complained of the intransigence of socialists was not so much that they denied the practical advantages of family limitation but that they refused to acknowledge that Malthusian economic doctrines were inextricably associated with such advantages.

The League assumed that socialists would never accept the necessity of birth control but it did have hopes that the leaders of the women's movement would. As was seen in chapter five, the early birth control advocates all concerned themselves with the question of women's emancipation. The Drysdales were to be especially active in the feminist agitation of the late nineteenth century. C.R. Drysdale helped to establish a college for the medical training of women and participated in the campaign against the Contagious Diseases Act.[14] His wife, Alice Vickery, the first woman chemist admitted to the Pharmaceutical Society, was an outspoken defender of women's rights. The *Malthusian* applauded each and every advance in the feminist struggle. What disappointed the League was that the women's movement, in focusing attention on the issue of political rights, appeared to be ignoring the vital problem of fertility control. In articles such as 'On the Position of Women, as Affected by Large Families' Alice Vickery argued that women would never be fully emancipated until they controlled their own bodies.[15] Indeed in the feminist review, the *Freewoman,* C.V. Drysdale suggested that the late nineteenth-century women's movement only emerged because the birth rate by its previous decline permitted women to interest themselves in politics.[16]

Since the English women's movement was intent on securing the vote, the Malthusian League's writers were willing to concede that it was understandable that suffragists would avoid the potentially explosive issue of birth control.[17] Yet at the same time the *Malthusian* carried the names of a number of European women – Aletta Jacobs of Holland, Maria Stritt of Germany, Madeleine Pelletier and Nelly Roussel of France, Anna Wicksell of Sweden, Rosika Schwimmer of Hungary – who were both feminists and avowed neo-Malthusians. The implication was clear; the suffragists were, in the eyes of the League, pursuing the will-o-the-wisp of political power and losing sight of the far more significant problems of motherhood. The League was never to attack feminists as it belaboured socialists but it did not hide its disillusionment that after having championed emancipation it should find its message spurned by the leading women activists.

The Malthusian League sought to win English feminists to the cause of birth control by showing them that the leaders of the continental women's movement supported it; in a similar fashion the League wooed the British medical profession. Any sympathetic reference to birth control by an European physician was quickly reported in the *Malthusian.* It gave an account, for example, of the International Medical Congress of 1879 at which Drs Leblond, Lutaud, and Aran denied that contraception was medically harmful. In *The Small Family System: Is it Injurious or Immoral* (1913) C.V. Drysdale cited Dr Hector Treub and Dr Aletta Jacobs of Amsterdam, Jan Rutgers of the Hague, Dr H. Rohleder of Leipzig and Dr Auguste Forel of Zurich as doctors of note who were declared neo-Malthusians. But the fact that the League had to look outside England to find distinguished practitioners who dared to defend birth control publicly was the most eloquent expression of its failure to convert its own medical profession.[18] The Drysdales were themselves active in medical circles and did have the support of a few individual doctors such as Drs Kate Mitchell, William Hitchman, and

Walter Dunstan. The vast majority of doctors refused to commit
themselves.

The treatment meted out by the medical profession to Dr Henry
Allbutt provided a warning to others. Allbutt, a secularist and organiser
of the Leeds neo-Malthusian movement, had the League establish a
medical section in 1880 in order to attract the support of physicians.
That support was not to be forthcoming was made abundantly clear
when Allbutt was himself removed from the medical register for having
published *The Wife's Handbook.* Like Knowlton before him Allbutt
was convinced that his 'crime' had been to make knowledge too cheap.
In *Artificial Checks to Population: Is the Popular Teaching of Them
Infamous?* (1888) he concluded that morality was graded according to
price. If a doctor wrote in technical terms in books restricted to an
educated elite he could freely broach the question of sexuality. It was
providing a clearly written pamphlet on birth control for six pence that
occasioned persecution.[19] The fairness of this characterisation of the
profession's attitude will be judged in chapter seven.

The League was itself extremely reluctant to provide practical
information on fertility control; its goal was to educate doctors so
that they would in turn provide their patients with the help they
required. For the moment the League found it necessary to recommend
the pamphlets of Allbutt, Standring, and Besant but these were not
official publications of the movement. Here again the League
demonstrated its innate conservatism. Though continually opposed by
the medical profession it was only with the greatest reluctance that the
neo-Malthusians considered the option of circumventing this problem
by establishing their own clinics. It was not until 1913 that it took the
step of offering information directly to couples and even then it
required them to fill out an elaborate form in order to receive a
pamphlet on *Hygienic Methods of Family Limitation.*[20]

The fact that many doctors would declare themselves eugenists and
yet refuse to defend birth control was in some ways the final proof of
the ineffectiveness of the Malthusian League's attempt to win
respectability. The eugenic crusade received the imprimateur of the
British Medical Association in 1912 when its president Sir James Barr
was reported in a speech at the annual general meeting as stating,

No serious attempt had yet been made to prevent the race from
being carried by its least worthy citizens. If such an attempt was to
be successful we must begin with the unborn. The race must be
renewed from the mentally and physically fit, and the moral and

physical degenerates should not be allowed to take any part in adding to it.[21]

It was a curious situation and one that will be discussed at length in chapter eight that the medical profession while still regarding the voluntary restriction of fertility as a tabooed subject was willing to debate the sterilisation of the 'unfit'.

The Malthusian League remained in existence until 1927. In its last years its survival depended more and more on the personal financial support of the Drysdales.[22] It became increasingly clear with time that the rigid Malthusianism of the organisation had crippled its effectiveness as a populariser of birth control. In 1919 George Standring made an attempt at creating an alternative to the *Malthusian* by establishing a new journal, *Birth Control.* This periodical would present, declared Standring, the arguments of 'mere birth controllers,' not the 'strong and sometimes even aggressive Individualism' of the Malthusian League.[23] Standring's *Birth Control* only had two issues but his effort to free the subject from the thrall of Malthusian economics was to be achieved in 1921 by Marie Stopes' Society for Constructive Birth Control.

What were the results of the Malthusian League's activities? If success were measured simply in numbers of neo-Malthusian tracts produced and distributed the work of the Drysdales and their colleagues could be viewed as a triumph. It has been estimated that between 1879 and 1921 the League issued about three million pamphlets and leaflets.[24] However, the League did not pride itself on the provision of practical information. If it had it would not have waited until 1913 − thirty-six years after its founding − before beginning the circulation of its own leaflets on contraception. The interests of the League were primarily economic; the vast majority of its publications were simple recapitulations of population theory. What it sought and what it failed to achieve was the conversion of the British public to a belief in Malthusian economics. The League's most striking success was in making the defence of birth control appear to be the monopoly of a conservative coterie. If it could not coax even doctors into an acceptance of its tenets what reception could it expect to meet from the leaders of labour?

Notes

1. On family size see N.L. Trantner, *Population Since the Industrial Revolution* (London, 1973), p.98; for an optimistic account of the League's role see Peter Fryer, *The Birth Controllers* (New York, 1966), p.189.
2. The term 'neo-Malthusian' which is a more accurate description of the League's position was first used in English in the early 1880s by J.M. Robertson. Norman E. Himes, *Medical History of Contraception* (New York, 1936), p.257 n.64.
3. Angus McLaren, 'George Jacob Holyoake and the Secular Society: British Popular Freethought, 1851-1858,' *Canadian Journal of History*, 7 (1972), pp.235-51; Edward Royle, *Victorian Infidels: The Origins of the British Secular Movement* (Manchester, 1974).
4. George Drysdale's work first appeared as *Physical, Sexual, and Natural Religion* (London, 1855) and was as the title suggests religiously heterodox. Drysdale attacked 'spiritualism' for hindering a true appreciation of the body and called for a 'physical religion.' The book was to become one of the neo-Malthusian classics and go through thirty-five editions and 80,000 copies by 1905 – despite the fact that only six of its four hundred and forty-nine pages concerned contraception.
5. David Tribe, *President Charles Bradlaugh M.P.* (London, 1971), pp.69-80; see also the *National Reformer*, 2 (1861), 3 (1862).
6. Arthur H. Nethercott, *The First Five Lives of Annie Besant* (Chicago, 1960), 90 ff.
7. The presidency of the League was handed down from Charles R. Drysdale (1877-1907) to Alice Vickery Drysdale (1907-1921) to Charles Vickery Drysdale (1921-1927).
8. Rosanna Ledbetter, *A History of the Malthusian League 1877-1927* (Columbus, Ohio, 1976).
9. *Malthusian* (December, 1879), p.90.
10. *Malthusian* (November, 1885), p.649.
11. See also Bessie Drysdale, *Labour Troubles and Birth Control* (London, 1920).
12. See Standring's journal of the 1880s the *Republican* in which socialist and neo-Malthusian arguments are presented.
13. See Aveling, *Darwinism and Small Families* (1882) in which he writes (p.4) that large families imply '. . .a lowness of intellect on the part of the parents that goes as far down as wickedness.' Aveling later translated Marx's *Capital* but was to win fame by his scandalous personal behaviour which drove Eleanor Marx to suicide. See C. Tsuzuki, *The Life of Eleanor Marx* (Oxford, 1967).
14. See Charles R. Drysdale, *Medicine as a Profession for Women* (London, 1870). For Allbutt and Drysdale in the C.D. agitation see Benjamin Scott, *A State Iniquity* (London, 1890), pp.116, 119, 217.
15. *Malthusian* (September, 1880), pp.154-5. See also Marie Fisher, 'Ought Women to be Punished for Having too Many Children?' *Malthusian* (August, September, October, 1888), pp.58-60, 68-9, 75-6.
16. *Freewomen* (30 November, 1911), pp.36-7, (4, 25 January, 1912), pp.128, 194.
17. *Malthusian* (January 1909), p.4.
18. Drysdale did acknowledge that the South West branch of the B.M.A. had passed a motion against birth control as late as 1905. See also Charles R. Drysdale, *The Population Question* (London, 1892) and *Medical Opinions on the Population Question* (London, 1901).
19. Allbutt, *Artificial Checks to Population* (London, 1909 14th edn.), pp.8-9. See also Allbutt, *Evils Produced by Over-Childbearing and Excessive Lactation* (London, 1878).

20. *Malthusian* (June, 1914), p.41.
21. *The Times* (24 July, 1912), 7 ff.
22. On the personalities in the London movement see Margaret Sanger, *An Autobiography* (New York, 1938), 129 ff.
23. *Birth Control* (February, 1919). Standring had earlier attacked the conservatism of the League in a lecture at Finsbury, 'Neo-Malthusianism, the Handmaiden of Socialism,' *Malthusian* (June 1906).
24. D.V. Glass, *Population Policies and Movements in Europe* (Oxford, 1940), pp.42-3.

7 BIRTH CONTROL AND THE BRITISH MEDICAL PROFESSION, 1850-1914

Until this point the main focus of the discussion has been on the way in which the birth control issue was manipulated for political purposes. An analysis of the hostile response of doctors to the question, a subject touched on in chapter four, makes it clear that concerns for professional interest and status would also play a major role in the birth control debate. The decline of the British birth rate in the latter half of the nineteenth century (from 34.1 per thousand in 1870-72 to 24.5 per thousand in 1910-1912)[1] appears all the more remarkable when it is recalled that it occurred despite the continued opposition of the medical profession to the use of contraceptives. Medical practitioners spent the better part of a century in turning a deaf ear to the appeals of the advocates of birth control. In 1848 George Jacob Holyoake, while advancing John Stuart Mill's economic arguments in favour of family limitation, called in vain on doctors to complement his activities.

> We want a physician of authority to treat the medical view of the question with the same power and boldness with which Mill treats its bearings on Political Economy. . .I publish these chapters of Mill, in the hope of stimulating the further compliance consistency demands — the want of which is a disgrace to the medical reputation of the age.[2]

At the famous meeting of the Dialectical Society in 1868 Lord Amberley declared that women were anxiously looking for safe ways in which to limit their families and that it was the responsibility of doctors to suggest the appropriate measures. Charles Drysdale seconded Amberley's plea in agreeing that it was a medical problem.[3] In 1873 Holyoake returned to the question.

> The decrease of large families among the rich and middle classes in every great country shows that limitations are known; and it is the disgrace of medical men that no college of physicians give proper information to the poor, in language which the pure might read; and not leave them victims of the verbiage or pollution of quacks.[4]

Some doctors recognised the problem. Dr Henry Oldham, lecturer on midwifery at Guy's Hospital, was presumably expressing the feelings of fellow physicians when he wrote in 1849,

> It constantly happens that cases come before us where either from disease of the uterus or pelvis, or sexual organs, or exhaustion from frequent abortions or protracted labours, − that it would be most desirable to suspend for a time or altogether prevent pregnancy.[5]

Similar sentiments were expressed by American physicians whose works circulated in Britain. Dr George H. Napheys in *The Physical Life of Women* (1869) stated that patients who found their doctors unresponsive sought help from others: '. . .numberless wives and husbands who turn a deaf ear to the warnings of doctors and the thunders of divines, and, eager to escape a responsibility they have assumed, hesitate not to resort to the most dangerous and immoral means to accomplish this end.' Much the same concern was voiced by Mrs E.B. Duffey in *What Women Should Know* (1873) in a chapter entitled 'Enforced Child Bearing': 'But how this evil of too large families is to be avoided is a question asked by many, especially suffering wives. They ask their physician during the pains and terrors of delivery, and they are answered flippantly, if not indelicately.'[6] Thus, even within the medical profession, it was acknowledged that doctors should express an opinion on contraception, if only to warn patients against the dangers it entailed.

A handful of physicians did support the campaign for birth control in the last decades of the nineteenth century but the medical profession as a whole remained adamantly opposed to contraception. Sensitive to the explosive nature of the issue and anxious to establish its respectability, the profession's initial response was to declare that control of fertility was not a medical problem. Such a stance could not be long maintained. The growing public awareness that the upper and middle classes were artificially regulating family size, the concern expressed that working-class women were resorting in ever greater numbers to abortion, and the interest shown in neo-Malthusian propaganda, especially after 1877, all combined to force upon the medical world the recognition that its involvement in the birth control controversy could not be avoided. Finally, compelled in the last decades of the nineteenth century to take a stand on an issue that it would have preferred to ignore, the profession declared that contraception, because of the physical and psychological damage it occasioned, could not be sanctioned by medical practitioners. Why did the medical profession adopt such a stance? The traditional response given to this question — that doctors were motivated primarily by ethical concerns — provides only part of the answer. Medical opposition to contraception was not gratuitous; the profession's opinion on this specific issue throws light on some of the general characteristics of its approach to health care. First, doctors were slow to interest themselves in preventive medicine. Birth control was just one of its many forms long ignored by doctors. The medical profession only hesitantly came to grips with such problems as high infant and maternal mortality, alcoholism, and tuberculosis. The temperance movement had to emerge as a self-help medical crusade to deal with the problems of drunkenness. In a somewhat similar fashion the birth control campaign surfaced outside the realm of professional medicine in order to deal with the problem of undesired pregnancies. Both movements were, to varying degrees, opposed to and opposed by official medical science which, because of its pathological orientation, under-emphasised preventive strategies. This led to the second reason why doctors opposed contraception: they viewed it as an inappropriate subject for study by respectable physicians because it was associated with the activities of non-professionals — the quacks, the retailers of rubber goods and the midwives — who challenged their professional monopoly in medical science. Thirdly, doctors, because they did not seriously study the question, continued to confuse abortion and contraception. The fears they felt concerning the dangers of the former practice spilled over into their condemnations of the latter. Fourthly, many doctors were sincerely convinced that contraception was dangerous to the health. To suggest, as some historians have done, that physicians simply made up horror stories to frighten patients is to credit them with an unlikely degree of cynicism and hypocrisy.[7] A doctor opposed to contraception would not be informed by patients of their success in limiting family size; he would probably only have to deal with the unsuccessful and his fears and prejudices would thus be confirmed. In short doctors did not have to fabricate accounts; they were told what they wanted to hear. It was true that in the last decades of the nineteenth century they increasingly downplayed the physical damage caused by 'conjugal onanism' and accentuated the psychological. Of course if a patient who adopted such practices showed signs of 'nervous complaints' it was for the very reason that doctors had repeatedly informed him that they could result in sterility, amnesia, insanity and suicide. Finally, the doctor saw himself as family confessor and counsellor. Assuming the role of public censor once fulfilled by the priest he advanced medical evidence to support what were basically moral arguments against contraception. He felt particularly duty-bound to rebuke women who, in their attempts to limit their own fertility, challenged him as a male, a medical scientist, and a moral arbiter.

The importance of the above prejudices and preconceptions will be made clear in this chapter in which doctors' attitudes towards specific types of birth control — male and female contraception, abortion, physiological checks, and abstinence — are analysed. Although John Peel in 'Contraception and the Medical Profession' and J.A. Banks in *Prosperity and Parenthood* both give the impression that medical hostility to contraception only surfaced after 1877, in the first part of this chapter it will be shown that such opposition can be found much earlier.[8] It is true that the appearance of the neo-Malthusian movement from the late 1860s on did drive the medical profession into making increasingly hysterical attacks on family limitation; this literature will receive special attention in the latter half of the chapter.

Nineteenth-century physicians assumed that the male took the decision on whether or not to limit family size and their attitudes towards contraception as a whole can be best begun by a discussion of male contraceptive tactics. The two most commented on by the medical profession were coitus interruptus and the use of the condom or sheath. The former, the withdrawal method of birth control, was the oldest and most widely known of contraceptive measures. Evidence abounds that the stratagem of Onan, condemned in the book of Genesis, was well known to nineteenth-century Englishmen. In the *1811 Dictionary of the Vulgar Tongue* under the term 'Coffee House' one can read: 'To make a coffee-house of a woman's ****; to go in and out and spend nothing.'[9] A correspondent of Francis Place in the 1820s wrote that the French referred to the practice as '. . .*la Chamade,* the Retreat, but most commonly by the softer name of *la Prudence,* or *la Discretion.* . .'[10] A century later this method was still relied upon, even in the upper classes, if one is to believe Oswald Mosley's memoirs. He writes that after his wife, Cynthia, daughter of Lord Curzon, had her first child she was visited by Margot Asquith, wife of the former Liberal Prime Minister, who imparted the following advice: '"Dear child, you look very pale and must not have another baby for a long time. Henry always withdrew in time, such a noble man."'[11]

The medical profession took a much more jaundiced view of coitus interruptus. It attributed to the practice a variety of physical and psychological complaints and in the main treated it as a form of masturbation or onanism.[12] Indeed the term 'conjugal onanism' was used to describe this type of birth control.[13] Both marriage partners were said to suffer as a result of such practices: the woman, because she was raised to a high pitch of excitement but then deprived of the 'vital fluid'; the man because his expenditure of energy was not compensated by a creative act. For most doctors it was the damage done to the male that was most distressing. In Naphey's words, 'Nervous prostration, paralysis, premature debility and decay, are its inevitable consequences. No wife who loves her husband will ask or permit him to run this danger.'[14] There were advocates of birth control such as George Drysdale and Annie Besant who were also critical of coitus interruptus but in their case the concern was motivated by the belief that it was the woman who suffered. The man would achieve orgasm; the woman was excited but deprived of full satisfaction.[15]

Coitus interruptus was opposed by doctors because it was assumed to be simply a form of masturbation; the condom was opposed because it was associated in their minds with prostitution and venereal disease. In Robley Dunglinson's *A Dictionary of Medical Science* (1853) condoms were described as still being made of sheep gut; their chief purpose was to prevent venereal infection.[16] According to George H. Napheys' *The Transmission of Life* (1872) their only legitimate use within marriage was to prevent the wife from catching an infection picked up by the husband.

> We therefore believe such instructions [on the use of sheaths] should be kept for individual instances, and reserved for those cases, in married life, where, on the one hand, an abstinence on the part of the husband might lead to bitter feeling, or destruction of domestic ties from suspicion and jealousy; and on the other, should he not abstain, he might involve her in his own misfortunes.[17]

In fact the evidence suggests that sheaths were already used, by those who could afford them, as contraceptives. By the 1870s they were being produced in large numbers by the vulcanisation process and retailed by that peculiarly British outlet for contraceptives – the barbershop.[18] A French writer, Frederic Buret, referred to them in passing: 'These little contrivances, employed more especially in bourgeois households, where a fear exists of the multiplication of mouths to feed, are too well known for us to dilate on them.'[19] Another French observer, Hector France in *Les va-nu-pieds de Londres* (1883) wrote that in Petticoat Lane one could even find '. . .*French letters* avec le portrait du ministre Gladstone ou de la reine Victoria. . .'[20]

Doctors regarded the condom or male 'covering,' even when emblazoned with the portrait of Gladstone, as a sordid instrument. They warned their patients that it deprived the sexual act of pleasure, lessened the virility of the male, and like coitus interruptus, by depriving the female of vital fluid, occasioned nervous complaints.[21]

Turning to female forms of contraception, the medical profession held up for special scrutiny the use of the sponge or pessary and the employment of the douche or syringe. The sponge was recommended as a contraceptive by all the birth control advocates — Place, Owen, Knowlton, Drysdale, Besant, and Allbutt. Doctors also prescribed the use of sponges or pessaries but not for the purpose of limiting fertility. Believing as they did that most female complaints stemmed from a malfunction of the reproductive system doctors had long spoken of the problem of 'displacement' of the womb. The medical profession of the mid-nineteenth century revealed its mechanistic penchant by responding to the problem by recommending the readjustment and manipulation of the womb by the insertion of pessaries.[22] A typical account of the usefulness of pessaries to support the uterus and vagina was included by James Blundell in *Observations on Some of the More Important Diseases of Women* (1837). He noted in particular the efficacy of a sponge pessary popularised by a Dr Haighton.

> He recommended tapes to facilitate is [sic] removal, and was of the opinion that some advantage might be derived from imbuing the instrument daily, with some astringent lotion, alum, for instance, the strength of which should be gradually increased.[23]

Such pessaries were not a new idea. Dr Edward John Tilt in *A Handbook of Uterine Therapeutics* (1863) noted that a wide variety of articles had been used to adjust the angle of the womb. Hippocrates had used a pomegranate; some contemporary French surgeons used small lemons. Sponges and India-rubber appliances which were steeped in alum and inserted on strings in order to be removed and cleaned at night were now gaining in popularity. Tilt, for his part was sceptical of their utility. He sniped at Dr J.Y. Simpson's interest in them which he likened to his '. . .enthusiastic spirit that made him take up chloroform for midwifery.'[24] In Tilt's opinion the idea of the womb being displaced was a myth and the insertion of devices thus useless or even, in the case of the interuterine stemmed pessary, dangerous in that it could cause death by acute peritonitis.[25]

Strangely enough it was some time before doctors addressed

themselves to the question of the use of sponges and pessaries as contraceptives. Their tardiness was perhaps due to the assumption that the woman would not play an active role in limiting births but leave the initiative to the male. Yet the pessaries described in the medical texts are so similar to the devices recommended by the birth controllers that it is difficult not to believe that some women were using them early in the century for contraceptive purposes. One of the first public condemnations of such tactics was made by the American physician John Cowan in *The Science of a New Life* (1869).[26] He warned his readers that the sponges and rubber pads widely advertised by quacks deprived the sex act of all pleasure and were moreover no guarantee against conception. Dr C.H. Routh followed up Cowan's attack in a speech before the obstetrical section of the British Medical Association in 1878. He informed his listeners that even doctors were implicated in the use of pessaries for contraceptive purposes.

> It has been reserved, however, for some of our own people to discover a fifth method [of birth control]. In a debate before the Medical Society of London last session on the use of intra-uterine stems, devised originally for uterine diseases, we were credibly informed that they were also used by some ladies of high positions, and continually worn by them, with a view to *prevent* conception. . . To find them placed in proper position, and with this intent, implies the assistance of a person of some skill, and shows to what degree of degradation some men have fallen.[27]

Medical men had not only made the public aware of the use of the pessary; they had also broadcast the hygienic benefits of douching. E.J. Tilt recommended the use of Coxeter's vulcanised India-rubber siphon syringe to counter vaginal inflammation; E. Ruddock noted the effectiveness of a similar contrivance in dealing with leucorrhoea; P.H. Chavasse suggested that the monthly nurse attending young mothers equip herself with a Higginson syringe.[28] But the syringe, like the sponge pessary was an instrument which could be turned from its original 'innocent' purposes to contraceptive ends. W.T. Stead wrote in his diary 20 January 1899: 'I have from the birth of Willie (1875?) practised simple syringing with water. Of late always withdrawal. We never used anything but this. . .'[29] When such practices were brought to doctors' attention their response was to declare that vaginal injections immediately after intercourse caused serious shocks to the nervous system and accordingly posed grave dangers to health.[30]

Douching was held suspect in some doctors minds because it could be used both as a contraceptive measure and as a means to induce a miscarriage or, in the popular phrase, 'bring on a period'. The actual relationship of the period to pregnancy seems to have been clear enough to most married women, but for much of the nineteenth-century doctors were divided on the issue. As a result many medical texts, though they condemned recourse to abortion, did provide details on how the use of purgatives could elicit a late period. Ruddock, for example, warned against the use of 'forcing medicines' but then proceeded to list medications to be employed in the case of suppression of the menses.[31] George Tate in *A Treatise on Hysteria* (1830) attributed almost every female nervous complaint to faulty menstruation and recommended a mix of iron and aloes to ensure regularity.[32] Astringent douching, electrical shocks, and infusions of ergot of rye were prescribed by the anonymous author, 'A Physician', in *The Diseases of Women: Their Cases, Symptoms and Treatment* (1878).[33] Ergot of rye was also suggested by Tilt, along with savine and aloes, as the best purgatives with which to 'solicit the mense'.[34]

That many women did use such drugs to bring on their period was noted frequently in the medical press. The American physician Edward B. Foote in *Plain Home Talk* (1881) attributed leucorrhoea to '. . .bad habits for the prevention of offspring'.[35] Holmes noted in 1831 that old women advised the younger to employ '. . .*penny-royal,* and other herbs of a *forcing* character'. Such tactics were adopted, he lamented, even by *'good women'.*[36] Weatherly reported that the traditional remedy of taking 'gin and other alcoholic drinks' to bring on the discharge was still popular in the 1880 s.[37]

With the growing appreciation that women were using drugs in an attempt to control their fertility doctors began from mid-century onwards to attack practices which they had earlier tolerated. Thomas Bull in *Hints to Mothers* (1857) warned women that if 'strong purgative medicines' were used to induce miscarriage the result was almost inevitably death.[38] Bull singled out for particular condemnation savine, rue, iron filings, black hellebore and preparations of Spanish Fly. Similar warnings were included by Mrs Lydia F. Fowler, MD in *Woman, Her Destiny and Maternal Relations* (1864).[39] E.J. Tilt, though he prescribed some purgatives, recognised in *On Observations of the Health of Women at Critical Periods of Life* (1851) that many young women 'dread having children.' When their period did not arrive they took drugs, not realising such an action was equal to 'murder'. The fault was their mothers' who had not taught them the evil of the practice.[40]

That doctors and women had differing attitudes on the legitimacy of inducing miscarriage was made equally clear by the American physician Mrs R.B. Gleason who, in *Talks to my Patients* (1870), paraphrased the arguments of female patients who came to her seeking abortion.

> 'It must be done! You can do it better than anyone else, and now that it is so early, there is no life, hence no sin,' etc. . . [Gleason refuses] 'But', says our client, 'quickening is not till the four-and-a-half month, and so, abortion before that time is no sin.' 'But', someone says, 'what shall we poor, sick, overworked women do, who have now more children than we can well look after — more than our husbands can well provide for?' For such I have no advice.[41]

What is particularly interesting in Gleason's report is the statement that female patients assumed, because she was a woman doctor, she would provide abortions.

> In my early practice I was often asked to induce abortion, for the impression seemed to prevail then that the important part of a woman's work in the medical profession was to prevent pregnancy or procure abortion.[42]

P.H. Chavasse of Birmingham agreed with much of what Gleason had to say and attributed, as she and other doctors did, the extent of abortion to women's retention of the traditional notion that before 'quickening' it was permissible to take whatever means necessary to bring on a period.[43] These same doctors went on to state that the situation was being exacerbated by the appearance in the popular press of advertisements for abortificacients.

> With such temptations strewn in her path what will the woman threatened with an excessive family do? Will she not yield to evil, and sear her conscience with the repetition of her wickedness?[44]

Napheys stated that such a woman was often as not married and otherwise a virtuous matron. She was not to be moved by moral claims; the physician could only stop her by graphically portraying the disease, insanity and early death to which the use of abortifacients led.[45]

The fact that abortion figured centrally in the birth control debate was of significance on two counts. First, by failing to disentangle the issue of abortion from that of contraception the medical profession prevented the latter from receiving the dispassionate analysis which it warranted. Secondly, by withholding knowledge of contraception, the profession forced desperate women thus deprived of information on how to control their fertility to the very acts of abortion which doctors condemned.[46]

Condoms, sponges, douches, and drugs were all attacked by doctors as mechanical and artificial means of family limitation which by their unnatural nature could only damage and derange the user. This did not mean that the medical profession believed that no limit should be set to the size of the family; physicians implied that there were 'natural' methods which could be safely employed. In the first half of the century doctors showed little interest in such problems. For example, John Elliotson in *Human Physiology* (1835) stated that questions of generation were for a woman 'long and almost constant'.[47] In the second half of the nineteenth century, however, it was increasingly acknowledged by doctors that numbers should be regulated, that it was healthier if births were spaced, that there could be such a thing as 'over-production'.[48] To attain the limitation and spacing of births the medical profession proposed the adoption of three forms of 'natural' birth control: prolonged nursing, the rhythm method, and abstinence.

Prolonged nursing was a traditional means of attempting to prevent conception. Although doctors recognised that some mothers could conceive while nursing, lactation was advised as a way in which to limit births.[49] Cowan admitted that it was not reliable but followed this statement up with the claim that the woman who would not nurse was evil.[50] Napheys was confident that in nursing nature had provided a safe means by which to space births.[51] Lionel A. Weatherly in *A Young Wife's Own Book* (1882) reported that so convinced were the poor that nursing did provide such protection that they prolonged it up to two years.[52]

The second 'natural' method and one in which doctors had greater faith than in nursing was reliance upon the 'safe period' in a woman's ovulation cycle.[53] In fact the cycle was completely misunderstood and the so-called 'safe period' fell at mid-month but this did not stop several generations of physicians from vaunting its reliability. S. Mason in *The Philosophy of Female Health* (1845) stated that the fertile period consisted of the few days immediately before and after the catamenia.[54] Edward John Tilt in *On Diseases of Women and Ovarian Inflammation* (1853) cited Raciborski and Pouchet of France and Robert Lee and Martin Barry of England as authorities who established similar schedules.[55] Edward Ruddock of the Homeopathic Dispensary, Woolwich gave as his source the Frenchman, Cazeaux when writing in 1861 that,

. . .those who are anxious to increase their families should consider their hopes with this period [just before the mense], whilst they who for reasons of health, from poverty, or other circumstances do not wish to add to the number of their children, should then exercise particular caution and self-control.[56]

J. Marion Sims, the father of American gynaecology, was, as he made clear in *Clinical Notes on Uterine Surgery* (1861), of the same opinion.[57]

With the benefit of hindsight and the knowledge that doctors were proposing a method of fertility control that was completely unsound it is all the more disturbing to see with what enthusiasm the 'safe period' was hailed. George H. Napheys in *The Physical Life of Woman* declared that now the woman weary of child-bearing had a way out: 'To such sufferers we reply that Nature herself has provided to some extent against over-production, and it is well to avail ourselves of her provisions'.[58] Indeed Napheys suggested that marriages be scheduled for the middle of the woman's cycle to prevent immediate conception. In one of the most popular sex manuals of the nineteenth century, R.T. Trall's *Sexual Physiology and Hygiene* (1891) the rhythm method was introduced by what might well be described as a 'feminist' manifesto:

> No truth is more self-evident, no rule of right more plain, no law of Nature more demonstrable, than the right of a woman to her own person. Nor can this right be alienated by marriage. . .Restore woman to health, and give her what God has ordained as her birthright — the control of her own person — and the trade of the abortionist will soon cease; but until then not only will the abortionist flourish, but the larger race of empirics in every city, who sell useless or injurious specifics for the prevention of pregnancy, will derive a profitable trade.[59]

The question of abortion has been dealt with; here it is only necessary to note that, despite the verbiage, Trall was simply recommending reliance on the safe period; all other forms of contraception were skirted.

As long as birth control was achieved by the use of the sheath, douche or sponge — all non-medical appliances associated in the public's mind with the libertine, the prostitute, and the midwife — it lay outside the realm of respectable medicine. The importance of the rhythm method and the reason why it was greeted by doctors with enthusiasm was that it was not tainted by such associations; it had been scientifically determined and so opened up an avenue by which the medical profession could legitimately extend its expertise into the most intimate area of human life. The discovery of the 'safe period' was used by the profession to exalt its pretensions; thus despite the fact that this form of fertility control was completely unreliable it would continue to be advised by doctors for over sixty years.[60]

Doctors such as Trall who defended the rhythm method regarded themselves as daring for the reason that some of their colleagues opposed even such a 'natural' means of family limitation. T.L. Nichols in *Human Physiology* (1872) condemned the tactic in no uncertain terms.

> To select for union the period when conception is least likely to occur, or to use any means whereby the masculine and feminine elements cannot unite, are unnatural practices, clearly akin to the solitary vices which are so abhorrent and so destructive; and there is no doubt that every practice of this kind is a physical injury.[61]

For purists such as Nichols the only safe and sure method was abstinence. He declared that it was not as difficult to maintain as some thought; high moral culture naturally led to love of chastity. Obviously borrowing from Spencer, Nichols declared that in all animals families grew smaller as the organism reached a higher development. He pointed to the small numbers of the peerage to prove that the same occurred in humans.[62] Several variants of this idea enjoyed a certain popularity in the latter half of the nineteenth century. Ruddock attributed infertility to '. . .a luxurious or *inactive* mode of life, the hardworking and the poor classes being much more prolific than the rich, the indolent, and the free liver'.[63] Chavasse picked up on Doubleday's theory and held wine-drinking responsible for family limitation; he cited the small families of France as evidence of this phenomenon.[64]

Those doctors who advanced abstinence as a form of birth control had to deal eventually with the problem of whether or not the sexes had differing sexual needs. In *The Functions and Disorders of the Reproductive Organs* (1857) William Acton, the best known nineteenth-century writer on sexual complaints, had provided medical justification for the Victorian view that the female did not enjoy the sexual passions felt by the male.

> As a general rule, a modest woman seldom desires any sexual

gratification for herself. She submits to her husband's embraces, but principally to gratify him; and, were it not for the desire of maternity, would far rather be relieved of his attentions.[65]

It followed that the female could tolerate abstinence; Acton did not feel the same was true of the male. Indeed the doctor devoted much of his book to sympathising with those men who faced such a fate.

I almost daily witness such ill consequences as the following very painful case, in which the patient's wife — to whom he is passionately attached — is the real cause of serious illness in her husband, by obdurantly refusing to allow marital intercourse, for fear of having any more children (she had perhaps had several), although she otherwise keeps up a semblance of familiarities and affection, and thus adds very greatly to his suffering.[66]

Though Acton denied that he was suggesting that such husbands find consolation elsewhere it was assumed by a number of observers, chief of whom was Professor Francis Newman, that the medical profession was going so far in its defence of the double standard as to recommend recourse to prostitutes.[67] Doctors who lauded the benefits of abstinence were thus obliged to prove that it would not lead to either physical illness or immorality. The case was most strongly advanced by Dr Elizabeth Blackwell in *The Human Element in Sex* (1885). Blackwell's book is perhaps best known for the fact that it contains a reply to Acton's charge that women had little in the way of sexual feelings. Blackwell insisted that women did seek physical pleasure; if they appeared at times indifferent to '. . .the special act of the male. . .' it was as much due to the husband's clumsiness and brutality as to the wife's sensitivity.[68] Some historians have taken such statements to mean that Blackwell favoured a greater expression of sexuality but it is quite clear from her writings that her goal was a move towards greater chastity by both sexes.[69] The double standard was to be destroyed by convincing men as well as women of the benefits of abstinence. It was abstinence, wrote Blackwell, which permitted nervous force to be turned to intellectual and practical pursuits and avoided its being squandered in promiscuity. Moreover such a life was not as onerous to bear as some pretended.

The utmost devotion to intellectual life, to lofty thought, to beneficent action, never injures the procreative power, which always remains intact, capable of its special faculty throughout the virile age. But the active exercise of the intellectual and moral faculties has remarkable power of diminishing the formation of sperm, and limiting the necessity of its natural removal, the demand for such relief becoming rarer under ennobling and healthy influences.[70]

The civilisation of western Europe and the 'social power' of the individual could only be sustained by the institution of such rational checks.

In a society in which it was still difficult for the lower classes to obtain contraceptives it was obviously necessary for large numbers of couples to rely on abstinence as the only totally safe form of birth control. To suggest, however, as many doctors did that the upper and middle classes had limited the size of their families solely by restraint — a restraint made easy because of their superior morality — was to create a self-serving class doctrine which enjoined the public to view the unnecessarily large and unhealthy family as the necessary consequence of the unbridled lusts of poor parents.

For the first two-thirds of the nineteenth century all artificial means of contraception were condemned by the medical profession but usually only in passing during general discussions of health problems. From 1868 on one witnessed the appearance of a new medical literature which was written with the specific ends in mind of attacking the advocates of birth control and disassociating respectable physicians from their activities. This heightened sensitivity on the part of the profession was sparked by the discussion in July, 1868 by the Dialectical Society of James Laurie's paper 'On the Happiness of the Community as Affected by Large Families.' In the ensuing debate Lord Amberley and Charles Drysdale declared that the control of family size was a medical problem. The medical press was quick to respond. The *British Medical Journal* carried an editorial on 1 August which declared, 'We believe that our profession will repudiate with indignation and disgust such functions as these gentlemen wish to assign to it.'[71] On 8 August the *Medical Times and Gazette* accused Amberley of insulting the profession, degrading women, and seeking to coerce doctors into becoming accomplices in unnatural crimes. Returning to the attack on 15 August the same publication announced:

We cannot find words sufficiently strong to express our utter abhorrence and condemnation of the idea of discussing such a question as a purely Medical one. It is *not* a Medical question, and will never become so until others, some of which we shall attempt to indicate, shall have been established in the affirmative.[72]

The sort of question asked was: did man have the right to control life? Once again the medical press purposely confused contraception, abortion and infanticide. Amberley found himself having to deny that he was in favour of 'unnatural crimes' but hostile comments continued to appear in 1869 in the columns of the *Lancet* and the *British Medical Journal.*

The fury with which the medical profession assaulted the defenders of birth control was motivated in part by the knowledge that though no medical man yet dared to pronounce himself publicly in favour of contraception some had done so in the privacy of their consulting rooms. T.L. Nichols in *Human Physiology* (1872) bemoaned the fact that '. . .not a few of the more ignorant and unprincipled members of the medical profession' had adopted such a tactic. Nichols reminded them that 'Free Love' or 'Sexual Religion' or 'Social Science' which held that it was a right to enjoy sexual union while avoiding the responsibility of parenthood was a doctrine which led inevitably to unrestrained promiscuity.[73]

Nichols' appeal to his colleagues was echoed by C.H. Routh in a speech before the Obstetrical Section of the British Medical Association in 1878. Routh accused the advocates of birth control of advancing an ideology which was simply 'vice, clothed in a misnamed Malthusian garb,' 'sexual fraudulency, conjugal onanism,' and 'indirect infanticide.'[74] Relying heavily on the French physician L.F.E. Bergeret's *Des fraudes dans l'accomplissement des fonctions génératrices* (1868), Routh informed his audience that conjugal onanism led to acute metritis, leucorrhoea, cancer, ovaritis, insanity, and death — not infrequently by suicide.[75] France stood as an example of how the attempt at family limitation resulted in individual degeneration and national humiliation. Fortunately in England moral restraints were still in force. The unmarried could keep their lusts at bay by 'athletics, hard mental work, and industrial occupations'. As for the married, if they were worried by the prospects of an overly large family they had only to have faith in nature: 'Let the mothers do their duty by their children, and suckle them as they are bound to do, and so they shall not procreate more frequently than is consistent with health.' If this proved unsuccessful Routh advised 'methodise your conjugal relations'. He was referring to the rhythm method; he assured women they could not conceive from mid-month to the beginning of menstruation. Yet even with these natural methods of family limitation Routh was concerned lest they serve to teach women how they might escape their natural duties.

> For conjugal onanism is not only criminal in men, it must tend to demoralize women. If you teach them vicious habits, and a way to sin without detection, how can you assure yourself of their fidelity when assailed by a fascinating seducer? And why may not even the unmarried woman taste of forbidden pleasures also, so that your future wife shall have been defiled ere you know her?

In conclusion Routh appealed to his colleagues:

> Shall we now remain silent where attempts are made to introduce into our happy homes, habits of immorality, which are so vile in their character, so dishonourable in their development, so degrading in practice![76]

His professional peers assured Routh in the ensuing discussion that they shared his concerns. Dr Sims stated that it was his experience that women had their nerves shattered by conjugal onanism but were promptly restored by child bearing. Dr George Brown of Islington reported that since the appearance of the birth control tract *Fruits of Philosophy* and the consequent employment of sponges and douches he had to treat an increasing number of complaints caused by sexual excesses. Dr McClintock of Dublin captured the tone of the meeting when he stated that doctors found it,

> . . .satisfactory to have it demonstrated in a conclusive manner, that the methods employed to frustrate the physiological object of sexual intercourse were capable of giving rise to various evils, social and physical, of a serious kind, so that in this, no more than in any other instance, can the physiological laws of our body be violated with impunity.[77]

Francis William Newman, brother of Cardinal John Newman, had, as seen above, protested against Acton's implication that the male sex drive could not be stayed. In *The Corruption Now Called Neo-Malthusianism* (1889) Newman in conjunction with Dr Elizabeth Blackwell continued Routh's onslaught against the birth controllers.

The gist of Newman's argument was that, just as some held that men had to have recourse to prostitutes and therefore the Contagious Diseases Act was necessary to protect health, so too some held that men had to have access to their wives at all times and therefore birth control was necessary to avoid unwanted pregnancies. In each case a 'control' was instituted so that impure acts could be indulged in with impunity. The neo-Malthusians were castigated by Newman as a '. . .materialistic clique of false science, which passed off unnatural and detestable arts as the way of health, which now strives to misguide and pollute marriage.' Their strategies could only result in evil. For Newman and Blackwell the only way forward was through abstinence: 'No considerable improvement which may be called National can be hoped for, until women insist on exacting from men the chastity which we claim of them.'[78]

It was the appearance in 1877 of an official neo-Malthusian movement, the Malthusian League, which goaded Routh and Blackwell into attacking both the morality and safety of contraception. They feared that the fact that a physician, Dr Charles R. Drysdale, was president of the League would be taken by the public as a sign of the medical profession's approbation of the movement. Their fright was premature; the League through its mouthpiece, *The Malthusian,* confined itself almost solely to economic arguments in favour of population control.

It was not until 1885 that an English doctor put his name to a birth control tract. In that year Dr H.A. Allbutt of Leeds published *The Wife's Handbook* which in addition to describing the already well-known contraceptives such as the condom, douche, and sponge contained an account of the use of the Mensinga diaphragm. Allbutt's contribution to the birth control campaign has already been touched on. For the purposes of this chapter it is only necessary to note that his activities led to his being prosecuted and found guilty by the General Medical Council in 1887 of, first,

. . .having published, and publicly caused to be sold, a work entitled *The Wife's Handbook,* in London and elsewhere, at so low a price as to bring the work within the reach of the youth of both sexes, to the detriment of public morals. Secondly, the offence is, in the opinion of the Council, 'infamous conduct in a professional respect'. Thirdly, the Registrar is hereby ordered to erase the name of Mr. H.A. Allbutt from the Medical Register.[79]

The Council's actions failed completely to stem the tide of neo-Malthusian propaganda. As a consequence of the notoriety won by the trial, *The Wife's Handbook* was to be sold by the hundreds of thousands. But the Council could count itself successful inasmuch as by making Allbutt a martyr it dissuaded other physicians from publicly defending contraception.

The turn of the century saw no change in the medical profession's attitude towards contraception. The experience of the Boer war had, if anything, made doctors even more vehement in protestations of opposition to a practice which threatened to sap the strength of the nation. John W. Taylor, president of the British Gynaecological Society spelled out his organisation's views in *On the Diminishing Birth Rate* (1904). He began by lamenting the fact that instead of the family of six, twelve or eighteen children one was reduced in England to 'the so-called family of three or two or one'. Even this diminished task was increasingly shirked by the fittest and handed over to 'the lower classes of our population and to the Hebrew and the alien'.[80] It was contraception which posed such dangers, not just to the nation but to the individual. According to Taylor the douche could cause acute peritonitis and the 'mechanical shield' purulent vaginitis. There were moreover the long term problems to which sexual excess led.

> This chronic impairment of nervous energy of which I am now speaking, often referred to under the name of neurasthenia, and still more recently under that of 'brain fag', has many causes, and may be produced whenever there has been too great a tax or drain upon the nervous system, and too short a time for recuperation; but it is especially marked in many of these cases of sexual onanism.[81]

The symptoms were the same as those of the school boy addicted to self-abuse: loss of memory, unreasonable fears, inability to fix attention, mental depression. Taylor concluded that, since women were especially affected, seminal fluid '. . .must therefore have some function beyond and in addition to its power in the reproduction of the species'. Without it women flagged.

> It is quite possible, then, that in one or both of these suggested ways [of semen being absorbed by uterine glands] some tonic constituent of the seminal fluid may be taken up by the uterus, and thus affect the general organism; and there is nothing unreasonable in the suggestion that such absorption may allay the exhaustion which,

without it, is liable to follow the act of connection.[82]

The healthiest women were in short the ones with the largest families.
Their husbands benefited as well because the man needed '. . .recurring
periods of abstinence and restraint induced by each pregnancy'. It was
therefore the doctors' duty to deny to couples any information on
how to limit their family.

> . . .it is not the time for the fairly healthy parents of one child to
> shelter themselves behind the terrors and troubles of a first
> confinement, and demand some easy but evil way of further
> immunity.[83]

Indeed such couples had to be warned that if they attempted by
artificial means to limit the size of their family the children they would
eventually produce would bear the scars of such actions.

> Artificial prevention is an evil and disgrace – the immorality of it,
> the degradation of succeeding generations by it, their domination or
> subjugation by strangers who are stronger because they have not
> given way to it, the curses that must assuredly follow the parents of
> decadence who started it – all of this needs to be brought home to
> the minds of those who have thoughtlessly or ignorantly accepted
> it.[84]

Given the fact that the medical profession's public hostility to birth
control continued unabated in the first decade of the twentieth century
there was a certain irony in the fact that the 1911 census revealed it to
have the smallest families of all occupational categories.[85] Indeed it was
a cruel irony because, as the National Birth Rate Commission noted in
its findings, doctors were in many cases advising women to space their
births but refusing to tell them how. The report of the Commission
which includes the last words of doctors on birth control before the
first World War was edited by James Marchant and published as *The
Declining Birth Rate: Its Causes and Effects* (1917). Its chief interest
is that it indicates how little progress had been made since 1850 in the
rational examination of the pros and cons of contraception.
Dr Schofield declared that there was a common consensus that the use
of preventives led to nervous disorders. Sir Francis Champneys assumed
that lengthy use of contraceptives reduced fertility.[86] Dr Armand Routh,
consulting obstetric physician to Charing Cross Hospital, maintained

that artificial forms of fertility control invariably produced physical, mental and moral harm.[87] Dr Mary Scharlieb agreed and referred to such practices as 'race suicide'.[88] The Commission did hear evidence that some medical men were advising the use of checks and felt they posed no threat to health. The witness who made this statement was not a typical member of the medical profession; it was Dr C.V. Drysdale, the foremost advocate of birth control and Secretary of the Malthusian League.

Of all the evidence collected by the Commission perhaps the most dramatic was that which indicated that women were not passively waiting for either their doctor or their husband to enlighten them on the question of contraception; they sought in many instances to control their own fertility in their own ways. Dr Armand Routh confirmed Scharlieb's account.

One frequently hears that a woman refuses to have any children for a time, or even to have any children at all, and even unknown to her husband, she will either introduce into the passage some chemical agent which will destroy the spermatozoa, or she will sometimes wear a cap over the neck of the womb, which takes the place, in the female, of the 'letters' that men wear. . .the husband will bring his wife to the doctor to know why they do not get a child, and the wife will tell the doctor privately that this is what is going on.[89]

Sir Thomas Oliver stated that similar situations were found when a woman had recourse to abortion.

I think there must be many cases where the husband does acquiesce in the act done by his wife; but at the same time I am perfectly certain from several patients I have attended in the infirmary and in the case of others whom I have seen with doctors outside, that the husband was perfectly ignorant of what his wife had taken.[90]

This sort of evidence suggests that the medical profession's failure to supply contraceptive information may have had little impact on women firmly resolved to limit family size. The decline of the birth rate in Britain as in France and America was accomplished mainly by the employment of 'pre-industrial' techniques such as coitus interruptus and abortion which owed nothing to nineteenth-century medical science. The real importance of doctors' hostility was not that it forced couples to rely on unsafe methods; it was that it burdened them unnecessarily with feelings of fear and guilt.

It required the first World War to provide the social solvent to destroy much of the official medical antagonism to fertility control. It was fitting that the first contraceptive to be accepted by a still overwhelmingly male profession was the condom. Because it fulfilled an obvious prophylactic function in protecting the male from venereal disease it was finally to enjoy a tolerance which practitioners offered no other contraceptive. The necessity of such devices was brought fully home by the war bulletins. In 1917, 54,884 British soldiers were hospitalised by venereal disease and the columns of the most staid medical journals were devoted to discussions of the problem.[91] The government, on medical advice, eventually approved the policy of issuing protective sheaths to the troops. It was the first time in history that the state had seen fit to instruct the masses in the use of prophylactics and marked more clearly than any other single event the end of 'Victorian England'.[92]

The attitude of the British medical profession towards birth control prior to 1914 was more complex than later commentators realised. The historian has first to grapple with the interpretative problem posed by the lack of representativeness of doctors who either opposed or defended birth control. Although the former were predominant both groups were atypical in tnat they differed from the vast body of the profession in dealing with a subject which their colleagues carefully avoided. Then there is the confusion in the minds of nineteenth-century physicians which an analysis of their response to the issue of birth control reveals. The questions of the difference between artificial and natural means of fertility control, between male and female forms of contraception, between abortion and contraception, between prophylactics to prevent disease and those to prevent births continued to be regurgitated decade after decade. But it was hardly surprising if it appeared at times that the profession was seeking to make the issues needlessly complicated. It had never adopted as its task the provision of a technically effective form of contraception. Its first responsibility was the maintenance of a professional monopoly in the realm of medical science. The fact that the monopoly was being in part challenged by the advocates of birth control, by the retailers of contraceptives, and by ordinary men and women seeking to regulate their own fertility, meant that, until doctors came up with their own medically-approved contraceptives, they would approach the question with suspicion and hostility.

Notes

1. D.V. Glass, *Population Policies and Movements in Europe* (New York, 1967), p.5.
2. *Reasoner* (1848), p.84.
3. Bertrand and Patricia Russell, (eds.), *The Amberley Papers* (New York, 1937), pp.170-1.
4. G.J. Holyoake, *John Stuart Mill as Some of the Working Classes Knew Him* (London, 1873), p.22.
5. Henry Oldham, 'Clinical Lecture on the Induction of Abortion in a Case of Contracted Vagina from Cicatrization,' *London Medical Gazette,* 9 (1849), p.48.
6. Napheys, *The Physical Life of Women* (Philadelphia, 1869), p.91. The British edition was published in Edinburgh in 1872. Duffey, *What Women Should Know: A Woman's Book About Women Containing Practical Information for Wives and Mothers* (Philadelphia, 1873), p.133.
7. See for example Alex Comfort, *The Anxiety Makers: Some Curious Preoccupations of the Medical Profession* (London, 1967).
8. John Peel, 'Contraception and the Medical Profession,' *Population Studies,* 18 (1964), pp.133-46; J.A. Banks, *Prosperity and Parenthood* (London, 1954).
9. Robert Cromie, (ed.), *1811 Dictionary of the Vulgar Tongue* (Northfield, Ill., 1971).
10. 'I.C.H.' to Francis Place (1823?), Place Papers, 68.
11. Oswald Mosley, *My Life* (London, 1969), p.114.
12. On the confusion concerning masturbation and coitus interruptus see Richard Dawson, *An Essay on Marriage. . .with Observations on Spermatorrhoea* (London, 1845).
13. On the same problem in France see Angus McLaren, 'Some Secular Attitudes toward Sexual Behaviour in France, 1760-1860,' *French Historical Studies,* 8 (1974), p.605.
14. Napheys, *Physical Life,* p.98. John Cowan described coitus interruptus as 'beastly': *The Science of the New Life* (New York, 1869), p.110. The British edition was published by Fowler and Company in 1897. Dr Mary Scharlieb referred to the practice as 'masturbation à deux' in James Marchant, (ed.), *The Declining Birth Rate: Its Causes and Effects* (London, 1917), p.63.
15. George Drysdale, *Physical, Sexual and Natural Religion* (London, 1855), p.347; Annie Besant, *The Law of Population* (London, 1884), pp.33-4.
16. See also James Thorn, *An Attempt to Simplify the Treatment of Sexual Diseases* (London, 1831), p.11.
17. *The Transmission of Life, Counsels on the Nature and Hygiene of the Masculine Function* (Philadelphia, 1872, 13th edn.), p.108.
18. John Peel, 'The Manufacturing and Retailing of Contraceptives in England,' *Population Studies,* 17 (1963), pp.113-25. Curiously enough the fact that a husband possessed several 'French Letters' was to figure centrally in one of the century's most famous murder cases. See Yseult Bridges, *Poison and Adelaide Bartlett* (London, 1962), p.228.
19. Frederic Buret, *Syphilis in the Middle Ages and in Modern Times,* trans. A.H. Ohmann-Dumesnil (London, 1892), I, pp.287-8.
20. *Les va-nu-pieds de Londres* (Paris, 1883), p.65. See also 'On the Use of Night Caps by a Married Man,' in Peter Fryer, *The Man of Pleasure's Companion: A Nineteenth Century Anthology of Amorous Entertainments* (London, 1968).
21. Cowan, *Science,* p.110.
22. See for example J.P. Holmes, *Popular Observations on Diseases Incident to Females* (London, 1831), pp.39-40; Sir Charles Mansfield Clarke, *Observations*

on those Diseases of Females Which are Attended by Discharges (London, 1831).

23. *Observations on Some of the More Important Diseases of Women* (London, 1837), p.50.

24. *A Handbook of Uterine Therapeutics* (London, 1863), pp.196-201, 169.

25. Tilt, *Handbook,* p.204. Displacement of the womb could be a serious problem; by the 1860s surgery was employed by gynaecologists to deal with birth injuries.

26. Cowan, *Science,* p.111.

27. C.H. Routh, *The Moral and Physical Evils Likely to Follow if Practices Intended to Act as Checks to Population be not Strongly Discouraged and Condemned* (London, 1879), pp.9-10.

28. Tilt, *Handbook,* pp.20-21; E. Ruddock, *The Common Diseases of Women* (London, 1888, 6th edn.), pp.87-8; Pye Henry Chavasse, *Advice to a Wife* (Toronto, 1879), p.197.

29. Cited in J.W.R. Scott, *The Life and Death of a Newspaper* (London, 1952), chap.19.

30. On the dangers of the douche see Marchant, *Medical Aspects,* pp.94-5; Napheys, *Physical Life,* p.98; Cowan, *Science,* p.111; Duffey, *Women,* p.134. See also the plea made by Marc Colombat de l'Isère: '. . .all these toilet vinegars, these essences, the astringent compositions and all these mysterious waters that perfumers have the talent to produce, under a variety of picturesque titles, should be proscribed by females who attach any importance to the conservation of their health. . .' *A Treatise on the Diseases and Special Hygiene of Females,* trans. Ch. Meigs (Philadelphia, 1845), p.556.

31. Edward Ruddock, *The Affections of Females* (London, 1861), p.28.

32. *A Treatise on Hysteria* (London, 1830), p.11.

33. A Physician, *The Diseases of Women: Their Causes, Symptoms, and Treatment* (London, 1878), pp.41-2.

34. Tilt, *Handbook,* pp.154-5.

35. *Plain Home Talk* (New York, 1881), p.463.

36. Holmes, *Popular Observations,* pp.13-4.

37. Lionel A. Weatherly, *A Young Wife's Own Book* (London, 1882), p.75. On home remedies see also Robert Abercrombie, *The New Self Doctor or Medical Referee* (London, 1879), p.43.

38. Bull's *Hints to Mothers* was a best seller, going through fourteen editions between 1837 and 1877. Little attention was paid to abortion in the first edition (London, 1837), p.103 but greater notice was given in the later issues; see for example the eleventh edition of 1857, p.124.

39. *Woman, Her Destiny, and Maternal Relations; or Hints to the Single and Married* (London, 1864), pp.37-38.

40. *On the Preservation of Health of Women at Critical Periods of Life* (London, 1851), pp.73-4.

41. *Talks to My Patients; Hints on Getting Well and Keeping Well* (New York, 1870), pp.158-9. British edition published by Fowler in 1895.

42. Gleason, *Talks,* p.161.

43. Chavasse, *Advice,* p.119. Chavasse's work enjoyed large sales; *Advice to a Wife* went through seventeen editions, *Counsel to a Mother,* nineteen.

44. George H. Napheys, *Physical Life of Woman* (London, 1895), p.98. See also Duffey, *Women,* pp.124-5.

45. Napheys, *Physical Life,* pp.93-4.

46. On the confusion which continued on into the twentieth century see the *Lancet,* 2 (1905), pp.1496-97.

47. *Human Physiology* (London, 1835), p.700.

48. See for example Napheys, *Physical Life*, p.86; Fowler, *Woman*, p.3; Elizabeth Blackwell, *How to Keep a Household in Health* (London, 1870), p.8.
49. T. Laycock, 'On the Influence of Lactation in Preventing the Recurrence of Pregnancy,' *Dublin Medical Press*, 199 (1842), pp.263-4; John Robertson, *Essays and Notes on the Physiology and Diseases of Women and Practical Midwifery* (London, 1851), pp.187-95; Bull, *Advice*, (1857), p.49.
50. Cowan, *Science*, iii, p.117.
51. Napheys, *Physical Life* (1869), pp.96-97.
52. Weatherly, *Young Wife*, p.83.
53. Thomas Laycock, *A Treatise on the Nervous Diseases of Women* (London, 1840), pp.42-3; Napheys, *Physical Life* (1869), p.89.
54. *The Philosophy of Female Health* (London, 1845), pp.50-1.
55. *On the Diseases of Women and Ovarian Inflammation* (London, 1853), pp.27-8.
56. Ruddock, *Affections*, pp.74-5; and see Ruddock, *Common Diseases*, pp.87-8.
57. *Clinical Notes on Uterine Surgery* (London, 1866), pp.381-3. James Reed of Rutgers University has informed me, however, that some American physicians such as Frederick Hollick did have a clear idea of when conception occurred and that, ironically, confusion in this area was greater at the end of the century than in the 1840s. See Reed's forthcoming *Private Vice to Public Virtue: The Birth Control Movement and American Society, 1830-1975* (New York, 1978).
58. Napheys, *Physical Life* (1895), p.92.
59. R.T. Trall, *Sexual Physiology and Hygiene* (Glasgow, 1891).
60. For continued support of the 'safe period' see Dame Mary Scharlieb, 'The Medical Aspects of Contraception,' in Sir James Marchant, (ed.), *Medical Views on Birth Control* (London, 1926), p.60.
61. *Human Physiology: The Basis of Sanitary and Social Science* (London, 1872), pp.310-11.
62. Nichols, *Physiology*, p.295.
63. Ruddock, *Common Diseases*, p.85.
64. Chavasse, *Advice*, pp.21, 40-43.
65. *The Functions and Disorders of the Reproductive Organs* (London, n.d., 6th edn.), p.213.
66. Acton, *Functions*, p.139.
67. On Newman's attack in *The Relation of Physiology to Sexual Morals* see Acton, *Functions*, pp.209-10.
68. *The Human Element in Sex* (London, 1885), p.45. See also Carl Degler, 'What Ought to Be and What Was: Women's Sexuality in the Nineteenth Century,' *American Historical Review*, 79 (1974), pp.1467-90.
69. See for example Patricia Branca, *Silent Sisterhood: Middle Class Women in the Victorian Home* (London, 1975), pp.122, 126.
70. Blackwell, *Human Element*, pp.29-30. See also the chapter on the 'Law of Continence' in Cowan, *Science*, p.116. On the way in which women would use such 'laws' to protect themselves from pregnancy see John J. and Robin M. Haller, *The Physician and Sexuality in Victorian America* (Urbana, Illinois, 1974), p.102 and chapter eleven below.
71. Russell, *Amberley Papers*, p.173.
72. Ibid., p.174.
73. Nichols, *Physiology*, p.301.
74. Routh, *Physical Evils*, iii, pp.8, 9.
75. Bergeret's book, which was to go through eighteen editions by 1910, had a major impact in Britain and America. See McLaren, 'Some Secular Attitudes,' pp.612-3.
76. Routh, *Physical Evils*, pp.16, 17, 18.

77. Routh, Ibid., pp.21, 21-4. In 1879 Charles Drysdale brought the question of birth control to the attention of the Medical Society of London. In the discussion of his paper 'Morality of the Rich and Poor' the hostility of the doctors to the subject was made clear. In a report of the meeting the *Lancet* (8 November, 1879) stated that it was 'humiliating' to envisage the necessity of birth control. See C.R. Drysdale, *Medical Opinions on the Population Question* (London, 1901).
78. *The Corruption Now Called Neo-Malthusianism With Notes by Dr. E. Blackwell* (London, 1889), pp.5, 8.
79. Cited by Norman E. Himes, *Medical History of Contraception* (Baltimore, 1936), p.251.
80. *On the Diminishing Birth Rate* (London, 1904), pp.11, 12, 13. That religious concerns affected Cox's appreciation of contraception is suggested by the fact that he also authored *The Coming of the Saints: Imaginations and Studies in Early Church History and Tradition* (London, 1906).
81. Taylor stated that coitus interruptus was a vice 'but slightly removed from that of self-abuse and is open to the same criticisms and strictures.' *Birth Rate,* p.13.
82. Taylor, *Birth Rate,* pp.14, 15.
83. Ibid., pp.16, 23.
84. Ibid., pp.24-5.
85. The British Medical Association supported Lord Braye's 1909 bill to stop the sale of contraceptive devices; it failed to pass. Peel, 'Contraception,' p.136.
86. Marchant, *Declining Birth Rate,* pp.135, 136. Champneys was the author of a tract put out by the Society for the Propagation of Christian Knowledge, *Address on Chastity* (London, 1909).
87. Marchant, *Declining Birth Rate,* pp.252-7. The fact that Routh was an advocate of Caesarian sections presumably prejudiced him against contraception.
88. Ibid., p.271. Scharlieb produced an enormous number of books on women's health and marriage in addition to sex education manuals for children. See *How to Enlighten Our Children: A Book for Parents* (London, 1917).
89. Marchant, *Declining Birth Rate,* p.247.
90. Ibid., pp.318-9.
91. See for example the *Lancet* 13 October, 1917; 20 April, 27 April, 5 October, 1918.
92. For post 1914 developments see the special number on contraception of the *Practitioner,* 111 (July 1923).

8 BIRTH CONTROL AND EUGENICS

As noted earlier there were doctors who supported eugenic programmes but opposed birth control. One of the obvious ironies of the population debate at the turn of the century was that, though the question of the voluntary limitation of the family remained very much a tabooed subject, the question of the forcible sterilisation of the unfit was widely discussed. The two issues were related. Because the upper and middle classes were restricting their fertility, social commentators raised the alarm that the nation faced 'race suicide' and national degeneration. If a healthy demographic balance was to be maintained it would be necessary to entice the 'fit' to breed or take measures to restrict the births of the 'unfit'. The upsurge of concern was triggered by the social investigations made from the 1880s onward – in particular those of Charles Booth and Seebohm Rowntree – which revealed the wretchedness of the lives of a substantial portion of the urban working class. These reports supplemented those that demonstrated that the poorest portions of the population were contributing the largest additions to the national birth rate. Political concerns were added to social fears by the Boer war crisis; the chronic ill health and physical weakness of the English working class revealed by the recruitment programme and the subsequent 1904 Inter-Departmental Committee on Physical Deterioration brought forcibly home to the public the seriousness of the situation. It was in this period of anxious reappraisals of population policies that the eugenics movement blossomed.

Eugenics, the science of the production of fine offspring, was the creation of a cousin of Charles Darwin, Francis Galton. Galton (1822-1911) wrote on a vast range of subjects from finger printing to 'Statistical Inquiries into the Efficacy of Prayer.' His dictum, 'Whenever you can, count,' reflected his mystical faith – and one shared by many late Victorians – in the explanatory powers of statistical analysis. In an autobiographical passage which cries out for a Freudian interpretation Galton even confessed to his habit of counting and classifying the women he passed in the street.

> Whenever I have occasion to classify the persons I meet into three classes, 'good, medium and bad,' I use a needle mounted as a pricker, wherewith to prick holes, unseen, in a piece of paper, torn rudely

into a cross with a long leg. I use the upper end for 'good', the
cross-arm for 'medium', the lower end for 'bad'. The prick holes
keep distinct, and are readily read off at leisure.[1]

It was Galton's belief that the statistical approach — if used to
encourage selective breeding — could solve the social ills that beset
Britain. Following the tables produced by Charles Booth he graded
citizens according to their civic worth — desirable, passable, and
undesirable. It was his hope that a national biographical index could
then be established listing those fit and those unfit — the inmates of
prisons, hospitals, and asylums — to breed. Amongst the former he
hoped to elicit a 'sentiment of caste' which in time the state would
officially recognise by the provision of 'eugenic certificates'.

Galton's idea that the first condition of any process of natural
selection in a race was to determine the existence of differences was
taken up and made scientifically respectable by Karl Pearson, professor
of Applied Mathematics and Mechanics at University College London.[2]
Pearson developed the science of biometry by applying statistical
methods to the study of biology. Between 1891 and 1906 he launched
a series of investigations into such questions as differences in stature,
cephalic index, eye colour, fertility, and longevity. At the same time he
served as the statistician of the Evolution Committee of the Royal
Society set up by Galton and the biologist W.F.R. Weldon.

One weakness in the eugenists' attempt to use statistics to determine
the direction in which evolution was moving was their ignorance of
Mendel's work on heredity which was only rediscovered in 1900. It
was in part due to the difficulty of working with Mendelian-minded
biologists more interested in chance mutations than in actuarial tables
that Galton abandoned the Evolution Committee and established the
Eugenics Record Office. This he in turn handed over to Pearson in
1906 to form part of the Biometric Laboratory at University College.
Its purpose was to make the academic reading public aware of the
dangers of hereditary illnesses through two series of publications —
'Studies in National Deterioration' and 'Eugenic Laboratory Memoirs' —
while the Eugenics Educational Committee, established by Galton in
the same year, was to bring the message to both the politicians and the
public.

The rise of eugenics was a sign of the general decline of faith in
nineteenth-century liberalism and the growing belief in the need for
'interventionist' policies. Under the aegis of Herbert Spencer who
coined the term, 'survival of the fittest,' mid-century liberalism held

that competition was the key in an age of greater specialisation, differentiation, and interdependence.[3] Those who were poor and unsuccessful had proved themselves 'unfit' for the struggle and would, by the free working of natural laws, be removed from the contest. Spencer's doctrine was — for the fit — basically optimistic for he assured them that they would continue to prosper and had no need to seek assistance from the state. The population theories of the first half of the nineteenth century mirrored the model of the laissez-faire economy. It was generally accepted that it was only possible to establish the 'laws' of population; such laws could not be countered by institutional interference. This line was followed by the most pessimistic Malthusians and the most optimistic Spencerians. Both accepted a passive approach because they believed that population arrived naturally at its correct level.

Old-fashioned Social Darwinists were true to these beliefs and were willing to let the struggle for existence continue; the eugenists called for a halt. They took this step because the social investigations from the 1880s onwards made it clear that the unfit were not being eliminated from the market. A glance at the birth rate showed that it was the fit who were failing to reproduce. Whereas the Malthusians — including those in the Malthusian League — only concerned themselves with the quantity of the population, the eugenists concerned themselves with its 'quality'. It was not that some survived but *who* survived; it was the process of selection, not elimination, that had to be controlled. The Malthusian and utilitarian concept of 'static adjustment' was thus replaced by the eugenists with an evolutionary model in which heredity and environment, rather than reasoned self-interest, fired the engine of progress. It followed that decisions on breeding could no longer be left to individual whim or chance; an outside agency was required to monitor actions which affected the entire community.[4]

This belief that some order had to be brought to the question of breeding motivated not only eugenists but social scientists and politicians who in the 1880s were moving away from the Malthusian hedonistic model and the atomistic individualism of Spencer and adopting a 'collectivist' or 'interventionist' approach to social problems.[5] This new activism was a sign, first, of an optimistic belief in the possibility of social manipulation. Eugenics was rooted in a belief in perfection which could be traced back to Rousseau and Condorcet. The triumphs of the industrial revolution furthered the faith in the ability to create new men. K.M. Ludmerer has suggested that, 'In 1848, John Humphrey Noyes, a Perfectionist preacher, was the first in modern times to support the possibility of improving the human race by judicious breeding.' But as we have seen even earlier in England, Robert Owen, industrialist and socialist, had speculated on the state's supervision of births to attain '. . .improvements of the organization of man.'[6] The later eugenists' activism was a sign, secondly, of a new fear of the lower classes. Terrified by the prospect of the unfit multiplying thoughtlessly while the prudent restricted family size the eugenists called for state controls. Whereas the Malthusian attributed the poverty of the poor to their lack of foresight and addressed to them moral appeals, the eugenist attributed their plight to environmental and hereditary factors which could not be attenuated by individual prudence. The poor were not demoralised; they were degenerate. If their degeneration was due to environmental causes it could be cured by social programmes; if it was due to heredity the state could only limit the problem by restricting their breeding. According to the older liberal interpretation the poor were seen as morally irresponsible but at least it was presumed they could, if they saw the evil of their ways, escape their lot. The eugenists adopted a more brutal attitude — if lack of fitness was attributed to a hereditary taint there was no reprieve.[7]

The 'brutal pessimism' developed by the eugenists in their dealings with the working class seems to be at first glance at odds with the fact that Pearson and others active in the movement described themselves as socialists. The term is misleading. Pearson was close in spirit to the American 'progressives' — the professional upper-middle class Anglo-Saxons who felt threatened by the rise of labour.[8] His 'socialism' was that form of government which would empower the technocrat with means of social control. Though at times sounding radical Pearson and the eugenists sought to protect the values, virtues, and social structure of the society in which they had a vested interest. They claimed to be protecting 'quality' of race but failed to acknowledge that their own criterion of 'fitness', namely high socio-economic status, predisposed them to categorise the lower classes in general as genetically inferior.

What attitude did the eugenists take towards birth control? This depended on whether they put greater emphasis on inducing the fit to breed (Positive Eugenics) or in preventing the unfit from multiplying (Negative Eugenics). Those who, like Galton and Pearson, favoured the former policy, opposed the neo-Malthusians on the grounds that only the fit adopted the practice of restricting family size. 'I protest', wrote Galton in *Hereditary Genius*, 'against the abler races being encouraged to withdraw in this way from the struggle for existence.'[9] Charles Drysdale, thinking he recognised in Pearson's writings an implicit sympathy for the Malthusian League, wrote asking that he declare himself. Pearson replied,

> I am certainly in favour of rational limitation. None the less, I believe in the efficiency of society largely depending on the selection of better stocks, the removal or destruction of the less fit stocks. Now my grave difficulty about Neo-Malthusianism is simply this. It tends to act in the better, in the physically or mentally fitter, ranks of society, among the educated and thrifty of the middle and working classes. It does not act, so far as I can see, at all on Mr. Booth's 'Class B.'. . .While limiting the population we must, at the same time, ensure that the worst stock is the stock which is first and foremost limited. . .I do not see how, without a strong Socialistic State it will be possible.[10]

Even within the small family of the upper classes Pearson detected a danger. In 'On the Handicapping of the First Born' he argued that it was statistically provable that the first child did not do as well as its siblings; thus if the family size was limited the dangers of degeneration were raised.[11]

Rejecting as they did the neo-Malthusian's argument that the individual's self-interest in matters of family planning inevitably coincided with the interests of the community, it followed that the eugenists would also question the advantages birth control purportedly offered society in sparing women unwanted pregnancies. The leading neo-Malthusians adhered to John Stuart Mill's feminist line of reasoning that women had the right to advance as far as their individual capacities admitted. The eugenists replied that sex differences were based on biological facts which could not be over-ridden by appeals to justice.[12] Woman's role was determined by her reproductive function. Biology, not politics, subjected her to man. If she was unhappy the answer was not to wrench her from her natural calling and plunge her into an unequal contest from which she could only emerge defeated and embittered. The answer was to provide her with the support necessary to permit her to fulfill more completely her function as child-bearer. In one of his earliest essays Pearson asserted that before woman's 'rights' were debated it was first required to establish her physical capabilities by a science of 'sexualology'.

> We have first to settle what is the physical capacity of woman, what would be the effect of her emancipation on her function of race-

production, before we can talk about her 'rights', which are, after all, only a vague description of what may be the fittest position for her, the sphere of her maximum usefulness in the developed society of the future.

Higher education could, for example, raise the intelligence of women or lead to her degeneration. Feminists had the duty to advance their ideas with caution.

They must face sex-problems with sexualological and historical knowledge, and solve them, before they appeal to the market-place with all the rhetorical flourish of 'justice' and of 'right'. They must show that emancipation will tend not only to increase the stability of society and the general happiness of mankind, but will favour the physique and health of both sexes.[13]

The question of woman's emancipation, he insisted, had to be decided not on whether it was good or bad but if it was social or anti-social.

The greatest anti-social act that, in the eyes of the eugenists, the better stock of women were committing was the avoidance of pregnancy. Pearson described as tragic the fact that the finer females in restricting family size were permitting the acquired characteristic of intelligence to be lost. He was willing to recognise that some women regarded child-bearing as a form of subjection but he was willing to accept it as a price paid for the 'race instinct for reproduction'. In the future women would be rewarded and honoured for their sacrifice.

. . .it will be simply based upon the recognition that women's child-bearing activity is essentially part of her contribution to social needs; that it ought to be acknowledged as such by the State; that society at large ought to insist, exactly as in the case of labour, that the condition under which it is undertaken shall be as favourable as possible that *pro tanto* it shall be treated as part of woman's work for society at large.[14]

The fact that activists in the woman's movement did not respond to such an offer, that they refused to measure women's rights against the touchstone of 'general social efficiency', that many were 'out-and-out individualists' was for Pearson a source of regret.

The belief that feminism actually posed a danger to the eugenics movement was shared by many of its adherents. Galton was himself a well-known anti-feminist, a supporter of the Anti-Suffrage Society and a defender of the Contagious Diseases Act. W.C.D. Whetham, the Cambridge scientist and agriculturalist, wrote that it was no coincidence that the feminist movement emerged as the birth rate of the upper classes fell. The better sort of woman was shirking her maternal duty.[15] C.W. Saleeby, a populariser of eugenic doctrines, led an all out attack in *Woman and Womanhood: A Search for Principles* (1911) on the 'dysgenic consequences' of women's education, the 'intolerable evil' of married women's work, and the high rate of *male* infant mortality which he referred to as 'infanticide'. He called for a 'Eugenic Feminism' which would lure back to their natural roles the 'incomplete and aberrant women' who were 'ceasing to be mammals'. The real divisions in society, according to Saleeby, were not along class or sex lines; they were between parents and non-parents. 'Women's rights' could only be considered after those of, first, mothers' and secondly, fathers'.[16]

In the writings of Havelock Ellis, the 'sexual sage' of Edwardian England one finds perhaps the most determined attempt to balance the demands of eugenists, feminists, and birth controllers. Fertility control he declared to be a fact and indeed a concomitant of a higher civilisation. The claim that it threatened 'race suicide' was matched by the argument that it prevented unwanted births and infant deaths. Ellis was even willing to broach the question of abortion and suggest that in some situations it was an understandable tactic to adopt.[17] What interested Ellis most in the question of contraception, however, was the possibility of employing it to achieve 'selection in reproduction'. This concern for reproduction coloured his appreciation of feminism. The campaign for women's suffrage he considered unimportant. He was much more enthused by the 'Mutterschutz' movement in Germany in which the defence of motherhood was given priority over political questions.[18] Ellis believed that Galton and the Swedish feminist Ellen Key had arrived independently at the same conclusion as to the religious importance of procreation. As long as there were no children lovers could live as they pleased; once offspring appeared the state had an obligation to intercede. Only in eugenics could the competing claims of the race and the individual be reconciled.[19]

Instead of encouraging, as did the neo-Malthusians, the best stock to restrict births the eugenists supported schemes to promote their fertility. Galton suggested that a policy of 'befriendment' of thriving families be adopted to encourage reproduction of the fit. Whetham proposed that old age pensions be based on the number of children raised, that scholarships be set aside for the children of the middle class,

and that posts in the empire be guaranteed to the sons of the gentry.
The discussions of the 'endowment of motherhood' and child welfare
in the first decade of the twentieth century naturally attracted the
attention of the eugenists. Such aid, stated Pearson, could only be
socially useful if care was taken that the right sorts of families were
supported: 'Yet the time is approaching when real knowledge must take
the place of energetic but untrained philanthropy in dictating the lines
of feasible social reforms.'[20]

The problem with the 'Positive Eugenics' stance was that it appeared
more difficult to determine who should breed than who should not.
Moreover it was the danger of the growth of degeneracy as documented
by the Boer war crisis, rather than the possibility of more conscientious
breeding by the middle classes, which excited attention. By the time of
his 1901 Huxley Lecture Galton was calling for negative forms of
eugenics including the segregation and sterilisation of the 'undesirable'.
Pearson sounded the same note in his 1903 lecture: social reforms could
not repair the defects of heredity. 'No scheme of wider or more
thorough education will bring up in the scale of intelligence hereditary
weakness to the level of hereditary strength.'[21]

The direction in which the eugenists were moving was made clear by
their studies, many of which appeared in the appropriately named series,
'Studies in National Deterioration'. Alien immigration, feeble-
mindedness, alcoholism, insanity, and women's work were all presented
by researchers as having a nefarious influence on fertility. The eugenists
responded in two ways to the perceived threat of biological
deterioration. Some, out of a fear of a contagion of tainted 'germ
plasm', called for campaigns against alcoholism and venereal disease.[22]
Others adopted the opposite tack, arguing against preventive medicine
on the grounds that it kept alive the diseased and debauched who
would inevitably infect the innocent.

The Malthusian League which could not support the eugenists in
their pro-natalist policies did follow them in calling for the restriction
of the breeding of the unfit. By the 1890s the *Malthusian* began to
print letters from League members suggesting that it range its support
behind Galton and by 1897 Charles Drysdale was insisting that his
movement was not opposed to some form of state regulation of births.
In *Neo-Malthusianism and Eugenics* (1912) C.V. Drysdale claimed that
the League had always been eugenically-minded inasmuch as its main
goal was to limit the births of the poor.[23]

The neo-Malthusians were not alone in capitulating to the eugenists'
spectre of 'race suicide'. The fear of lower-class degenerates swamping

civilised society by simple force of numbers precipitated a deluge of books and articles at the turn of the century calling for policies to check their breeding. In these works the authors' belief that they were dealing with a contagion that had to be put down at all cost was amply demonstrated by the brutality with which they speculated on repressive measures. Victoria C.W. Martin in *The Rapid Multiplication of the Unfit* (1891) bewailed the burden that paupers in Britain, as Blacks in America, placed on society. Henry Smith agreed that the marriage of such specimens had to be prevented; prevention was better than cure. Just as the state took sanitary measures in questions of sewage and drainage, so too it would have to interfere in breeding. Such was Smith's fear of the ill that he declared that the mother who smothered her deformed child deserved to be honoured – a curious argument to make in a book entitled *A Plea for the Unborn* (1897).

Another negative eugenist, Dr John Berry Haycraft, argued in *Darwinism and Race Progress* (1895) that tuberculosis was society's 'friend': 'If we stamp out Infectious Diseases we perpetuate Poor Types.' According to Haycraft there were 'types' susceptible to crime, insanity, TB, and alcoholism and to attempt to protect them by preventive forms of medicine was to create an unhealthy 'hothouse' race. In his opinion laws against drink were a symbol of not merely ineffectual but counter-productive legislation. The goal had to be to let alcoholics drink themselves to death and so rid the world of their kind. No charity could be offered the criminal, the insane, the epileptic. 'The incapables' had to be segregated; the task of the state was to ensure the 'non-perpetuation' of the 'worse strains'.[24]

Arnold White, a leading light of the school of yellow journalism, followed Haycraft in asserting that hospitals were 'manufacturing' unemployables. The state was actually abetting the multiplication of the unfit by assisting those who should never have married: 'Parental neglect, premature and reckless marriage leading to the multiplication of tainted brains and rickety frames, are matters of indifference to practical politicians.' White accused bureaucrats of soaking the rich in order that the diseased poor might languish comfortably in clinics. There was, he stated, something, '. . .revolting in our tendency to overwhelm the strong and healthy with the ever-growing demands of profligate, thriftless, and prolific invalids'. The state had no duty to treat 'avoidable' disease. If the people of the street fell ill as a consequence of their penchant for alcohol and tinned food it was their own fault. What the nation required was a healthy citizenry, not a diseased rabble of 'pauper voluptuaries'. Therefore actions had to be

taken to prevent the propagation of such types; White called for the
tightening of marriage laws and the sterilisation of the incapable. A
smaller, more efficient population would be far superior to the
unhealthy masses currently existing. 'We must abandon the formulae
that the increase of a decayed population is a popular boom; that every
poor man in need of help is an innocent victim.' In the face of outside
threats England could no longer afford such philanthropic luxuries:
'The Empire will not be maintained by a nation of out-patients.'[25]

G. Lowes Dickinson echoed the assertion that the old prejudices
against interference in marriage had to be put aside. In *Justice and
Liberty: A Political Dialogue* (1909) he stated that the 'production of
children is a private and irresponsible function' but thanks to Galton's
work it was being recognised that restrictions had to be put on
criminals, lunatics, and the syphillitic.[26] Carveth Read, Grote Professor
of Philosophy at the University of London, declared that he was at least
'consoled' by the fact that the lower classes who had the highest birth
rate also had the highest death rate. But even so nature would have to
be assisted in her task: 'Whether anything can be done to weed the
population by permanently segregating criminals and quasi-lunatics
and imbeciles, by preventing marriage amongst certain classes of invalids
and hereditary suspects, by euthanasia of certain idiots and incurable
sufferers, time will show.'[27] W.C.D. and C.D. Whetham were already
calling, in *The Family and the Nation* (1909), for the 'extinction of the
tribe' of the criminal and feeble-minded — not by death as in the past —
but by institutionalisation. 'We must attain the same result by the
longer, gentler system of perpetual segregation in detention colonies,
with all the mitigations that are practicable.' C.W. Saleeby showed
himself to be similarly sensitive. 'Painless extinction' was, he declared,
unacceptable but 'permanent care' and sterilisation in effect offered
the same advantages.[28]

The question of just who would be sterilised was discussed by Robert
Reid Rentoul in *Proposed Sterilization of Certain Mental and Physical
Degenerates* (1903). Declaring that the asylums *produced* lunatics
Rentoul called for the sterilisation of their 107,944 inmates. The
morality of the act he defended on the grounds that it was a policy of
self-defence adopted by the community. Thus justified in his own mind,
Rentoul went on to propose the same operation for those with
congenital heart and lung complaints, the carriers of venereal disease,
the 36,000 to 50,000 tramps and the 60,000 prostitutes, the latter two
groups having demonstrated by their choice of profession their mental
defectiveness. W.A. Chapple in *The Fertility of the Unfit* (1904) went

into some detail on how such a programme could be carried out. Anaesthetics and antisepsis made it far simpler than some thought; vasectomies for men and tubo-ligatures for women could be accomplished with a minimum of inconvenience.[29]

The logic of the eugenic argument led naturally to 'mercy killing'. Passing references were made in the literature to euthanasia but few English writers were prepared to defend it openly. One of the rare discussions of the question was in *The Elements of Child-Protection* (1912) by the Hungarian physician Sigmund Engel, translated into English by Dr Eden Paul. Engel argued that if a child was judged by a panel of doctors to be potentially harmful to the species it should be destroyed; to keep it alive was useless.

> This procedure is a grave infringement of the law of parsimony if only for the reason that in other departments of social life, with the same expenditure of effort, far greater and more valuable results could be obtained. When such children, for one reason or another, find their way into the world, they should be quickly and painlessly destroyed. What method should be adopted to attain this end is a minor consideration.[30]

Engel concluded his case by asking why, if one killed the criminal who could harm only one generation, one should not eliminate those who could harm several.

Given the fact that so much of the eugenists' writings read like science fiction (that they played a role in H.G. Wells' fantasies will be discussed in chapter ten), it was inevitable that they should have influenced tne literary portrayals of modern life. The influence is most apparent in the surge of turn-of-the-century novels depicting the slum culture of East London. For example, in Arthur Morrison's *A Child of the Jago* a doctor asks the local priest,

> Is there a child in all this place that wouldn't be better dead — still better unborn? But does a day pass without bringing you just such a parishoner? Here lies the Jago, a nest of rats, breeding, breeding, as only rats can; and we say it is well. On high moral grounds we uphold the rights of rats to multiply their thousands. Sometimes we catch a rat. And we keep it a little while, nourish it carefully, and put it back into the nest to propagate its kind.[31]

The priest has no answer.

Not surprisingly fear of other races as well as of other classes was evident in much of the eugenic literature. Arnold White was the best-known of the anti-semite propagandists. In *Efficiency and Empire* (1901) he warned, 'Rule by foreign Jews is being set up.' In his vivid imagination the invaders formed a motley army of wealthy financiers and 'diseased aliens'.[32] The fact that the Jewish birth rate remained higher than that of Anglo-Saxons was commented on sourly by other observers. According to the Whethams reproduction of such 'thriftless stock' posed a real danger. 'Whatever good qualities these aliens may possess, they are not those typical of the Anglo-Saxon; and these immigrants cannot be regarded as a satisfactory equivalent to the native population.' The appearance of a Yiddish translation of Allbutt's birth control tract was thus greeted in the *Malthusian* with the pious hope: 'We trust that this may convert many of that people to less fatal traditions than those they have hitherto trusted to in the matter of population.' It was in the context of such concerns that the 'anti-alien' agitation culminated in the passage of the 1905 Aliens Act aimed at preventing the entry into England of Jewish refugees.[33]

In an age in which the freedom of the poor to live and breed was no longer viewed by the middle class with indifference but fear eugenics seemed,by the very ruthlessness of its scientism, to offer a way out. It appealed to those of every political persuasion who saw themselves struggling to maintain the rule of the fit and proper. Pearson's belief that fertility could pose a danger if not checked by 'extra-group selection' led him to call himself a socialist.

> The real solution is simply that the limitation of population without loss of national vigour is possible in a socialistic community, but not in a capitalistic one. In our present capitalistic society the neo-Malthusians have by their teaching very sensibly lowered the birth rate, but all the evidence I can collect seems to show, that this lowering of the birth rate is at the expense of national vigour, for it has taken place among the physically and mentally fitter. . .It will profit little, however, that the social man and woman without state-interference limit the number of their offspring, if large anti-social sections of society still continue to bring any number of unneeded human beings into the world. Society will have in some fashion to interfere and to restrict the anti-social in the matter of child-bearing.[34]

These sentiments were shared by some socialists. The response of the

Fabians will be examined in chapter ten but here it can be noted that the idea that in the collectivist society the state would assume the role of policing reproduction appealed to the bureaucratically-minded.[35]

Even liberals were infected by the eugenist contagion. J.A. Hobson in *The Social Problem* (1901) agreed with Pearson that 'natural selection' was no longer operating in its crude, effective fashion. Some attempt had to be made to prevent the rapid growth of the weak and diseased.

> But a social policy of veto upon anti-social-propagation, however difficult of enforcement it may seem, and whatever moral risks it may involve, is really essential. . .When it is once plainly recognized that the production of defective children is the worst crime which anyone can commit against society, the necessary penalties will be attached, and will be as effective as other coercive measures can be in repressing the particular crimes to which they are directed.[36]

C.F.G. Masterman, the coiner of the term 'New Liberalism', made the same point in *The Condition of England:* 'The nation must inevitably suffer from an artificial restriction of children amongst those very classes and families who should be most encouraged to produce them. . . And a nation is in a serious condition if its better stocks are producing smaller families or no families at all, and its least capable are still raising an abundant progeny.'[37]

The actual number of members of the Eugenics Society may have represented only a small proportion of all English social theorists but their concerns were widely shared. Attributing to the poor the responsibility of their own plight was a temptation which, as the socialist Robert Blatchford remarked, few middle class social scientists could resist.

> The poor! The poor! The poor! The thriftlessness of the poor! The intemperance of the poor! The idleness of the poor! How long do we have to listen to these insults? How long have we to hear men prate about the poor and about the working class who never knew what poverty is, who never knew what hunger means, who never did a stroke of manual work, and whose knowledge of 'the poor' is got from poems and novels and the essays of university men, or from furtive and uncharitable glances at the public house steps or the pawnshop door as their excellencies' carriages are hurrying them through the outskirts of the slums.[38]

Even H.G. Wells who was drawn to the idea of breeding a super race
was dismayed by the transparency with which sociologists and
anthropologists turned quantitative analyses to the purpose of
legitimising the powers of the middle class while denigrating those of
the workers.

> Just as in the early days of British Somaliland, rascals would descend
> from nowhere in particular upon unfortunate villages, levy taxes
> and administer atrocity in the name of the Empire, and even, I am
> told, outface for a time the modest heralds of the government, so in
> this department of anthropology the public mind suffers from the
> imposition of theories and assertions claiming to be 'scientific',
> which have no more relation to that organized system of criticism
> which is science, than a brigand at large on a mountain has to the
> machinery of law and police, by which finally he will be hanged.[39]

But the 'hanging' Wells prophesised was not to occur for some time.
The Eugenics movement was at its height at 1912; Arthur James
Balfour, the leader of the Conservative party, was only the best known
of the many public personalities who supported its policies. More
importantly, eugenics was to have a major influence on the social
sciences. Despite its peculiar preconceptions eugenics had developed
through rigorous empirical methods of data gathering and statistical
analysis, a methodology that made competing schools of British
sociology appear dilettantish in comparison.[40] Eugenic considerations
were going to colour the discussions of the reform of the Poor Law,
the protection of children, and the incarceration of the feeble-minded
in the upsurge of social legislation that marked the first decades of the
twentieth century.

For the purposes of this study the importance of the eugenics
movement is that its basic ideas seeped into the birth control debate.
It shifted attention from the rights of the mother to those of the state;
from the quantity of the work force to its quality. The rise of eugenics
was but one facet of the shift from an individualist to a collectivist
biologism by those who sought to turn the population problem to
their own purposes of social control. Finding in the most advanced
studies in social research new justifications for social inequalities, the
eugenists advanced fresh, powerful arguments to explain why women
and workers could not be left to determine their family size for
themselves.

Notes

1. Cited in C.P. Blacker, *Eugenics: Galton and After* (London, 1952), p.65; see also Karl Pearson, *The Life of Francis Galton* (4 vols., London, 1914-1930); D.W. Forrest, *Francis Galton: The Life and Work of a Victorian Genius* (London, 1974).
2. On Pearson see E.S. Pearson, 'Karl Pearson: An Appreciation of Some Aspects of his Life and Work,' *Biometrika,* 28 (1936), pp.193-257; 29 (1938), pp.161-248; Bernard Semmel, *Imperialism and Social Reform: English Social Imperial Thought 1895-1914* (New York, 1968), pp.24-42.
3. J.D.Y. Peel, *Herbert Spencer: The Evolution of a Sociologist* (London, 1971).
4. The idea that evolution could be leading in the wrong direction was popularised by Benjamin Kidd, *Social Evolution* (London, 1894) and *Principles of Western Civilization* (London, 1902). Kidd saw religion serving as the necessary check; attacked on this point by Galton and Pearson he replied in *The Science of Power* (New York, 1918). See also C.W. Saleeby, *Evolution: The Master-Key* (London, 1906); O.C. Beale, *Racial Decay: A Compilation of Evidence from World Sources* (London, 1911).
5. Bentley B. Gilbert, *The Evolution of National Insurance in Great Britain: The Origins of the Welfare State* (London, 1966); Jose Harris, *Unemployment and Politics: A Study of English Social Policy* (Oxford, 1972).
6. Ludmerer, *Genetics and American Society: A Historical Appraisal* (Baltimore, 1972), p.10; Robert Owen, *Lectures on the Marriages of the Priesthood of the Old Immoral World* (London, 1840, 4th edn.), p.32.
7. See Gareth Stedman Jones, *Outcast London* (Oxford, 1971).
8. See Richard Hofstadter, *Social Darwinism in American Thought* (Philadelphia, 1945).
9. Cited in Forrest, *Galton,* pp.99-100.
10. Pearson to Drysdale (1894) cited in the *Malthusian* (December 1897), p.90. See also Karl Pearson, *The Ethic of Freethought* (London, 1901 [1st edn. 1887]), p.371.
11. Pearson, *Pearson,* (1938), 189.
12. See also Frederic Harrison, *Realities and Ideas* (London, 1908); Jill Conway, 'Stereotypes of Femininity in a Theory of Sexual Evolution,' in Martha Vicinus, (ed.), *Suffer and Be Still* (Bloomington, 1972), pp.140-54.
13. Pearson, 'The Woman Question,' *The Ethic of Freethought,* p.355. Similarly Charles Darwin expressed the concern that birth control might pose the danger of 'extreme profligacy amongst unmarried women'. Darwin to G.A. Gaskell (15 November, 1878) in *More Letters of Charles Darwin* (London, 1903), II, p.50.
14. Pearson, *The Chances of Death* (London, 1897), p.251.
15. Whetham, 'The Extinction of the Upper Classes,' *Nineteenth Century and After,* 66 (1909), pp.105-6.
16. Saleeby, *Woman and Womanhood* (London, 1901), pp.6, 13, 262, 333.
17. Ellis, *Studies in the Psychology of Sex* (Philadelphia, 1910), VI, 588 ff.
18. Ellis, *The Task of Social Hygiene* (London, 1912), 88 ff.
19. Ellis, *The Problem of Race Regeneration* (London, 1909); 'Eugenics and St. Valentine,' *Nineteenth Century and After,* 59 (1906), pp.779-87; the *New Age* (11 April, 1908), p.469.
20. Whetham, 'Inheritance and Sociology,' *Nineteenth Century and After,* 65 (1909), pp.85-7; see also Rev. R.F. Horton, *National Ideals and Race Regeneration* (London, 1912), pp.37-8; C.W. Saleeby, *Parenthood and Race Culture: An Outline of Eugenics* (London, 1909). Pearson cited in Pearson, *Pearson,* (1938), p.172.

21. Forrest, *Galton,* p.250; Pearson, *Pearson,* (1936), p.238.
22. See C.W. Saleeby, 'Racial Poisons: Alcohol,' *Eugenics Review,* 2 (1910-1911), pp.30-52; Charles H. Harvey, *The Biology of British Politics* (London, 1904).
23. The two movements were linked by Montague Crackenthorpe who was active in both the Malthusian League and the Eugenics Educational Society. See his *Population and Progress* (London, 1907).
24. Haycraft, *Darwinism* (London, 1895), p.108; see also F.W. Headley, *Darwinism and Modern Socialism* (London, 1909); L.G. Chiozza Money, *Riches and Poverty* (London, 1906 3rd edn.), p.172.
25. White, *Efficiency and Empire* (London, 1973 [1st edn. 1901]), pp.97, 99, 100, 117.
26. Dickinson, *Justice and Liberty* (London, 1909), p.45.
27. Read, *Natural and Social Morals* (London, 1909), p.159.
28. Whetham, *The Family* (London, 1909), 215; Saleeby, *The Methods of Race Regeneration* (London, 1911), p.43.
29. Rentoul, *Proposed Sterilization* (London, 1903), p.17; Chapple, *The Fertility of the Unfit* (Melbourne, 1904), p.107.
30. Engel, *The Elements of Child Protection* (London, 1912), p.257.
31. Morrison, *A Child of the Jago* (London, 1969 [1st edn. 1896]), p.171. See also Morrison, *Tales of Mean Streets* (London, 1894); Rudyard Kipling, *The Record of Badalia Herodsfoot* in *The Writings in Prose and Verse* (London, 1899), XIV, pp.185-221.
32. White, *Efficiency,* p.80; see also White, ed., *The Destitute Alien* (London, 1892).
33. Whetham, *The Family,* p.147; *Malthusian* (March 1897), p.22; and see Bernard Gainer, *The Alien Invasion* (London, 1972).
34. Pearson, *Chances,* 129 ff; Pearson, *The Ethic,* p.423.
35. See Eden Paul, *Socialism and Eugenics* (London, 1911); Eden and Cedar Paul, (eds.), *Population and Birth Control: A Symposium* (New York, 1917); George Whitehead, *Socialism and Eugenics* (London, 1907); Alvan A. Tenney, *Social Democracy and Population* (New York, 1907).
36. Hobson, *The Social Problem* (London, 1901), pp.216-7.
37. Masterman, *The Condition of England* (London, 1909), p.78; see also Alfred Marshall, *Principles of Economics* (London, 1890), p.256.
38. Blatchford, *Merrie England* (London, 1894), pp.202-3; see his *Not Guilty: A Defence of the Bottom Dog* (London, 1906).
39. Wells, *Mankind in the Making* (London, 1903), p.52.
40. Such was the importance of eugenics that L.T. Hobhouse devoted a portion of each of his seven major works to it. See especially *Social Evolution and Political Theory* (New York, 1911) chapter three; *Democracy and Reaction* (London, 1904), chapters three and four. See also Philip Abrams, *The Origins of British Sociology* (Chicago, 1968), p.90.

SOCIALISTS AND BIRTH CONTROL: THE CASE
OF THE SOCIAL DEMOCRATIC FEDERATION

In May of 1887 Beatrice Potter, the future Beatrice Webb, passed a
Sunday at Speakers' Corner in Hyde Park listening to the amateur
orators. The largest crowd, she wrote in her diary, was drawn by a
socialist condemning birth control.

> From a platform a hoarse-voiced man denounced the iniquities of
> the social system; in one hand he held Malthus, in the other, *Fruits
> of Philosophy*. The subject was a delicate one — the rival methods
> of checking population, late marriage versus preventive checks. He,
> however, joined issue with both methods, for he asserted that
> neither was needed. There was bread enough for all if it was equally
> distributed. Men starving while warehouses were stocked to
> overflowing; it was the commercial system that was at fault, not
> the laws of nature.[1]

It comes as something of a surprise to read that a respectable young
woman could, at the height of the Victorian age, listen to a public
discussion of family limitation. It is equally interesting to discover that
at the turn of the century the socialists in large part ignored the threat
posed by eugenist teachings and continued — as had the Chartists and
Owenites — to do battle with the Malthusian spectre of over-population.[2]
Socialist sensitivity in this area was sustained by the activities of the
Malthusian League which violently opposed socialism of any stripe and
presented, in orthodox neo-Malthusian fashion, the restriction of family
size as the only way in which the working class could escape poverty.[3]
One of the League's adherents, Mrs Fenwick Miller, spelled out the
alternatives: 'What are the remedies that are offered to modern society?
There are only two: Neo-Malthusianism and Socialism; and who would
hesitate between the two?'[4] The English public was thus presented with
the simplistic notion that self-improvement and social reform were
mutually antagonistic goals. Given the fact that the public defenders of
birth control were social conservatives many socialists felt they had no
alternative but to oppose it. To accept the notion of the social necessity
of either contraception or postponed marriage would, they feared, be
tantamount to acknowledging that unemployment and poverty were

not the artificial products of a capitalist society but the natural
consequence of over-breeding. In *Contemporary Socialism* (1884) John
Rae noted that socialists '. . .utterly ridicule [the] Malthusian horror of
a progressive population'.[5] In 1885 John Robertson made the same
observation in *Socialism and Malthusianism:* 'A remarkable feature in
current Socialist propaganda is the almost complete unanimity with
which the doctrines of Malthus are there derided, denounced, and
repudiated.'[6] Thirty-five years later when the American birth control
propagandist Margaret Sanger was lecturing in Britain she noted that
workers came out to listen to her, first because it was rare to hear a
woman speaker and secondly because they were drawn '. . .to fight the
ancient battle of Marx against Malthus'. In her opinion the 'Efforts of
the English neo-Malthusians to introduce birth control to the masses
had been hampered not only by the opposition of the upper classes,
but more especially by the persistent hostility of the orthodox
socialists.'[7]

The opposition of socialists to the discussion of fertility control was
motivated by two major concerns. The first was the belief that the
'population question' was a false issue manufactured by reactionaries
to turn attention away from the need for social reform. The second was
the fear that an examination of the ways in which limitation of family
size might effect the health and happiness of the individual woman
could impede the progress of labour.

As was seen in the earlier discussion of Owenism and Chartism all
questions of population control in the nineteenth century were
inextricably associated in English men's minds with the doctrines of
Malthus. No major change was to occur in the course of the century.
Socialists could, no more than the Owenites, accept a doctrine that
attributed poverty simply to the 'over-breeding of the poor'. Marx
himself wrote:

> The hatred of the English working class against Malthus — the
> 'mountebank parson', as Cobbett rudely calls him — is therefore
> entirely justified. The people were right here in sensing instinctively
> that they were confronted not with a *man of science* but with a
> *bought advocate,* a pleader on behalf of their enemies, a shameless
> sycophant of the ruling class.[8]

Marx had, however, little interest in the population debate and English
socialists relied on the traditional assertion that the organisation of
labour and the redistribution of resources could meet any challenge

posed by demographic pressures.

The population debate died down at mid-century only to re-emerge in the 1880s as a consequence of the 'Great Depression'. On the one hand an organised movement arguing in favour of the limitation of family size appeared; on the other the first English socialist parties in favour of massive social reforms emerged. In his *Memoirs* the labour leader Tom Mann wrote that the trial of Charles Bradlaugh and Annie Besant in 1877 for distributing birth control literature had focused the attention of all political activists on the question of population.[9] English anarchists republished Proudhon's attack in which the Frenchman declared: 'The theory of Malthus is the theory of political murder; of murder from motives of philanthropy and for love of God.'[10] Slightly less vitriolic arguments against the Malthusians were presented by Joseph Lane of the Labour Emancipation League in his *An Anti-Statist Communist Manifesto* (1887) and N. Kempner's *Commonsense Socialism* (1887).[11] 'Justitia,' the anonymous author of *Emigration and the Malthusian Craze in Relation to the Labourer's Position* (1886) declared that the real answer to existing poverty was the redistribution of wealth; the bogey of population pressure had been simply raised by political economists in order to avoid dealing with the basic problem:

> Emigration and checks to population are quack remedies too often preached by the partisans of the *'Laissez-faire'*, or 'Let Alone Policy', in opposition to any unpopular scheme of reform that may be proposed.[12]

The land nationalisation schemes of Henry George represented just such reforms and the popularity of his theories in the 1880s was due in large part to the belief that he had silenced the Malthusians.[13]

Hostility to Malthus was thus endemic to the left but it was most noticeable in the small group of self-proclaimed Marxists who made up the Social Democrat Federation created in 1884. I say 'self-proclaimed Marxists' because the policies followed by the SDF, as will be shown, owed more to the idiosyncrasies of its leadership than to the teachings of Marx. The SDF was the creation of H.M. Hyndman, a wealthy, Cambridge-educated society man whom Marx found 'self-satisfied' and 'garrulous' and Engels described as '. . .a frock-coated playboy agitator with a gift for instant viturperation'.[14] Hyndman did have a natural bent for rubbing people the wrong way and this penchant was to play no small part in limiting the numbers drawn to what the

Pall Mall Gazette witheringly referred to as 'The Democratic Federation, as Mr Hyndman persists in calling himself'.[15] According to the mechanistic model of social change adopted by Hyndman all meaningful reforms had to await the revolution; he was accordingly scornful of the short-term goals pursued by trade unionists, feminists and the like. On occasion such movements would even be labelled as diversionary by the SDF journals, *Justice* and the *Social Democrat.* The failure of the SDF to recognise the potential importance of birth control to working-class families was but one example of its rigid opposition to anything its leadership regarded as mere palliatives.

In his own work Hyndman scoffed at the 'foolish theories of Malthus' and derided John Stuart Mill's suggestion that workers could improve their situation by limiting their numbers.

> Under our system of unregulated competition, the worker on the average gains nothing, and if he limits his family as a class and reduces the numbers of available hands — a thing practically impossible — he but accelerates the introduction of new machines, and in due time the re-creation of a relative over-population.[16]

But having said that it was futile to attempt to restrict numbers Hyndman then went on to state that capitalists were in fact interested in 'over-population' because it did provide them with a 'reserve army' of labour which they could bring in at times of high demand in order to keep down wages.

In the SDF's *The Socialist Catechism,* drawn up by J.L. Joynes, a one time master of Eton, arguments for restricting family size were presented as a ploy by which the bourgeoisie sought to make the worker assume responsibility for poverty that was in reality a consequence of class exploitation. Socialists were seeking to overturn this system; the Malthusians were seeking to maintain it.

> Q. How does the standpoint of the Malthusian differ from that of the socialist?
> A. The former accept the basis of capitalist society, namely, the existence of two distinct classes of wage-payers and wage-earners, and merely advise the workers to attempt to secure a larger wage.
> Q. How do Socialists regard this advice?
> A. They consider the discussion as whether the workers shall enjoy one-half or one-third of the wealth which they produce is relatively unimportant, and they continue to urge the rightful

claim of the workers to the full value of their own productions.[17]

In a letter to the *Malthusian* (April 1883) Joynes insisted that poverty was caused, not by over-population but by inequitable distribution. Even if the population was reduced no meaningful change could occur because the workman would be still subject to the 'iron law of wages' that forced salaries down to a subsistence level. Birth control was thus useless. Joynes, a confirmed vegetarian, stated that even if those whom he called his 'corpse-eating friends' adopted his diet the social problem would still remain unresolved; adoption of birth control, he declared, would be just as ineffective.[18]

William Morris, a founding member of the SDF who led a break-away group to form the Socialist League, nevertheless continued to follow Hyndman's line that population control was like thrift, self-help, and cooperation a simple stop gap measure thrown up by the capitalists in a vain attempt to stave off the inevitable triumph of the proletariat.

> . . .others beg the proletariat not to breed so fast; an injunction the compliance with which might be at first of advantage to the proletarians themselves in their present condition, but would certainly undo the capitalists, if it were carried to any lengths, and would lead through ruin and misery to the violent outbreak of the very revolution which these timid people are so anxious to forego.[19]

The spokesmen of the SDF and the Socialist League never tired of asserting that the population question was a social, not an individual, issue. The argument was put perhaps most forcefully by a young member of the London SDF, Guy Aldred in a 1906 pamphlet, *The Religion and Economics of Sex Oppression.*

> An economic disease [poverty], its remedy is not individual, but social; not racial, but class; not a question of birth-rate, but one of wealth-distribution; not lack of production, but fluctuation in existence. And this disease, a scourge of capitalism, will not be remedied with poison in the womb or even a palliative continence that really thrives at the expense of others' lust.[20]

Being opposed to birth control did not mean that the socialists assumed that the population would increase interminably. Marx himself believed that each society had its own population law. 'Overpopulation' took place in capitalist society because 'variable capital' (that which went to pay for labour) tended to increase more slowly than did population. Thus 'overpopulation' really signified surplus labour which was in fact essential to capitalism. It was Marx's belief that in the socialist society a higher standard of living would lead to a decline of the death rate; he did not say what would happen to the birth rate.[21] Bebel, Nitti and other Marxists tended to adopt Herbert Spencer's optimistic view that with a better distribution of wealth the birth rate would fall.[22] This standard of living argument presented the socialists with one problem. If they were to be consistent they would have to admit that the drop in fertility that was occurring in the last decades of the century signified improvements in the conditions of the working class; this they were, for political reasons, loth to do.

The opposition of the English Marxists to the Malthusian League was logical enough; as proponents of social reform they had no choice but to attack those who held that only restriction of population would improve the condition of the masses. The problem was that the socialists, having demolished the argument of the social necessity of birth control, then took the unfortunate and unnecessary step of suggesting that individual attempts to limit family size were in some way anti-social acts. Given the fact that birth control was being employed by ever larger numbers of couples such pronouncements by the SDF appeared increasingly out of touch with reality. By the 1890s observers such as the Webbs were drawing attention to the fact that working as well as middle-class women were limiting the size of their families.

> We attribute this adoption of neo-Malthusian devices to prevent the burden of a large family. . .chiefly to the spread of education among working-class women, to their discontent with a life of constant ill-health and domestic worry under narrow circumstances, and to the growth among them of aspirations for a fuller and more independent existence of their own.[23]

Despite such testimony the SDF continued to oppose birth control, a tack adopted in part because of the simple anti-feminism of men such as Hyndman and Bax. There was always a strong misogynist current evident in the writings of the SDF and it followed that birth control, which was already suspect because of its Malthusian connotations, would be open to further attack when viewed as a means by which women sought to escape their natural duties. The SDF, which prided

itself on its political radicalism, revealed a pronounced social
conservatism when dealing with any issue relating to women. To put
the party's attitude towards birth control in context a word or two
must be said of its response to the questions of women's paid
employment, prostitution, and the vote.

According to Marx the emancipation of women would only be
possible when they could take part in production on a large scale and
free themselves from domestic drudgery. In a famous passage in *Capital*
he stated:

> However terrible, however repulsive, the break up of the old family
> system within the organism of capitalist society may seem; none
> the less, large scale industry, by assigning to women and young
> persons and children of both sexes, a decisive role in the socially
> organized process of production, and a role which has to be fulfilled
> outside the home, is building the new economic foundation for a
> higher form of the family and of the relations between the sexes.[24]

If the SDF were to have followed Marx's analysis it would have
demanded increased female employment and the support facilities and
birth control which would permit such employment to take place
outside the home. In fact the SDF followed just the opposite policy.
It asked women to remain at home and avoid competing with men for
jobs. It asked for social benefits which would permit women — not to
leave the traditional sphere of their activities — but to remain as
primarily wives and mothers.

Hyndman and his followers in the SDF assumed an 'organic' view
of society, much like the positivists, in which the sexes had supporting
and complementary roles. This in turn meant that they could not
entertain the notion of a struggle between the sexes. They resolved
the problem of men and women competing in the market place by
declaring that women had to be restricted to jobs for which they were
'fit'.[25] Capitalism was held responsible for plunging women and girls
into objectionable forms of employment such as that of the 'pitbrow
lasses'.[26] The questions of whether women needed or wanted to work
were hedged.

Married women's work in particular raised the ire of the SDF. It
attributed the drop in the birth rate to this phenomenon and in the
columns of *Justice* contributors argued that the protection of the race
necessitated the restriction of women's work. This approach found
support in the works of the Italian Marxist Enrico Ferri who in

Socialism and Positive Science (1905) declared that women could only be permitted work '. . .in keeping with sacred motherhood'.

> Society ought to put woman, as a human being and as a creator of men — more worthy consequently of love and respect — in a better legal and moral condition than she is at present — too often a beast of burden or object of luxury.[27]

Such a simplistic approach to women's labour raised protests even from within the SDF. Dora B. Montefiore, future secretary of the Women's Social Democratic Party, asked how the SDF, which claimed to believe in majority rule, could ask for legislation restricting women's work, when women were disbarred from political activity. She could only view it as an attempt by men to keep women in subjection:

> As capitalism and modern conditions developed and prevailed, the wage earner became the slave of society; and in proportion as he is striving to shake off his fetters he is attempting (unconscientiously in many cases, I know) to enslave women through forcing economic dependence on them either in 'the seclusion of the home' or in the worst paid and harder employments, in which the man does not care to compete.[28]

The SDF leadership could not understand this sort of argument. It assumed that if a woman were married to a worker with a decent wage the problem would disappear. At the moment such marriages were not possible because labour was forced to accept low salaries. The efforts of the SDF had to be aimed first at raising men's wages; secondly, at restricting women's work which provided cheap, 'blackleg' competition.[29]

The SDF's attitude towards women's work was parallelled in an interesting way by its view of prostitution. According to Harry Quelch, editor of *Justice,* capitalism forced all working-class women to sell themselves in one way or another — prostitution was only the most glaring example of class oppression. The problem was exacerbated moreover by Victorian middle-class males' tendency — following Malthus' advice — to postpone marriage until 'settled in life'. In the meantime these men satisfied their sexual desires by taking advantage of working-class women driven by poverty onto the streets. A contributor to *Justice* declared that all middle-class young men were 'fornicators'; the Dilke and Parnell cases were advanced as proof.[30]

Viewing prostitution as a case of class rather than sex exploitation led to some rather curious results. In the first place it meant that the SDF viewed with relative indifference the efforts of moral reformers seeking both to protect young girls from seduction and to end the Contagious Diseases Act which in effect legalised street-walking. In the columns of *Justice* 'The Prostitution Crusade' was classed as an example of nineteenth-century 'humbug'.[31] It was declared that it was impossible to rescue or reform prostitutes; prostitution as a product of class exploitation would only be ended when the system was overthrown. Secondly, the class approach of the SDF to the practice resulted in it showing surprisingly little sympathy for the working-class women who were its victims. From the male point of view of the writers of *Justice* it was the working-class men who suffered most: 'Prostitutes are bought with the wealth wrung out of the underpaid of these prostitutes' fathers and brothers.'[32] Once more the problems of women were underestimated.

Having opposed women's work and ridiculed the efforts of feminists to end prostitution the SDF went on to counter the efforts of the suffragettes. The opposition of Hyndman to 'the fine lady suffragettes' who wanted a limited propertied vote could be defended as a logical stance for a socialist but many of the contributors of the movement's journal, *Justice,* indulged in simple-minded anti-feminism. One writer stated that women could not be given the vote because they were '. . .Conservative by heart. . .' Others referred to the suffragist struggle as '. . .agitation for sex privileges'.[33] Some repeated the old saw that the only women interested in the vote were bitter, disappointed old maids. The leading anti-feminist of the SDF, E. Belfort Bax became a member of the Men's Anti-Suffrage League and attempted to rationalise his contempt for women by arguing that feminism like birth control or temperance were 'diversions' which could only impede the growth of socialism. He expressed outrage that attempts were made to 'smuggle' feminism into the working class movement by those who claimed that women formed an exploited class.[34] In Bax's view the opposite was the case. The suffragettes were 'vampires' seeking complete power; because women made up more than fifty per cent of the population to give them the vote would be to create a female dictatorship. Bax, who revealed an amazing ability to ignore facts, declared that women had already enslaved their husbands.

The inequality in question presses, as usual, heaviest upon the working-man, whose wife, to all intents and purposes, now has him completely in her power. If dissolute or drunken, she can sell up his goods or break up his home at pleasure, and still compel him to keep her and live with her to her life's end. There is no law to protect *him*. On the other hand, let him but raise a finger in a movement of exasperation against this precious representative of the sacred principle of 'womanhood', and straightway he is consigned to the treadmill for his six months. . .for the law jealously guards the earnings or property of the wife from possible spoliation. She on any colourable pretext can obtain magisterial separation and 'protection'.[35]

The tedious anti-feminist tone of *Justice* would not deserve further comment if it were not for the fact that in the very same columns in which women were derided it was asked why they were not joining the socialist cause. Perhaps the best example of such pig-headedness was an article on 16 June, 1894 entitled 'How to Induce Women to Become Socialists' in which both anti-semitic and anti-feminist slurs were combined. Women were by nature half-Jewish, stated the contributor, and hence the only way to lure them into socialism was to appeal to them as consumers.[36]

As one peruses the columns of *Justice* it becomes increasingly clear · that the SDF's conception of the role of the woman was drawn not from Marx and Engels, but from a distinctly British line of moralists running from Carlyle to Ruskin to Morris. More than one observer of the British left has remarked on the fact that these were the writers who provided the young socialist movement with its sense of moral purpose, its indictment of individualism, and its aspirations for a reformed society.[37] What has been glossed over and what for the purposes of this chapter is of particular interest is that their critique of the modern world — larded as it was with a religiosity, a medievalism, and a gospel of masculine work — explicitly denigrated women's efforts to limit the burden of child-bearing.[38]

It was Ruskin, the self-styled 'old Tory', who provided the socialists with many of their arguments against the crass materialism of industrialised society. He held up for special ridicule the premises of the Malthusian economists: in response to their insistence that population pressure posed a danger he replied,

That country is the richest which nourishes the greatest number of noble and happy human beings; that man is richest who, having perfected the functions of his own life to the utmost, has also the

widest influence, both personal and by means of his possessions,
over the lives of others. . .There is not yet, nor will yet for ages be,
any real over-population. . .[39]

Indeed Ruskin sketched out plans for a revival of medieval ceremonies
in order to increase the solemnity of marriage.[40] His concern was that
women in particular were no longer willing to carry out their natural
functions of wife and mother. According to his scheme woman was to
be the angel of the house. Her work was: 'I. To please people. II. To
feed them in dainty ways. II. To clothe them. IV. To keep them orderly.
V. To teach them.'[41] To learn such tasks she was in turn to receive a
special education.

> All such knowledge should be given her as may enable her to
> understand, and even to aid, the work of men; and yet it should
> be given, not as knowledge, not as if it were or could be an object
> for her to know, but only to feel and judge.[42]

The problem was that women were rebelling against such training and
duties. The self-renunciation to which Ruskin condemned them was
no longer accepted. Ruskin could only express his revulsion: 'I cannot
find words strong enough to express the hatred and the contempt that
I feel for the modern idea that a woman must cease being a mother,
daughter or wife in order to become a clerk or engineer.'[43] Attributing
much of the blame to John Stuart Mill's feminist writings Ruskin
complained that English young women found '. . .the "career" of the
Madonna is too limited a one, and that modern political economy can
provide them. . .with "much more lucrative occupations than that of
nursing the baby" '.[44]

This same combination of anti-Malthusianism and anti-feminism can
be found in the works of William Morris, the artistic heir of Ruskin and
founding member of the Social Democratic Federation. Morris' views
are most clearly set out in *News From Nowhere.* In this utopian novel
he portrays London as it will be after the socialist revolution
marvellously transformed it into an Arcadian paradise. Everyone is
healthy and happy. There is no property and hence no poverty or crime.
Work is a pleasure because each man is a skilled craftsman pursuing an
art he enjoys. But, asks the hero, are not the women dissatisfied with
the fact that they continue to do the housework? An old man replies
that the 'advanced' women of the nineteenth century felt that such
tasks won no respect but they were wrong. 'Come, now, my friend',

quoth he, 'don't you know that it is a great pleasure to a clever woman to manage a house skilfully, and to do it so that all the house-mates about her looked pleased, and are grateful to her?'[45] The narrator then broaches the question of sex.

> '. . .don't you remember that some of the "superior" women wanted to emancipate the more intelligent part of their sex from the bearing of children?'
> 'I *do* remember about that strange piece of baseless folly, the result, like all other follies of the period, of the hideous class tyranny which then obtained. . .How could it possibly be but that maternity should be highly honoured amongst us?. . .For the rest, remember that all the *artificial* burdens of motherhood are now done away with. A mother has no longer any more sordid anxieties for the future of her children. They may indeed turn out better or worse; they may disappoint her highest hopes; such anxieties as these are part of the mingled pleasure and pain which goes to make up the life of mankind. But at least she is spared the fear (it was most commonly the certainty) that artificial disabilities would make her children something less than men and women. She knows that they will live and act according to the measure of their own faculties. In times past, it is clear that the "Society" of the day helped its Judaic god, and the "Man of Science" of the time, in visiting the sins of the fathers upon the children. How to reverse this process, how to take the sting out of heredity, has for long been one of the most constant cares of the thoughtful men amongst us. So that, you see, the ordinarily healthy woman (and almost all our women are both healthy and at least comely), respected as a child-bearer and rearer of children, desired as a woman, loved as a companion, unanxious for the future of her children, has far more instinct for maternity than the poor drudge and mother of drudges of past days could ever have had; or than her sister of the upper classes, brought up in affected ignorance of natural facts, reared in an atmosphere of mingled prudery and prurience.'[46]

The assumption of Morris that if the state provided the support facilities women could be expected to welcome each and every pregnancy was shared by the leading contributors to *Justice*. In socialist society maternity was to be honoured and rewarded; there would thus be no need to discuss the unpleasant subject of artificial restriction of family size.

It was the very individualism — in particular the female individualism — of birth control which obviously most bothered many socialists. They feared that the restriction of family size entailed a lack of class solidarity. According to Enrico Nitti, an Italian Marxist whose works on population were frequently cited by the SDF:

> No society is less disposed to solidarity than that in which individual idealism is powerful; and nothing predisposes more to individual idealism than practices destined to restrict the family.[47]

The adoption of such tactics symbolised, for Nitti, a pessimism, a lack of faith in the eventual social revolution. Shifting the focus of the attack on birth control from the realm of the economic to that of the moral he condemned it as a form of 'monogamic prostitution' which was both psychologically and physically dangerous: 'Voluntary prevention simply leads to the degeneration of the senses, and the decadence of the race.'[48] This line of argument was followed by J.L. Joynes who declared that if the goal was to restrict family size the only moral means was by practising continence:

> ...while if this were, indeed, the case, I should prefer to teach conjugal continence, rather than those checks on the results of incontinence, which are precisely the same in principle as the emetics which the Romans used at their dinners as checks on the results of their gluttony.[49]

This strain of ascetic moralism was to be found in much of the writings of the socialists. It was pushed to its extreme by Guy Aldred who looked forward to the day when celibate comradeship would replace the sensuality of existing sexual relationships. Reflecting more the influence of Spencer than of Marx he stated: '...it is a psychological and physiological fact that the tendency of the race, in proportion as it becomes more truly intellectual, is away from sexual passion.'[50]

The SDF's suspicion that birth control propaganda was aimed in part at lulling the working class into believing social reforms were unnecessary was not unwarranted. Outside England this threat had been countered by radicals who made birth control part and parcel of their political programmes — Emma Goldman in America, Paul Robin in France, Karl Kautsky in Germany. Such a move was not contemplated by the SDF; it contented itself with stridently condemning the Malthusians who were presented as the sole public defenders of

contraception. The leaders of the SDF could congratulate themselves
on maintaining the doctrinal purity of their party; they failed to
appreciate how their stand on birth control as on women's work,
prostitution and the vote alienated them from potential sources of
popular support. The women within the SDF did not allow the views
of the male leadership to go unchallenged. Dora B. Montefiore defended
women's right to work.[51] Marion Coates attacked *Justice*'s portrayal of
females as idle consumers.[52] Eleanor Marx responded to Bax's ravings
by reminding the SDF of Marx and Engels' feminism: 'It is well
therefore, that readers of *Justice* should know Engels by no means
agreed with Bax's morbid views about women. As to Bax himself, he
surely does not need to be reminded of what Engels thought of his
womanphobia.'[53] S. Gardiner defended birth control. Citing Bebel, she
wrote, 'For ages men have taken advantage of a woman's physical
weakness, causing dependence at times, and made them the slaves of
slaves; and it will take generations to make us once again natural.' Part
of this struggle towards liberation would be control of one's own
fertility. It was, wrote Gardiner, the unremitting stream of babies which
cut women off from the outside world.

> Socialists should teach the women comrades how to lessen their
> families, have fewer children, and healthy ones, and then perhaps,
> more women would join our ranks, as they would have more time
> to learn about socialism.[54]

Such a positive view of birth control was rarely permitted to appear in
the columns of *Justice;* it provides one of the rare glimpses of a new
radical approach to sexual politics which the SDF leadership, because
of its preconceptions and prejudices was intellectually incapable of
pursuing. The situation was most succinctly summed up by a working
woman who, when asked what the letters SDF stood for, replied 'Silly
damn fools.'[55]

Notes

1. Beatrice Webb, *My Apprenticeship* (London, 1920), pp.258-259.
2. On the general issue see J. Peel and R.E. Dowse, 'The Politics of Birth Control,'
   Political Studies, 13 (1965), pp.181-97; Sheila Rowbotham, *Hidden from
   History* (London, 1974), pp.95-107.
3. For the situation on the continent see R.P. Neuman, 'The Sexual Question
   and Social Democracy in Imperial Germany,' *Journal of Social History,* 7

(1974), pp.271-86; Angus McLaren, 'Sex and Socialism: The Opposition of the French Left to Birth Control in the Nineteenth Century,' *Journal of the History of Ideas,* 37 (1976), pp.475-92.

4. Cited by O.C. Beale, *Racial Decay: A Compilation of Evidence from World Sources* (London, 1911), p.31.
5. *Contemporary Socialism* (London, 1884), p.387.
6. *Socialism and Malthusianism* (London, 1885), p.3.
7. *An Autobiography* (New York, 1971 1st edn. 1938), p.275.
8. Cited by L. Meek, (ed.), *Marx and Engels on Malthus* (New York, 1954), p.22.
9. *Memoirs* (London, 1923), p.27.
10. *The Malthusians,* tr. Benjamin R. Tucker (London, 1886), p.6.
11. *An Anti-Statist Communist Manifesto* (London, 1887), pp.22-3; *Commonsense Socialism* (London, 1887).
12. *Emigration and the Malthusian Craze in Relation to the Labourer's Position* (London, 1886), pp.1-2.
13. John Saville, 'Henry George and the British Labour Movement,' *Science and Society,* 24 (1960), pp.321-33.
14. Cited by W.O. Henderson, *The Life of Friedrich Engels* (London, 1976) II, p.682. See also H.M. Hyndman, *The Record of an Adventurous Life* (London, 1911), 252 ff.; and Chushichi Tsuzuki, *H.M. Hyndman and British Socialism* (Oxford, 1961).
15. Cited by Laurence Thompson, *The Enthusiasts: A Biography of John and Katherine Bruce Glasier* (London, 1971), p.34.
16. *The Historical Basis of Socialism in England* (London, 1883), p.254.
17. *The Socialist Catechism* (London, n.d.), p.13.
18. *Malthusian* (April, 1883), p.387.
19. *The Hopes of Civilization* in *Collected Works* (London, 1912 [1st edn. 1885]) XXIV, p.77. The liberal theorist C.F.G. Masterman wrote in a similar vein that birth control offered the establishment a means by which to avoid social reform and yet attain contentment by co-opting the historic leaders of all revolutions – the 'intellectual proletariat'. 'By such limitation of family the standard of comfort is reduced to the level of income, and the clerk and professional classes can be identified with the prevailing order, instead of becoming the centres of social upheaval.' *The Condition of England* (London, 1911 [1st edn. 1909]), p.79.
20. *The Religion and Economics of Sex Oppression* (London, 1906), p.36. Herbert Burrows was one of the SDF's most active campaigners against the 'Malthusian Delusion'. For reports of his speeches see the *Malthusian* (May, 1882), p.319; (March 1894), p.22. See also Arthur B. Moss and H. Quelch, *Malthusianism vs. Labour* (London, n.d.) and Edward Cannan, ' The Malthusian Anti-Socialist Argument,' *Economic Review,* 2 (January 1891), pp.71-87.
21. Meek, *Marx and Engels,* pp.58, 60, 100.
22. Francesco S. Nitti, *Population and the Social System* (London, 1894); August Bebel, *Women in the Past, Present and Future* (London, 1885) and see also the articles of A.P. Hazell in *Justice* (18, 25 December, 1897; 1 January, 1898).
23. B. and S. Webb, *Industrial Democracy* (London, 1897), II, p.658.
24. *Capital* (Chicago, 1908), p.536.
25. *Justice* (15 December, 1906); *Social Democrat,* 9 (1905), pp.620-24; 12 (1909), pp.45-458.
26. *Justice* (21 May, 16 July, 1887).
27. Enrico Ferri, *Socialism and Positive Science (Darwin, Spencer, Marx)* tr. Edith C. Harvey (London, 1905), p.11. See also *Justice* (15 March, 1890;

27 January, 1900; 23 August, 1902).

28. *Justice* (11 October, 1902) and see also the supporting letter of Elizabeth Elmy (18 October, 1902). Edward Carpenter's reference to women as a class in *Love's Coming of Age* also drew the criticism of *Justice* (6 May, 1899).

29. *Justice* (1 November, 1902); and see *Justice* (21 May, 16 July, 1887).

30. *Justice* (28 January, 1888; 11 January, 1890). See also E. Aveling and E. Marx, *The Woman Question from a Socialist Point of View* (London, 1886), a reprint of their article in the 1885 *Westminster Review*.

31. See the series of articles by Ernest F. Williams on 'The Prostitution Crusade,' *Justice* (12 March, 1892; 24 June, 1893; 29 December, 1894).

32. *Justice* (19 April, 1890).

33. *Justice* (23 January, 24 June, 1892; 18 August, 1894).

34. On Bax see his *Reminiscences and Reflections of a Mid and Late Victorian* (London, 1918); *The Religion of Socialism* (London, 1908); and Stanley Pierson, *Marxism and the Origins of British Socialism* (Ithaca, 1973), pp.89-97. By 1909 the SDF was finding Bax's strident anti-feminism was becoming such an embarrassment that it called on him to resign from the Anti-Suffrage League, Walter Kendall, *The Revolutionary Movement in Britain 1900-1921 (London, 1969), p.31.*

35. Bax, *Religion*, pp.115-6. See also his *The Fraud of Feminism* (London, 1917) and *The Legal Subjection of Men* (London, 1908).

36. *Justice* (16 June, 1894). Harry Quelch, editor of *Justice* and close friend of Bax, was of the opinion that the suffragist movement was 'wholly mischievous'. *Social Democrat*, 10 (1906), pp.713-6; 11 (1907), pp.456-63. There were men in the SDF who took a different line. Herbert Burrows, who helped Annie Besant organise the 1888 Bryant and May match girls' strike was a feminist and described Bax's tactics as 'sheer blackguardism'. *Justice* (20 February, 1897). H.H. Champion, according to Bax, was another 'fanatical feminist' active in the London dock strike of 1889 and in the formation of a 'Women's Trades Association'. Tiring of the rigidity of the SDF Champion emigrated to Australia in 1892. Tsuzuki, *Hyndman*, pp.80-90; Bax, *Reminiscences*, p.102.

37. For example Pierson, *Marxism* and E.P. Thompson, *William Morris* (New York, 1961).

38. No doubt the difficulties these men encountered in their own marriages coloured their attitudes toward birth control. See Frank Harris, *My Life and Loves* (New York, 1966 [1st edn. 1925]), pp.233-4; John Rosenberg, *The Darkening Glass: A Portrait of John Ruskin* (London, 1963); Oswald Doughty, *A Victorian Romantic: Dante Gabriel Rossetti* (Oxford, 1960).

39. *Unto This Last* cited by J.A. Hobson, *Confessions of an Economic Heretic* (London, 1938), p.38. See also *Munera Pulveris: Six Essays on Political Economy* (London, 1904), 52 ff.

40. *Time and Tide* (London, 1910), 146 ff.

41. *Fors* cited by J.A. Hobson, *John Ruskin: Social Reformer* (London, 1899), p.269.

42. *Sesame and Lilies* (London, 1865), p.155.

43. 'Arrows of the Chace' cited by Hobson, *Ruskin*, pp.266-7.

44. *Fors* cited by Hobson, *Ruskin*, p.266.

45. *News from Nowhere* in *Collected Works* (London, 1912 [1st edn. 1890]), p.60.

46. Morris, *News from Nowhere*, pp.61-2.

47. Nitti, *Population*, p.165.

48. Nitti, *Population*, p.165. The eugenists' concern for protection of the race begun to crop up in the SDF publications in the twentieth century. In *Justice*

(17 November, 1906), Bax declared that the state had a right to regulate
births; Reid Rentoul's 'Proposed Sterilization of Certain Degenerates' was
republished in the *Social Democrat,* 14 (1910), pp.374-80.

49. *Malthusian* (August 1883), p.434.
50. Aldred, *Religion,* p.37. See also Aldred's earlier essay in *Justice* (10 June,
    1904) on 'natural inequality'. Aldred was later to join the birth control
    movement; in 1922 he and Rose Witcop were prosecuted for selling Margaret
    Sanger's *Family Limitation: A Handbook for Working Mothers.* See his *No
    Traitor's Gate: The Life and Times of Guy Aldred* (Glasgow, 1955).
51. *Social Democrat,* 5 (1901), pp.48-9; see also 5 (1901), pp.367-9; 6 (1902),
    pp.50-1; 12 (1909), pp.537-44.
52. *Justice* (7 July, 1894).
53. *Justice* (21 November, 1896).
54. *Justice* (23 June, 1894). See also a letter asking for information on family
    limitation (5 August, 1893). On occasion *Justice* did carry advertisements
    for T.R. Allinson's *A Book for Married Women* and H.A. Allbutt's *The Wife's
    Handbook;* no explanation was given for their appearance.
55. F.C. Ball, *One of the Damned* (London, 1973), p.92.

10 SOCIALISTS AND BIRTH CONTROL: FREEDOM OR EFFICIENCY

Given the social conservatism of the Malthusian League — the only formal organisation to preach the benefits of birth control — the opposition of socialists to contraceptive propagandising was understandable enough. What the strident hostility of the SDF caused many to overlook was the fact that there were a number of men and women on the English left who did accept the importance of limitation of family size. They shared a common impatience with the simple-minded Malthusianism of the League but tended to divide themselves into two main camps: radicals who defended contraception on individualist grounds and collectivists who accepted it because of the greater social efficiency it promised.

In the activities of the little known London working-class agitator Daniel Chatterton can be found the first indications that socialists would not simply condemn birth control because of its association with the reactionary tenets of Malthusianism, but would seek to fit the practice into the context of their own programme. The *Malthusian* of July 1879 reported a discussion of population problems at the Phoenix Temperance Hall on Commercial Road in Whitechapel. The working-class participants included a Mr Archer who had read Robert Dale Owen and Chatterton who, identifying himself as a supporter of the Land and Labour League, agreed that the population question was crucial. In February of 1880 Chatterton again appeared at the Phoenix Hall when Charles Drysdale was speaking. On this occasion Chatterton ridiculed the notion of emigration as a solution to the social problem and called for the abolition of private property in land and capital. In August Edward Truelove, a man who had taken part in Owen's communitarian experiments in Hampshire and New Harmony and had been imprisoned for selling birth control tracts, spoke from the same platform and called for all reformers to act together. Chatterton's response was that such sentiments were all very well and good but the land issue had to be debated in conjunction with birth control. He kept up the same criticism at Malthusian League sponsored meetings at the Zetetical Society in 1881 and at Shakespeare Hall in

1883.[1]

The *Malthusian* of February 1884 reported a discussion held on
Poor Men's Politics' at the Speke Road Baths, Battersea. The chairman,
John Cleave, began the session by asserting that Malthus was not as
hard-hearted as the people assumed. T.H. Wickstead, a follower of
Henry George, retorted that it was necessary to separate the issues of
population and family. In other words he wanted the question of birth
control to be freed from its association with Malthusian economic
theory. This argument was to appear in *The Land for the People: How
to Obtain It and How to Manage It* which Wickstead was to bring out
in 1885. In it he attacked the idea that poverty was caused by
population pressure and expressed concern that the call for moral
restraint would only lead the public-spirited to refrain from breeding.
But having opposed the idea that population control was economically
necessary Wickstead went on to state, 'Urging a man to limit his family
for private motives is an entirely different matter; it is a private matter,
not a political.' The *Malthusian*'s correspondent reported that now
Mr Chatterton,

> . . .who announced that he hailed from the slums of Drury-Lane,
> said that 'Outcast London' [Andrew Mearns exposé of slum life] had
> made no 'bitter cry' at all. It went on the same as usual. . .Who had
> cried? Nobody but political capitalists and religious enthusiasts (hear,
> hear). The remedy was far away — because of the cruel apathy of the
> working classes. He had had two wives and ten children, and detailed
> the life he and his wives had led. He called upon his brothers and
> sisters of humanity not to breed like little bunny rabbits.
> Mr. Chatterton then went on to refer in a vehement and unreportable
> manner to the condition of the poor, remarking that he lived in a
> house in which every brick was loose, and yet the rental of it was
> £126 per year (shame), and not fit for a pig to live in. Sir Charles
> Dilke had been visiting round him, and a communication would no
> doubt go to the Vestry; but the Vestry would say 'You be blowed',
> and would put its fingers to its nose (laughter). Then they would go
> to the Board of Works, but the Vestry elected the Board of Works,
> and all were in the same swim (hear, hear).[2]

Chatterton followed up his hectoring of the Malthusians by producing
what appears to be the first birth control tract of the nineteenth
century written by a worker for other workers: *Babies and Bunny
Rabbits: A Popular Educator*. It should be recalled that the *Malthusian*

itself never carried direct information on birth control methods.
Nothing could have been further from its staid, restrained discussion of
population theory than Chatterton's tract which mixed practical
information with radical polemics. Citing cases of infanticide and
starvation he began by calling on the people to acknowledge that such
crimes were a consequence of over-population which the church and
the state sought to perpetuate: '. . .be you no longer hoodwinked by
the false teachings of the scoundrelly kingcraft and priestcraft, who
have ever cursed you by the enslavement of your bodies, the fearful
result of the encrampment of the brain power of millions of billions
of trillions of generations of peoples'.[3] Addressing then the mothers of
England, Chatterton stated that means of restriction which did not
blight pleasure were available, that two healthy children were the
delight of a family while twelve could be its destruction. Drawing from
Besant's work he described the use of the withdrawal method, the
sheath, the 'rhythm' method, the syringe, and the sponge. Returning
finally to the question of politics he ended his pamphlet with what
amounted to an appeal for a 'birth strike' against militarism and
capitalism.

> Women and Men of England — Marry young, enjoy the exquisite
> pleasure of food, of love, of leisure. Let the reproductions of your
> first sexual cohesions be the issues of womanly beauty, of manly
> vigour; let there be no more starving sempstresses, none of the
> horrors of the social evil which poisons the blood of the nation;
> do not breed your babies like bunny rabbits; do not go for soldiers;
> do not man the navy; do not yield the policeman's bludgeon, the
> sailor's cutlass, the soldier's bayonet.[4]

Chatterton advertsied his pamphlet and Marie C. Fisher's *Ought Women
to be Punished for Having Too Many Children* in a small sheet which he
published intermittently between 1884 and 1895 combatively entitled
Chatterton's Commune: The Atheistic Communistic Scorcher.[5] The
paper followed an aggressive line. The Queen Chatterton referred to as
a 'blood-stained old woman', charity he described as plunder and
starvation as murder by the rich. What was necessary was class war and
in one article at least he described how paraffin could be used in such
an eventuality.

The attempts of Chatterton, the aethestic agitator, to link birth
control and radical politics were curiously paralleled by the activities
of the Anglican clergyman — labelled by *Chatterton's Commune* as a

meddling 'sky pilot' — Stewart Headlam. Headlam was a marvellous crank who, though a high churchman, devoted his life to a wide variety of disreputable causes. In 1877 he formed the Christian Socialist Guild of St Matthew for the purpose of justifying God's ways to the population of East London. He came into contact with the secularists through his membership in the League for the Defence of Constitutional Rights and the National Association for the Repeal of the Blasphemy Laws. He supported Bradlaugh's attempts to gain entry to the House of Commons and backed Aveling's lecture courses at the National Secular Society School of Science. He had a special passion for the theatre and helped form a Church and Stage Guild at the annual dances of which Moncure Conway was '. . .amused to find that the ballet girls all came dressed with a certain prudishness in contrast to the *décolletage* of the clergymen's wives'.[6] Headlam — a man who was married to a lesbian, offered to act as surety for Oscar Wilde, and helped organise an Anti-Purity League — was in short not one to be overly concerned by what the Church hierarchy considered proper behaviour.

Headlam began to make known his support for birth control in the 1880s. He requested that the Malthusian League provide a clearly written pamphlet — much like that eventually produced by Chatterton — for use by the masses. But to the League's regret Headlam soon made it apparent that he considered the Malthusian economic doctrine as of little importance in the question. At a meeting of the Dialectical Society in July 1880 he declared that whether or not Malthus was correct women had to control their own fertility. By 1882 he was stating that after having read Henry George he was sure Malthus was wrong — land nationalisation could solve the poverty problem — yet birth control was still a basic right.[7] In 1885 he participated in a debate on the subject at the Junior Clergy Society. A. Lyttelton read a paper on 'Marriage and Neo-Malthusianism' in which he admitted, 'I know for a fact that these plans for checking conception are known and practised by many ladies in London society, and I believe doctors will tell you the thing is spreading.'[8] Lyttelton called for celibacy and purity in marriage; Headlam's response was that there was nothing in the use of such checks that could be considered either wrong or anti-Christian. Headlam's drift to the left took him finally into the Fabian Society; he was to sit on its executive from 1890 onwards.

Chatterton and Headlam showed that there was no reason why the defence of birth control and social reforms could not be combined. Such a realisation was to lead to the most sensational of the 'conversions' to socialism in the 1880s, namely Annie Besant's.[9]

Besant's initial Malthusian orthodoxy was fully revealed in her birth
control tract *The Law of Population* (1877) in which restriction of
family size was presented as the only way in which the lower classes
could improve their conditions. What her activities in the neo-
Malthusian campaign brought home to her, however, was the misery
in which many wives and mothers of all classes lived. It was their
response, she wrote, that shaped the course of her future activities:
'. . .there was the passionate gratitude evidenced by letters from
thousands of poor married women – many from the wives of country
clergymen and curates – thanking and blessing me for showing them
how to escape from the veritable hell in which they lived.'[10] Besant
entered the socialist cause out of her conviction that it alone could
bring women to full equality. She followed her friends Aveling and
Headlam at the prompting of Aveling's replacement on the Secular
Society board, John Robertson. It was with the encouragement of this
self-styled 'Socialist and Pessimist' that Besant finally 'came out' as a
socialist in 1885. But having taken up a position on the left, Besant
saw it as her duty to win her new companions' support for birth control.
In her journal, *Our Corner,* she sought to make it clear that fertility
control was not just a ploy of the upper classes. They might brandish
the doctrine of 'over-population', she wrote in 'The Law of Population
and its Relation to Socialism', but they employed every tactic to
postpone reforms.

> The unanimity with which they now cry out 'over-population is the
> cause of poverty' is only paralleled by the unanimity with which
> they denounced Mr. Bradlaugh and myself when we alleged ten
> years ago that over-population is a – not the – cause of poverty
> and when we recommended limitation of the family in addition to
> radical changes in the present system.[11]

Socialists were right to call for replacement of individual ownership but
were wrong, Besant insisted, to ignore the question of contraception.
She regretted the fact that save for Aveling no contributor to *Justice* or
Commonweal took the issue seriously. Seeing Malthus only as an
advocate of capitalism, the socialists failed to appreciate the benefits
that family planning could offer to individual workers and in particular
to working-class women exhausted by repeated pregnancies.

Besant expressed her opinions on birth control and socialism most
clearly in a debate with the secularist G.W. Foote in 1887 entitled
'Is Socialism Sound?' The main thrust of Foote's anti-socialist argument

was the familiar claim that Malthus' law of population doomed
socialism. In reply Besant agreed that it did pose an important problem
though many socialists '. . .ignore or deny that indisputable truth'.[12]
The point, however was that under capitalism the poor had no reason
to restrict their family size. Socialism would solve the problem by
raising living standards and so provide the working class with living
conditions they would have some reason to protect. Moreover the
restriction of family size would not represent simply a response to
economic rewards; it would be a result of the education of women.

> I believe that one of the strongest arguments in favour of the
> limitation of the population will come from women; as you educate
> your women more highly, as they take part in public life, as they
> become more economically independent than they are today, your
> women will refuse to be mere nurses of children throughout the
> whole of their active life. (Cheers). They will be willing to give all
> the care that is necessary for two or three children, but will refuse
> to have their health ruined, and the whole of public life shut to them,
> by having families of ten or twelve, which are practically destructive
> of motherly feelings as well as of happiness and comfort in the
> home.[13]

Foote in response declared that women's emancipation as it was
developing had nothing to do with socialism and pointed out that
socialists like Bax were reknowned for their anti-feminism. Besant
disagreed with Foote's first claim; in her opinion only socialists claimed
complete equality for women and it had been for this reason that she
had entered the movement.

Besant eventually abandoned both socialism and birth control for
theosophy but John M. Robertson, the man who was instrumental in
bringing her into the socialist camp, continued up to the First World
War to defend contraception from a radical position.[14] Like Besant he
set as his first task that of upbraiding socialists for their failure to
include the question of birth control in their programmes. 'Of these
socialists not a few practice the Neo-Malthusian principle which they
dishonestly disown. . .' claimed Robertson and proceeded to assert that
some were positively misleading the working class by repeating the old
cliches that 'luxury' or mental activity naturally restricted fertility.
And also like Besant he was most concerned that socialists were failing
to respond to the needs of women.

The truth is that, on the one hand, the lessons of Neo-Malthusianism are being widely learned in civilized countries; and that, on the other, women as they gain knowledge and status grow averse to making themselves the mere child-breeders they so commonly were in the past. They see that the old saws about olive branches and replenishing the earth and trusting in Providence have only served to keep them in a state of subjection and domestic martyrdom; and they desire to be something more than overworked nurses during the best part of their lives. And all men who desire to see women cultured and intelligent sympathise with them heartily. But while the more thoughtful men and women are thus practising parental prudence and deliberately limiting their families, sciolists and Socialists actually point to the results of their prudence as showing that no prudence is necessary, and tell the imprudent and the thoughtless among the working class that they need have no scruple about propagating in the freest fashion — that when they get good wages their fecundity will diminish to precisely the right point! Such advice may be the outcome of delusions; but it is none the less pernicious; and the delusion assuredly does small credit to the intelligence of those who cherish it.[15]

Robertson was particularly incensed by Henry George's advice that the working class rest its faith in an all-wise Providence and he went so far as to suggest that some hoped that misery itself would goad the masses into action.

Unhappily one cannot be sure that some agitators are not desirous of keeping up the pressure of over-population and misery in order to facilitate revolution; but there is no room to doubt as to the irrationality which such an aim — supposing it to exist — is promoted by the sentimentalists. Let a Malthusian advise some workers to keep their families small, and straightway some Socialist shrieks that the adviser is seeking to rob them of the one solace they had left — as if any good-hearted or sane workman could find pleasure in seeing around him a swarm of poorly fed children, presumably destined to a life of hardship like his own. Of course it is the men who talk so. The Socialist father — to judge by his utterances — is as far as the worst Philistine from proposing to restrict the animal and menial sphere of his wife's duties. She is to go on supplying him with 'solace' year after year, going through her eternal round of cooking, washing, mending, cleaning; passing periodically through long spells of weakness and pain; while her helpmeet, in his increased leisure, considers the present and future condition of socialism.[16]

He insisted that there was no reason why socialists should oppose birth control; indeed they would have to accept it if they were to be true to their principles: 'It is for Socialists to reconcile their professed championship of women with their repudiation of every suggestion for the alleviation of women's domestic burdens.'[17]

In *Over-Population* (1890), Robertson did concede that suspicion of the population issue was not unwarranted: 'It is not unnatural that when democratic reformers are told Malthusianism is against them, they should be against Malthusianism. In point of fact the law of population is no more opposed to any moral or social reform than is the law of gravitation.'[18] But instead of discussing the problem social reformers were, he claimed, assuming that the birth rate would fall spontaneously. The victims of these delusions were the working-class mothers who deprived of the knowledge and services of the middle classes were faced with unwanted pregnancies.

And the expedients to which many of them ignorantly resort to avoid maternity, just because knowledge of the right expedients is repressed by insensate pietism and Grundyism, for which the blame lies at the door of the middle and upper classes — the respectable classes — I say some of the expedients they do employ are injurious to a degree heart-breaking to think of.[19]

And if forcing women to such actions were not enough, Robertson objected, the state would now seek to punish such behaviour: '. . .we, in our wisdom, add to the misery of an abortion that of punishment (as if anybody would be tempted to abortion for its own sake), and so terrify others into undesired maternity, with the result sometimes of infanticide and often adding to the misery of the mother that of a child for whom there is no room.'[20]

Robertson sought to bully the socialist leadership into an acceptance of the importance of birth control. At the same time Julia Dawson, a regular contributor to the most successful of the socialist papers — Robert Blatchford's *Clarion* — brought the right of women to protect themselves from unwanted pregnancies to the attention of a large working-class audience. In 'Our Woman's Letter' column Dawson spoke warmly of Dr Allinson's birth control tracts, republished the addresses of the Malthusian League, and printed the arguments of Dr Alice

Vickery. Dawson emphasised that socialists could not accept the Malthusian economic argument but they did want information on contraception. She stressed the importance of the subject to women, especially working-class women, while noting that their needs were rarely taken into consideration by those who raised the spectre of the falling birth rate.[21]

Apart from Dawson's columns the *Clarion* carried only the occasional article dealing with the population issue. In 1903 A.M. Thompson and R.B. Suthers responded to the 'race suicide' fears expressed by President Roosevelt by asking why working-class women should be expected to have large families when the upper classes shirked such duties. Their answer was that the ruling strata favoured such a situation because it desired, first, a pool of cheap, excess labour, and secondly, it wished the poor to be too   preoccupied by domestic issues to address themselves to political problems.[22] Robert Blatchford was himself not advanced in his views on the subject of family restriction and in his own writings looked forward to the day when children would be released from schools and nurseries and creches and returned to their natural place — 'back to mother'.[23]

Those who were most responsive to the radical defence of birth control came not from the traditional socialist camp but from the fringes of what was known as the 'New Liberalism'. This school of thought attracted those who sought to provide liberalism with a social conscience and so rescue it from its association with the conservative doctrines of Malthus and Spencer. Representative of this approach were the works of David G. Ritchie, a tutor of Jesus College, Oxford. In *Darwinism and Politics* (1889) Ritchie attempted to exorcise the devil of biological determinism which increasingly plagued political discussions. Darwin's teachings had been misused, he claimed, by writers such as Spencer and Maine in order to deny the feasibility of socialism. Yet if Darwin had taught anything it was the importance of environment; by changing it you could change men. From this premise Ritchie drew three conclusions. His first was that state interference was necessary if waste and inequalities were to be avoided. The second, that biological arguments concerning women's inferiority were meaningless; differences were as much the result of socialisation and in any event there was no reason why such differences should result in social inequality. 'But the main point is really this: that society has enabled man to rise above the mere animal and, as has been pointed out, to be influenced not merely by natural pressure but by *ideas*.'[24] And here Ritchie singled out the socialists' view of women for particular criticism. In claiming that women were innately conservative such men were shutting their eyes to the limited life to which many women had been confined. It was the old story of caging a bird and then complaining that it could not fly. Moreover to suggest that women's condition would automatically improve along with that of the working class as a whole was, as Ritchie pertinently pointed out, an unproven assertion: 'It is not true to say that the *status* of women has *always* improved in direct ratio to the general advance.'[25] Ritchie's third conclusion was that social evolution necessarily involved restriction of family size and socialists made a grave mistake in ignoring the issue even though their suspicions of Malthus were well founded: 'Socialist views on the question have not always had so scientific a basis, but have often rested on nothing better than the popular superstition that where God sends mouths he sends the food to feed them, though this may be disguised in a non-theological form, such as "the earth is capable of producing abundance of food for all its inhabitants".'[26] Birth control symbolised the 'rational adaptation of means of ends'. Such a policy necessitated the full involvement of women which in turn required that options other than marriage and motherhood be offered them. Social Darwinists might belabour such tactics as a 'withdrawing from the struggle for existence'; this had to be the socialist goal.

George Shoobridge Carr approached the question of fertility control in *Social Evolution and the Evolution of Socialism* from much the same angle as did Ritchie. Carr's *bête noire* was Benjamin Kidd who had praised both the struggle for survival and the religious irrationality which sanctioned it. Carr noted that in *Social Evolution* Kidd had used the standard population pressure argument of the conservatives against the possibility of socialism: 'At the outset, underneath all socialist ideals, yawns the problem of population.'[27] Birth control, argued Carr, should be accepted by socialists as the answer to such challenges. The necessity of a ceaselessly increasing population he described as a 'barbaric and obsolete idea'. The chief aim of socialism had to be to give all an equal start in life and birth control offered such a 'provisional remedy'.[28] The working class could not be expected to approach political issues clearly and rationally as long as it were burdened with large families and inadequate housing.

John M. Robertson went further than either Carr or Ritchie in linking an apology for birth control to specific economic policies. He embraced what, following J.A. Hobson's work, would be called an

'underconsumptionist' interpretation of economics which attributed
depressions in trade, imperialist ventures, and poverty to maldistribution
of income. For the time the most radical point of this critique was the
claim that, given the initial inequities of the economic system, counsels
of thrift were pointless and could indeed be counterproductive.
Robertson made this case in *The Fallacy of Saving* (1892) as
G.A. Gaskell did in *The Futility of Pecuniary Thrift as a Means to
General Wellbeing* (1890) and J.A. Hobson and A.F. Mummery in *The
Physiology of Industry* (1889). The remedies proposed by these authors
were a redistribution of wealth through taxation, a policy of concessions
to labour, and an extension of social services. With living standards
raised and intensive exploitation of the nation's own resources the
dangers of both social unrest at home and foreign wars abroad could
thus be skirted.

Robertson's originality was to link this economic theory to birth
control. Whereas the Darwinists insisted that it was necessary to have
unlimited population growth in order that a 'struggle for existence'
could take place, Robertson maintained that in questions of
demography, as in economics, blind instinct was to be replaced by
'conscious progress'. If there were to be a struggle it would be a
struggle against the struggle for existence. Thus it would be necessary
to have on the one hand old age pensions to ensure the security of the
elderly and on the other contraceptive information so that children
need no longer be born simply as a form of 'insurance' against
destitution.

In *Patriotism and Empire* (1900) Robertson applied this
underconsumptionist argument to a criticism of the Boer war. The gist
of his thesis — like that of J.A. Hobson's better known *Imperialism:
A Study* (1902) — was that such foreign entanglements could be avoided
if capital were invested at home rather than abroad. In addition,
Robertson argued that over-population, or the fear of it, was a
secondary cause of foreign adventures. One of the stock apologies of
the imperialists was the need for space for emigration. Such reasoning
ignored the option of fertility control: 'It is implied that there is to be
no social science, no control of population by reason and knowledge,
no provision for it at home by better use of the land; nothing but a
fatal drift of blind instinct and blind competition so long as emigration
can take place and after that the deluge.'[29] Moreover Robertson
insisted that such pleas for space were in fact simply a blind for the
armed forces, the speculators, and the munition manufacturers whom
the state would subsidise at the very time it claimed it impossible to

aid paupers.

> . . .the central truth falls to be stated thus: imperial expansion is
> substantially a device on the part of the moneyed class, primarily
> to further its own chances, secondarily to put off the day of
> reckoning as between capital and labour. It does not and cannot
> bring a socially just solution any nearer: it does but secure a possible
> extension of employment for labour on old terms. In so far then as
> labour is led by any or all of the sophisms of imperialist patriotism,
> it is gulled to its ultimate perdition.[30]

Undeterred by what appeared to be working-class support for the Boer
war Robertson proclaimed his confidence that labour was not
imperialist though some who claimed to speak for it were. The way
forward for socialists, whom the imperialists recognised as their natural
enemies, was by a redistribution of wealth and a limitation of fertility:
'Against a policy of racial swagger, external force, expansion,
goldmining, and other exploitation of filched territory, a policy of
scientific social development, to the end of a maximization of real
wealth and a better distribution thereof. . .As against a perpetual
overbreeding which drives out yearly an army of exiles, a rational
control of population in all classes.'[31]

The efforts of Besant, Robertson and others to win the leaders of
labour to the birth control campaign met with little success. The SDF
remained violently opposed to such discussions; others were of the
opinion that it was a private, not a public, issue. John Burns, organiser
of the great dock strike of 1889 and future MP, was representative of
those who accepted limitation of family size as a legitimate solution
to individual domestic problems but denied that it could affect the
overall conditions of labour. ' "I am a trade unionist", he would say
[recalled Bax] , "a practical Malthusian [that is, he controlled the size
of his family] , a Teetotaller, and have always been so and yet I remain
for all these things what I was — a member of the working class,
subsisting on a weekly wage".'[32] Much the same line was taken by
Henry Seymour, editor of the *Anarchist*. He was responsible for
publishing the English translation of Proudhon's *The Malthusians* in
which birth control had been likened to murder. Attacked by Annie
Besant for condoning the 'idiocies' of the tract Seymour replied: 'We
Anarchists, while not urging the slightest objection to the limitation
of offspring where necessary or advisable, — nevertheless do flatly
deny that the increase of poverty and population *necessarily* go hand

in hand.'[33] In the same issue of the *Anarchist* two books which
favoured family limitation were reviewed: Henry Allbutt's *A Wife's
Handbook* — praised for its 'solid, practical information' — and
T.L. Nichol's *Esoteric Anthropology*. Yet if anarchists showed some
interest in birth control they continued to voice their suspicions of
any attempt to marry the Malthusian and socialist doctrines. Seymour
made the pertinent observation that the only faction which could
accept such a mongrel ideology would be the collectivist-minded
State Socialists. Seeking efficiency and order in every area of life they
would come to see the 'necessary correlative in the sovereignty of the
syringe'.[34]

The radicals defended the right to contraception on a variety of
individualist grounds: the right of the woman to control her own body,
the right of the worker to control the size of his family, the right of the
working class to stage a 'birth strike' against capitalists and militarists.
A second group of socialists interested themselves in the issue — the
collectivist-minded state socialists cited by Seymour — because of the
greater social efficiency fertility control could offer. This group was
represented by the best known of the Fabian socialists at the turn of
the century — Sidney and Beatrice Webb, George Bernard Shaw, and
H.G. Wells.[35] It is true that the Fabian Society also included at times
Besant and Headlam. Wells later wrote, 'Anti-socialists in those far off
days [circa 1900] used to accuse the Socialists, just as the pagans used
to accuse the early Christians, of having their wives in common. As a
matter of fact the Fabian socialists did not even have their ideas in
common.'[36] What is of interest here is that those Fabians who were
collectivist-oriented succeeded in dominating the organisation and
presented their views as those of the movement.

The Webbs, Shaw, and Wells shared a belief in what they called
'socialism' but which might have better been described as a form of
Comtean positivism which had as its goal not social revolution but social
reconstruction. They accepted, unlike the SDF, the Malthusian premise
that population pressures could jeopardise social reform. Their response
was to turn to a form of state-directed fertility control as the answer.
Central to their approach was the idea that the state could not remain
indifferent to this new form of social management; the crucial question
of reproduction was too important to be left to the decisions of
individuals.

State control was the touchstone of the Fabian form of socialism.[37]

They methodically sketched out what could be called a plan for the 'nationalisation' of the breeding industry. They reacted against the 'anarchy' of both the Malthusians, willing to let the laws of supply and demand have free reign, and the radicals, defending the individual's right to control fertility as he or she pleased. What the Fabians found distasteful in both schools of thought was the potential for struggle or conflict. It was their desire to avoid in particular the messy issue of class struggle and instead to make the existing system function more efficiently.

The Fabian distaste for class struggle evolved into a rejection of democracy itself and a growing obsession with expertise. Whereas the radicals sought to win for the poor the 'right' to limit births, the Fabians increasingly insisted on the poor's 'duty' to control family size. Moreover the Fabians went on to attack the irresponsibility of the middle class in matters of marriage and breeding. Influenced by the eugenic considerations of Galton and Pearson they expressed the fear that the lower classes would overbreed and the upper-class stock decline.

The Fabians were drawn to the population queston by their discovery of the fallacy of the Malthusian assertion that if the wages of labourers were increased so too would the size of their families; on the contrary it was made all too obvious to social investigators that it was the poorest who were the most 'reckless' in breeding. Sidney Webb, in *The Difficulties of Individualism* (1896), attributed the problem to the inequitable distribution inherent in capitalism. 'An inevitable corollary of this unequal distribution is wrong production, both of commodities and of human beings; the preparation of senseless luxuries whilst there is need for more bread, and the breeding of degenerate hordes of a demoralized "residuum" unfit for social life.'[38] From this statement it is clear that Webb's impatience with the clumsy workings of the economic system was matched by his contempt for the poor it produced. In his analysis there was no room for compassion; nor was there any hope expressed that the 'hordes of semi-barbarians' could save themselves. It was necessary for the state to intervene. 'It was largely the recognition that it was hopeless to expect to spread a Malthusian prudence among this residuum that turned John Stuart Mill into a Socialist. . .' declared Webb, implying that his own conversion had been similarly motivated.[39]

In *Industrial Democracy* (1897) the Webbs reiterated their concern that it was the 'prosperous and thrifty artisans' — not the improvident — who were limiting family size; they called for more detailed information on class fertility differentials. This request was in part answered by the investigations precipitated by the Boer war which revealed the intolerable living conditions of much of the working class. A rash of publications including L.S. Amery, *The Problem of the Army* (1904), J.B. Atkins, *National Physical Training* (1904), W.A. Chapple, *Fertility of the Unfit* (1904), and A. Watt Smyth, *Physical Deterioration* (1904) sought to bring home to the British public the point that the danger facing the nation was not that of a too large population but that of a weak and sickly one.

On 26 May, 1905 a sub-committee of the Fabian Society was formed to consider the question of the birth rate and infantile mortality. Its findings were reported by Sidney Webb in two letters to *The Times* under the headline 'Physical Degeneracy or Race Suicide' and in a Fabian tract entitled *The Decline of the Birth Rate* (1907). For most of the nineteenth century the fear had been that the population was increasing too rapidly but now, noted Webb, the concern was voiced that the birth rate was declining. Why was it? Webb swept aside the old notions that it was due to impersonal forces such as urbanisation, imbalance of the sex ratio or decline in marriages. Amongst the working class it was clearly a consequence of the 'inconvenience' of additional children in homes where the mother worked. Webb pointed out that the birth rate had dropped most noticeably in those towns — Northampton, Halifax, Burnley, Blackburn, Derby, Leicester, Bradford, Oldham, and Huddersfield — where there was a high level of employment of women in the mills. The situation had been aggravated, he asserted, by the enforcement of the 1891 and 1901 acts which required four weeks absence from work after birth and so added to the economic burden of motherhood. Amongst the servant-keeping class fertility was also down; here it was due to the attempt to maintain living standards in face of the rising costs of raising and educating the young.

What conclusions did Webb draw from these findings? He was initially optimistic. It was clear that the birth rate had declined as a result of 'volitional regulation'; there was no cause to fear the rise of some form of sterility. Moreover apart from religious qualms there was nothing morally objectionable in such practices. Indeed it was laudable that the prudent should seek to improve their situation and Malthusian economists such as Ricardo, Cairnes, and Fawcett should have been happy at such a result. But Webb sounded a warning. The problem was not so much that the nation was 'deprived' of 200,000 babies a year or one-fifth of the annual 'crop'. The danger was that the thrifty and foresighted restricted births; the population was thus increasingly recruited from 'our most inferior stocks'.

In Great Britain at this moment, when half, or perhaps two-thirds, of all the married people are regulating their families, children are being freely born to Irish Roman Catholics and the Polish, Russian and German Jews, on the one hand and to the thriftless and irresponsible — largely the casual labourers and other denizens of the one room tenements of our great cities on the other. This particular 25 per cent of our population, as Professor Karl Pearson keeps warning us, is producing 50 per cent of our children. This can hardly result in anything but national deterioration; or as an alternative, in this country gradually falling to the Irish and the Jews.[40]

Webb did not paint a totally gloomy picture. Since the restriction of births was a result of economic pressures it was only necessary for the state to implement social policies which would induce the right sorts of people to assume parenthood. On the one hand 'adverse selection' had to be ended and on the other encouragement was to be offered '. . .the self-controlled and foreseeing members of each class. . .' If motherhood was encouraged, praised, honoured, and freed of its economic penalties Webb was confident that it could be '. . .rendered part of the code of the ordinary citizen's morality.' Women, so he assumed, would willingly abandon all other careers for maternity if the rewards were sufficient. 'To the vast majority of women, and especially to those of the fine type, the rearing of children would be the most attractive. occupation, if it offered economic advantages equal to those, say, of school teaching or service in the post office.'[41]

This idea that if given the option most women would restrict themselves to the occupation of motherhood sprang from the Fabian's assumed division of labour along sex lines. It was best expressed by Beatrice Webb who was horrified by the propagandist Annie Besant: 'That woman with her blighted wifehood and motherhood and her thirst for power and defiance of the world.' Though carving out a career for herself in a male-dominated world Beatrice Webb considered it wrong for others to 'ape man and take up men's pursuits'.[42] She backed such beliefs by signing the anti-suffrage manifesto of Mrs Humphrey Ward. Her own life she justified on the grounds that it was not divided between duties but concentrated with religious-like zeal on social investigation. Early in her life she had made her feelings known to Canon and Henrietta Barnett:

I tried to explain to him my doctrine of nervous energy: that you are only gifted with a certain quantity, and that if it were spent in detail it could not be reserved for large undertakings. . .I told her that the only way in which we can convince the world of our power is to show it. And for that it will be needful for women with strong natures to remain celibate; so that the special force of womanhood — motherly feeling — may be forced into public work.[43]

Thus assured by this Spencerian analysis of her own intellectual superiority Beatrice Webb, the chaste social scientist, was to pontificate on the child-bearing *duties* of other women. In an article in the *New Statesman* entitled 'Personal Rights and the Women's Movement' she went so far as to warn American feminists that if they allowed the birth rate of the United States to continue to decline the nation would as a result of miscegenation eventually become a coloured state, fringed by Irish Catholics and ruled by Jews.[44]

The Webbs were circumspect when dealing with the issue of birth control; George Bernard Shaw expressed in a forthright fashion the ideas they harboured. On being read his *The Revolutionist's Handbook* Beatrice Webb confided to her diary, 'I was so delighted at his choice of subject — we cannot touch the subject of Human Breeding — it is not ripe for the science of induction, and yet I realize it is the most important of all questions, the breeding of the right sort of man.'[45] What Shaw called for in this work was, '. . .nothing but the replacement of the old unintelligent, inevitable, almost unconscious fertility by an intelligently controlled, conscious fertility, and the elimination of the mere voluptuary from the evolutionary process.'[46] The present society which inhibited good breeding by the restrictions of property and marriage relationships had to be replaced by one in which the bad stocks were weeded out. A 'State Department of Evolution' would be needed which would pay women for their child-bearing services and if necessary regulate a 'joint stock human stud farm' which would be preferable to the current unorganised forms of reproduction. Why was such planned breeding necessary? Because 'Proletarian Democracy' had proved its uselessness: 'But they [the workers] are still riff-raff; and to hand the country over to riff-raff is national suicide, since riff-raff can neither govern nor will let anyone else govern except the highest bidder of bread and circuses.'[47]

This Fabian vision of a world in which procreation would be overseen by the state came to full flower in the writings of H.G. Wells. It was his complaint that socialism in reaction to Spencer's individualistic brand of positivism had turned anti-scientific. As a consequence it refused to speculate on the workings of future society, a penchant aggravated by the effect of the 'uninventive' Marx's anti-utopian strictures. Even the Webbs, though they had turned away from a belief in 'crude democracy', had in Wells' opinion no other idea than to 'Fabianise' the existing governing class.[48] The real question, as Wells saw it, was how would a new, worthy elite — his 'competent receivers' — assume power. In effect he was talking, as Shaw was, of the necessity of creating and giving power to 'Supermen'.

In *Socialism and the Family* (1906) Wells defined socialism, not as a force in a class struggle, but as '. . .a plan for the reconstruction of human life, for the replacement of a disorder by order, for the making of a state in which mankind shall live bravely and beautifully beyond our present imagining.' Unfortunately the worker gave no thought to the creation of such a 'brave new world'. For him socialism meant only the expropriation of the rich, social services, and, 'A little home, a trifle larger and brighter than his present one, a more abounding table, a cheerful missus released from factory work and unhealthy competition with men. . .'[49] Such small-mindedness turned away potential recruits to the socialist cause — the middle-class professionals — whose attention Wells hoped to win. They were, he asserted, also perturbed by the belief that socialists favoured 'unconventional freedom of action in sexual matters'. Socialists had, on the one hand, to reassure the intelligent that the movement was not motivated by base desires for confiscation of property, and on the other show that it alone could deal with the population crisis. 'The birth-rate falls — and falls. The family fails more and more in its essential object. This is a process absolutely independent of any socialist propaganda; it is part of the normal development of the existing social and economic system. It makes for sterilisation, for furtive wantonness and dishonour.'[50] Socialism would not lead to greater moral laxity; on the contrary it would institute controls which would put an end to it: 'The modern tendency is all towards an amount of control over reproduction, if anything, in excess of that exercised by the state and public usage today.' Decay and moral collapse would be avoided when the government stepped in to assume its proper responsibility in the area of reproduction.

> The children people bring into the world can be no more their
> private concern entirely, than the disease germs they disseminate
> or the noises a man makes in a thin-floored flat. . .People rear
> children for the State and the future; if they do that well, they do

the whole world a service, and deserve payment just as much as if they built a bridge or raised a crop of wheat; if they do it unpropitiously and ill, they have done the world an injury. Socialism denies altogether the right of any one to beget children carelessly and promiscuously, and for the prevention of disease and evil births alike, the Socialist is prepared for an insistence upon intelligence and self-restraint quite beyond the current practice.[51]

Restraint had to be exercised most of all by the lower classes. Wells agreed with Shaw that they could not be trusted with power; their weaknesses were contagious and could tempt and demoralise even the civilised.

To give them equality is to sink to their level, to protect and cherish them is to be swamped in their fecundity. The confident and optimistic radicalism of the earlier nineteenth century, and the humanitarian philanthropic type of liberalism, have bogged themselves beyond hope in these realizations. The socialists have shirked them as he has shirked the older crux of Malthus.[52]

Wells, however, was willing to come to grips with the problem. He expressed his confidence that in time men would accept the death of the diseased or helpless as 'an act of love'. The new state could and would demand a 'minimum of personal efficiency' in its citizens. Both marriage and the bearing of children were to be privileges but motherhood would be recompensed. Those technocrats who rose highest in the meritocracy and whose offspring would naturally be most valued would form a 'voluntary nobility' or Samurai caste – in effect the Fabians – who would rule the socialist state.[53]

In the short term the necessity was to 'endow motherhood' so that child-rearing would no longer take place in poverty: 'So too the still more monstrous absurdity of women discharging their supreme social function, bearing and rearing children in their spare time, as it were, while they 'earn their living' by contributing some half mechanical element to some trivial industrial product, will disappear.'[54] Such maternity benefits could, claimed Wells, only be of use if they were employed discriminately. 'To endow poor and bad-class motherhood and leave other people severely alone would be a proceeding so supremely idiotic, so harmful to our national quality, as to be highly probable in the present state of our public intelligence.'[55] The socialist society could alone envisage the eugenic potential of such an instrument of social manipulation.

> It is manifest that no intelligent state would willingly endow the
> homes of hopelessly diseased parents, of imbecile fathers or mothers,
> of obstinately criminal persons or people incapable of education. It
> is evident too, that the state would not tolerate chance fatherhood,
> that it would insist very emphatically upon marriage and the purity
> of the home, much more emphatically than we do now.[56]

What was the final condition of men and women in the Wellsian utopia?
Women were to be restricted to mothering and their success closely
monitored.

> Frankly it [the state] will say to the sound mothering mother, not
> typewriting, nor shirt-mending, nor charring is your business, these
> children are. Neglect them, ill-treat them, prove incompetent, and
> your pay will cease, and we shall take them away from you and do
> what we can for them; love them, serve them, and through them,
> the state, and you will serve yourself.[57]

As for men, their interest in sex would decline, or should, because the
task of procreation would be less necessary. Wells conceded that some
might persist in wasting their time and energy in a non-productive
exercise but these were to be pitied more than anything else: 'An
able-bodied man continually addicted to love-making that had no
result in offspring would be just as silly and as morally objectionable
as an able-bodied man who devoted his chief energies to hitting little
balls over golf links.'[58] The tragedy, as Wells saw it, was that the man
not only wasted his own time but also that of his 'caddie'.

In the first decade of the twentieth century the crisis of the Boer war
divided the English left into those true to the older radical tradition and
the new adherents to a modern creed of amoral efficiency. This division
was mirrored in a curious way by the response of the left to birth
control. For libertarians such as Chatterton or Robertson contraception
was important because it offered the individual − in particular the
woman − greater personal freedom. For collectivists such as the Webbs
or Wells its attraction lay in its utility as a potential force for social
management. The debate over empire concerned a subject race; the
debate over birth control a subject sex.

Notes

1. *Malthusian* (February, 1883), p.387.
2. *Malthusian*, (February, 1884), p.483.
3. *Babies and Bunny Rabbits* (London, 1884?), p.3.
4. Ibid., pp. 5, 6-7.
5. *Chatterton's Commune* was a single sheet, hand-typed, tract.
6. Warren Sylvester Smith, *The London Heretics 1870-1914* (London, 1967), p.189; and see F.G. Bettany, *Stewart Headlam: A Biography* (London, 1906).
7. *Malthusian* (August 1880), p.146; (November 1882), p.361; (February 1883), p.387.
8. Reported in the *Malthusian* (February, 1888), p.12.
9. Arthur H. Nethercott, *The First Five Lives of Annie Besant* (Chicago, 1960).
10. Annie Besant, *An Autobiography* (London, 1893), pp.223-4.
11. *Our Corner* (June, 1886), p.324.
12. Annie Besant *Is Socialism Sound?* (London, 1887), p.23.
13. Ibid., p.98.
14. A life of John M. Robertson (1856-1918), MP for Tyneside (1906-1918) has not been written; see J.A. Hobson, *Confessions of an Economic Heretic* (London, 1938), 49 ff.
15. Robertson, *Socialism and Malthusianism* (London, 1885), pp.11, 13.
16. Ibid., p.15.
17. Ibid., p.15.
18. Robertson, *Over-Population* (London, 1890), p.10.
19. Robertson, *Over-Population,* p.14.
20. Ibid., p.15.
21. *Clarion* (24 February, 3, 10, 31 March, 1900; 12 August, 1904). The *Clarion* also carried advertisements for Marie C. Fisher's *Ought Women to be Punished for Having too Many Children?* (London, n.d.).
22. *Clarion* (24 July, 1903).
23. See Robert Blatchford, *The Sorcery Shop: An Impossible Romance* (London, 1909), p.57.
24. Ritchie, *Darwinism and Politics* (London, 1889), p.89; and for a criticism of Galton, pp.64-5.
25. Ritchie, *Darwinism,* p.89.
26. Ibid., p.92.
27. Kidd cited in Carr, *Social Evolution and the Evolution of Socialism* (London, 1895), p.59. Jane Hume Clapperton to whom Carr dedicated his book will be discussed below.
28. Carr *Social Evolution,* pp.66, 100.
29. Robertson, *Patriotism and Empire* (London, 1900), p.176.
30. Robertson, *Patriotism,* p.187; and see also Adelyn More [Charles Kay Ogden], *Fecundity versus Civilization* (London, 1916).
31. Robertson, *Patriotism,* p.202. In response to the eugenic argument Robertson stated, 'In fine the individualistic society of the past, so often credited with creating conditions favouring the "survival of the fittest" in the intellectual as in the physical life, is seen rather to have fixed conditions which theoretically are almost the least favourable to a maximum (numerical) development of potential mental faculty.' 'The Economics of Genius,' *The Forum,* 25 (April 1898), pp.188-9; see also Robertson, *A Short History of Morals* (London, 1920), p.436.
32. Cited in E. Belfort Bax, *Reminiscences and Reflections of a Mid and Late Victorian* (London, 1918), p.1905.
33. The *Anarchist* (1 June, 1886). Seymour was in favour of a vague form of

'free love' which he defended as editor from 1891 in *The Adult: A Journal for the Advancement of Freedom in Sexual Relations* and *The Anarchy of Love* (London, 1888) and *The Physiology of Love: A Study in Stirpiculture* (London, 1898).

34. The *Anarchist* (1 September, 1886).
35. On the Fabians see Willard Wolfe, *From Radicalism to Socialism: Men and Ideas in the Formation of Fabian Socialist Doctrines 1881-1889* (New York, 1975); A.M. McBriar, *Fabian Socialism and English Politics 1884-1918* (Cambridge, 1962); J.M. White, *Socialism and the Challenge of War: Ideas and Politics in Britain 1912-1918* (London, 1974).
36. H.G. Wells, *Experiment in Autobiography* (Toronto, 1934), p.202.
37. Sidney Webb, *Socialism in England* (London, 1890).
38. Webb, *The Difficulties of Individualism* (London, 1896 [Fabian Tract 69]), p.6.
39. Webb, *Difficulties*, p.12. See also Sidney Ball's complaint that 'quantity' was replacing 'quality' in population. *The Moral Aspects of Socialism* (London, 1896 [Fabian Tract 72]).
40. *The Times* (16 October, 1906), p.7. See the comment of one still true to Doubleday's theories: 'Mr. Webb, contrary it would seem, to his Socialistic principles, regrets the superior fertility of the poorer classes. . .because he anticipates national deterioration must be the result.' James W. Barclay, 'The Race Suicide Scare.' *Nineteenth Century and After*, 60 (1906), p.899.
41. Webb, *Decline of the Birth Rate* (London, 1907 [Fabian Tract 131]), p.19.
42. Kitty Muggeridge and Ruth Adam, *Beatrice Webb: A Life 1858-1943* (London, 1967), pp.166-7.
43. Beatrice Webb, *My Apprenticeship* (London, 1920), p.222.
44. *New Statesman* (11 July, 1914), p.429; on Fabians and race see Bernard Semmel, *Imperialism and Social Reform: English Social Imperial Thought 1895-1914* (New York, 1968); Bernard Porter, *Critics of Empire* (New York, 1960).
45. Cited by David Bowman, 'The Eugenicist's Handbook,' *Shaw Review*, 18 (1975), p.21.
46. *The Revolutionist's Handbook* (1903) in *Collected Works* (London, 1930), X, pp.188-9; on Shaw see Stephen Winsten, *Jesting Apostle: The Private Life of Bernard Shaw* (New York, 1957).
47. See Shaw's support for Galton in *Sociological Papers*, 1 (1904), p.74; see also Eden Philpotts call for a 'State Department for the Unborn,' *The New Age* (7 March, 1908), pp.368-9.
48. Wells, *Experiment*, pp.205, 215, 563.
49. Wells, *Socialism and the Family* (London, 1906), pp.6, 10, 48.
50. Wells *et al.*, *Socialism and the Great State* (London, 1912), p.27.
51. Wells, *Socialism and the Family*, pp.51, 48, 57-58.
52. Wells, *Anticipations* (London, 1901), p.314.
53. Wells, *A Modern Utopia* (London, 1925 [1st edn. 1905]), p.264.
54. Wells, *Socialism and the Family*, 59. See also 'A.M.,' *The Economic Foundations of the Women's Movement* (London, 1914 [Fabian Tract 175]), p.22; Henry B. Harben, *The Endowment of Motherhood* (London, 1910 [Fabian Tract 149]).
55. Wells, *Social Forces in England and America* (London, 1906), p.273.
56. Wells, *New Worlds for Old* (New York, 1913), p.125.
57. Ibid., pp.124-5. It might be noted that women have rarely fared well in English 'utopias'.
58. Wells, *Anticipations*, p.329. Not until 1906 did the Fabians amend the Basis to include the aim of equal citizenship between men and women; it was after

this that the Fabian women's group was formed. The Independent Labour Party under Keir Hardie's guidance showed greater concern for women's rights and included in its ranks such activists as Kathleen Glasier, Mary McArthur, Enid Stacey, and Mrs. Pankhurst. See chapter eleven.

11 FEMINISM AND FERTILITY CONTROL

The marked decline in the birth rate from the 1870s onwards coinciding as it did with the upsurge of the women's movement was taken by contemporaries — not least of all by eugenists and socialists — as sufficient proof of the interdependence of the two phenomena. But if the restriction of family size represented a 'revolt of women' how, asked later commentators, was one to explain the fact that few of the leading feminists publicly defended birth control while several opposed it? In chapter five it was shown that the question is misleading in that it misses the point that those working at mid-century for women's political and professional rights would naturally have avoided an issue which could have compromised their primary campaigns. Moreover it was demonstrated that all the leading birth control advocates were sympathetic to the women's cause. The argument which will be made in this chapter is that an examination of the writings of the women's movement in the late nineteenth century reveals that it was far from indifferent to the question of fertility control, that its interest is indeed one of the lost dimensions of Victorian and Edwardian feminism.

There was, of course, no single, consistent 'women's movement' at the turn of the century but several, each with its own particular goal — moral reform, political emancipation, economic independence.[1] Yet in separating the various strands of feminism and categorising activists as suffragists or purity campaigners or birth controllers there is the possibility of obscuring certain continuities in feminist thought. One implication of such demarcation is that the moral reformers and suffragists were, unlike the women in the Malthusian League, unmoved by the question of family limitation. Now while the former groups quite vehemently and logically reacted against forms of birth control which in their estimation increased male prerogatives it is not true that they were hostile to an alleviation of the burdens of motherhood. On the contrary they defended the woman's right of self-defence against undesired pregnancies as against other forms of male tyranny. The response of such reformers to the issue of restriction of family size is thus misrepresented if viewed as fundamentally antagonistic to that of the birth controllers. All feminists agreed on one thing: motherhood had to be voluntary. Unlimited, unwanted pregnancies could no longer be accepted. It was this common concern for a woman's 'right of

self-defence' be it against venereal disease, male sexual demands or
pregnancy which linked an apparently disparate force of purity
campaigners, moral hygienists, and birth controllers. James Marchant,
an opponent of birth control, noted in 1917 that the arguments against
the medical inspection of prostitutes and those in favour of limitation
of family size — questions which appeared at first glance to have
nothing in common — were necessarily linked as feminist concerns.

> In the early days of Mrs Josephine Butler's crusade against the CD
> Acts [which permitted state regulation of prostitution] she found
> it necessary to insist upon the right of every woman to the control of
> her own person. . .Now in the new Charter of Woman's Liberty that
> inviolable principle will be reasserted with this enormous extension
> in its application. Woman will claim full control over her person
> within the married state.[2]

Few feminists would in fact move all the way from attacking the double
standard to openly defending the woman's right to use artificial means
of fertility control. Nevertheless as will be shown in what follows it is
misleading to divide feminists simply into pro or anti-birth control
camps. Some called for complete chastity, others for periodic abstinence,
some for 'natural' means of birth control, others for contraception. The
response to the question of family limitation varied according to
preoccupation but the goal — to win for the woman the right to control
her own body — was the same.

The woman's first and elemental form of self-defence against
unwanted pregnancies was marital continence or the wife's right to
demand of her husband periods of abstinence. The feminist legitimation
of this demand turned in part on the Victorian middle-class myth that
the respectable woman's sexual needs were not as great as those of the
man. This plea for temperance was a more radical departure than it
first appears, however, for it was increasingly coupled with a new
insistence on men being as chaste as their spouses. Not only were extra-
marital relationships condemned but marriage itself was now declared
to be no longer a permit for sexual licence. Frigidity had been for many
Victorian wives the only means by which they could seek to limit their
husband's 'conjugal rights'. It did not mean, asserted Elizabeth
Blackwell, the leading purity reformer, that women were any less
passionate than men. It signified rather a rational fear of pregnancy and
its attendant dangers.[3] If men controlled themselves, if they raised their
conjugal relations to a higher level of continence women would at last

be able to fully express themselves.

This demand for greater sexual self-control by the male both within and without marriage became the central issue in the most dramatic of the nineteenth-century feminist campaigns — the social purity crusade against the toleration of prostitution. The danger posed by the venereally-diseased male to mother and child was the most striking argument employed by feminists in support of the woman's right of self-defence. The realisation at the end of the nineteenth century that syphilis could be carried even to the unborn spread fear and panic throughout society. But whereas the eugenists used the concept of bacterial infection to support the idea that prostitutes had to be controlled, the feminists used it to call for control of males. Support for such a case could be drawn from works such as Charles N.L. Shaw's 'The Supreme Menace' in which the 'father of the race' was depicted as picking up germs in the underworld and passing them on to his innocent loved ones.[4] Women had been told they had a duty to the race to breed but they now would respond that this same duty forbade them cohabiting with the potentially diseased.

The purity campaigns ranging from Josephine Butler's attack on the Contagious Diseases Act and its medical inspection of prostitutes to the White Cross Army which called on young men to pledge not to degrade women and keep themselves pure were manifestations of the attack on the double standard. Prostitution signified not simply the exploitation of women; it was portrayed by feminists as a physical as well as a moral threat. The man could be a 'carrier' of 'poisoned germ plasm' and the wife therefore had the duty and right to take whatever means necessary to protect herself and her children.[5] This was the context in which the slogan 'Votes for Women and Chastity for Men' was voiced by Christabel Pankhurst in *The Great Scourge and How to End it* (1913). Women were deprived of the vote, wrote Pankhurst, on the grounds that they were physically weak; what doctors would only reluctantly concede was that many female complaints were a consequence of disease brought home by the husband. Pankhurst claimed that 75.8 per cent of all men were infested before marriage and yet a conspiracy of silence prevented the truth being known. Such depravity was caused by men's 'sex instinct' being artificially cultivated; they now had to be re-educated and their minds freed of unclean superstitions. The cure could only take place in turn when women were fully equal and no longer had to pander to the desires of males. In the meantime it was only natural that the decline of the birth rate be viewed with disinterest by women. In a society in which the sexes were not equal neither marriage nor the bearing of children could be viewed as anything but degrading by the high-minded.[6]

Some even went further than Pankhurst and argued that any form of sexual encounter – even those untainted by venereal disease – necessarily resulted in the exploitation of the woman. The most extravagant example of this line of reasoning which reflected ancient prejudices and modern eugenic perceptions was Ellis Ethelmer's *Woman Free* (1893) in which it was asserted that if woman were weak it was because of the abuse of her body which had taken place at the hands of men over centuries. It had been discovered, wrote Ethelmer, that, '. . .nearly the whole of these special "diseases"., including menstruation, were due, directly or collaterally, to one form or other of *masculine* excess or abuse.' Citing T.L. Nichols' *Esoteric Anthropology* Ethelmer referred repeatedly to menstruation as '. . .this sign of his misdeed'.[7] According to this biological scenario the emancipated woman, freed of man's demands would lose this 'last abhorrent trace' of her subjection. Woman's plight was a consequence of both physical and psychological acquired characteristics. Doctors refused to acknowledge that her ills were 'an acquired painful consequence' of 'forced sexual abuse' but the proof would be provided by a 'rectification or reduction to pristine normality' as women emancipated themselves.[8]

Nichols' argument that the pain and dangers of childbirth were also unnatural was taken up by Frances Swiney in *The Bar of Isis: The Law of the Mother* (1907). Here the fear of poisoned 'germ plasm' was again turned against the eugenist. Semen was a poison, stated Swiney, and if there was race degeneration it was due to the incontinence of men. Epilepsy, idiocy, drunkenness were a result of 'sexual germs' spread by males.[9] Women had the right to protect themselves by either rejecting unfit males or carefully spacing sexual encounters. A similarly pathological view of intercourse was taken by Guy Aldred when shifting from a Marxist to an anarchist-feminist stance. He agreed with Swiney that sex was no more necessary than alcohol and just as harmful. It always led to inequities because the woman alone bore the child. Thus the feminist had to,

> . . .adopt the attitude of a celibate as a free lover and a believer in natural development and a deprecator of a passion founded on romantic ideals, corruptive of true purity, and degrading to womanhood, a passion only compatible with the continued suppression of women.[10]

The sacrifice would not be as demanding as some might think, declared Aldred, because sexual needs were artificially stimulated by a decadent life style and would accordingly wane with the rise of civilisation. He viewed the fall in the birth rate, like Pankhurst, with equanimity.

A fictional account suggesting the lengths to which the demand for celibacy could be pushed was provided in *The Strike of Sex* (1895) by George Noyes Miller, a member of the Oneida Community. A traveller to a small town arrives to find a 'Great Woman's Strike' in which not only votes, property rights, and equal wages are demanded but the woman's 'right to the perfect ownership of her own person'. Inspired by the success of the London dock workers' strike the married women form a united front with the 'courtesan class' and eventually force on the males a sexual Magna Carta.[11]

Turning from the feminist defence of abstinence to the response to the birth controllers' suggestion that artificial means of contraception be employed, it first has to be recognised that it would be natural for those campaigning against sexual excesses in general and prostitution in particular to condemn prophylactics associated with the demimonde. Such male forms of contraception if used in the home could, it was suggested, have the effect of reducing the wife's role to that of a whore and establish what James Hinton referred to as 'the enslavement of women under the name of wives'. In the feminist journal, the *Freewoman,* it was argued that contraception permitted men to over-indulge their passions both within and without marriage. Isabel Leatham described such practices as, '. . .a gross outrage on the aesthetic sensibilities of women'. Elizabeth Blackwell referred to wives whose bodies were ravaged by, '. . .the success of unnatural acts'. The excesses permitted by birth control were, according to F.W. Newman, more damaging to a woman's health than child-bearing ever could be.[12] For similar arguments the feminists could turn to Tolstoy's *The Kreutzer Sonata* (1889): a woman was forced, he wrote, to, '. . .destroy and go on destroying within herself to such a degree as may be necessary the capacity of being a woman, that is a mother, in order that a man may quietly and continuously get his enjoyment.'[13] And the child was, according to I.D. Pearce, as much a victim as the mother: 'For one child who in birth has suffered from his mother's need to work, how many I wonder, have suffered from their father's licentious indulgence of their so-called "rights".'[14] Though birth control could limit the number of a woman's pregnancies the point made by several feminists was that this in no way necessarily altered the fact of male dominance. Indeed some argued that in stripping the woman of her one unique power — the power of reproduction — birth control increased the influence of the husband.[15] George Bernard Shaw noted that many a middle-class woman married with the thought that if she did not love her husband at least she would have the affection of her children. If the husband chose to employ contraceptives, however, she could find herself reduced to 'a barren bodily slavery'. The perversity of the situation was that, by law, a marriage could be annulled if the man was naturally sterile but not if he artificially prevented conception.[16]

The fact that doctors constantly warned of the dire consequences of contraception might have reinforced feminist mistrust of artificial means of birth control. The actual effect is hard to gauge. One of the standard complaints of women activists was that the nineteenth-century medical profession was a male monopoly which used scientific arguments to maintain female subjection. Elizabeth Blackwell attacked physicians for their support of the double standard, Christabel Pankhurst claimed they lied about the true extent of venereal disease, Josephine Butler attributed the regulation of prostitution to an international league of doctors, and France Power Cobbe described them as being 'doubly treacherous' to women.[17] Given such suspicions it remains a moot point if feminists would be impressed by what doctors had to say about contraception. What is clear is that feminist hostility was aimed not so much at contraceptive practices as at the men who would employ them for the sole purpose of increasing their domestic powers and sexual pleasures. It is striking that, despite the vast amount of feminist activity, few direct attempts were ever made to ban birth control literature. The National Vigilance Association — the leading purity institution — debated the issue in May of 1887. Active in the discussion were Millicent Fawcett and several Christian feminists. Mrs Ormiston Chant (later to lead the attack on music halls), Mary Bunting (a leading Methodist social worker), and Elizabeth Lidgett (also active in social work) were against birth control literature *per se*. Elizabeth Blackwell favoured the prosecution of only 'promiscuous circulars of this kind of knowledge'.[18] The NVA which drew up the Indecent Advertisements Act of 1889 made no mention in it of such literature.

Many feminists who were opposed to birth control primarily because they viewed it as an unnatural practice employed for the benefit of men could contemplate the adoption of 'natural' methods designed to protect women. Here limitation of family size could be presented as a

sign of the greater seriousness with which women regarded their role
as mothers. Olive Schreiner declared in *Woman and Labour* that,

> . . .the New Woman's conceptions of parenthood differs from the
> old in the greater sense of the gravity and obligation resting on
> those who are responsible for the production of the individual life,
> making her attitude toward the production of her race widely
> unlike the reckless, unreasoning, maternal reproduction of the
> woman of the past. . .[19]

Insistence upon abstinence at least during pregnancy and nursing
was the oldest means of spacing births. One step beyond abstention
was reliance on what was thought to be the 'safe period' in the
woman's ovulation cycle. Elizabeth Blackwell, whose contribution to
the medical debate on birth control has been examined, was the most
vocal defender in the feminist ranks of this tactic. For her and other
feminists the obvious appeal of the discovery of the 'safe period' was
that now, '. . .woman assumes her due place as the regulator of sexual
intercourse. . .The forgoing law is a truth full of hope and promise of
infinite progress, for nations have hitherto perished in large measure
through the abuse and degradation of women.' Now it would be
possible to 'reconcile marriage with foresight', demand of the male
periodic continence, and deliver to the female full control of fertility.[20]
    Edward Carpenter, who wrote widely on questions of sexuality,
also favoured the 'safe period' as more in keeping with the religiosity
of marriage. As a feminist and homosexual he found contemporary sex
'slimed over with the thought of pleasure' and therefore in need of
rehabilitation to give it a sense of 'almost religious consecration'. But
this could not occur as long as woman was a 'mere machine for
perpetual reproduction'. Artificial checks were unsatisfactory because
of their uncertainty, 'their desparate matter-of-factness', and because
the man's satisfaction was achieved at the price of the woman's. The
answer was therefore to rely on the woman's monthly cycle.[21] In
addition Carpenter expressed his support for the method of coitus
reservatus —intercourse without ejaculation — practised in the American
Oneida Colony and made known in England by Alice B. Stockham's
Karezza: Ethics of Marriage (1896). It was, wrote Stockham,
'. . .especially necessary for the wife to be freed from the mental dread
of excessive and undesired child-bearing. . .' This could be attained,
not by employing artificial methods of control which only exaggerated
lusts, but by raising sexual intercourse to a higher plane and making it

distinct from race propagation: 'Copulation is more than a propagative act; it is a blending of body, soul and spirit, ennobling or degrading according to the attitude of the participants.' Such a practice required that the husband improve his powers of self-control so that 'through the power of the will, and loving thoughts, the final crisis is not reached'.[22] The same tactic was advocated by George Noyes Miller in *After the Strike of Sex or, Zugassent's Discovery.*

Feminist demands for an ascetic if not celibate life, their suspicions of and hostility toward artificial means of fertility control were but facets of what contemporaries and historians were to refer to as the 'sex antagonisms' if not the 'sex war' of the first decades of the twentieth century.[23] What has been ignored is that such a position was a logical if extreme response to the outrageous demands made for women's compliance to the sexual inclinations of men and the manipulative manner with which fertility was discussed by the eugenically-minded. Also overlooked was the fact that some feminists, recognising the unreliability of 'natural' methods of birth control and the crucial importance of limiting family size, did accept the necessity of women employing contraceptives. Their chief concern was neither . the neo-Malthusian population problem nor the eugenist fear of degeneration though they would turn both forms of arguments to their purpose; their concern was the health and happiness of the individual woman. The birth control and feminist campaigns were most clearly linked together in the last third of the nineteenth century in the activities of Annie Besant. Her contributions to the birth control debate and the importance she saw women playing in it were dealt with in chapter ten; here it is only necessary to note that she was not, as some assume, unique in holding such a position.[24] The increasing seriousness with which child-bearing was viewed was taken up by others as reason enough for its control. The thoughtlessness which gave rise to large families was declared by Jane Hume Clapperton in *Scientific Meliorism and the Evolution of Happiness* (1885) to be no longer acceptable.

If immature persons marry, deferred parentage is what society has a right to require, and it should exercise moral pressure, through an enlightened public opinion, to that effect, and bring home to all parents the social responsibility they incur by the birth of a child; whilst private action of social reformers should teach the rational methods by which, in this class, the populating tendency may be kept within due limits, and prudence, foresight, and self dependence be promoted.[25]

Clapperton pursued her defence of birth control as the 'new key to the social question' in her utopian novel, *Margaret Dunmore: or, A Socialist Home* (1888). Advancing what she referred to as 'meliorist' ideas she outlined the story of a commune, 'La Maison,' in which sex distinctions were put aside and domestic work socialised. A General Council administered the 'Unitary Home' which had as one of its main preoccupations the control of fertility. Older means, such as those suggested by the Oneida and Wallingford Perfectionists, Clapperton put aside as products of a 'childish Theology.' She had one of her characters declare that the problem had to be worked out by women: ' "These are delicate matters for mothers alone. They must limit their families. They must learn what their duty is to their own health, the health of their children, and the health of the nation. We women will instruct them in self-respect, and show them how to support one another in cases where men are brutal and ought to be resisted." '[26]

The idea that women should even discuss limitation of family goaded E. Lynn Linton into producing a series of sensational attacks on 'The Wild Women.' In response Mona Caird declared that women would continue to fill the role of mother but in reasonable proportions. There could not be a conscript army of mothers. Indeed Caird pointedly asked why, if motherhood was so 'natural,' did some feel it necessary to force it upon women? Ethel Snowden made many of the same points in *The Feminist Movement* (1911); the last and greatest of its demands was for '. . .a woman's absolute right over herself after marriage'. In the future declared Katherine Bruce Glasier, all children would be 'wanted', there would be no 'regrettable accidents'.[27] But to achieve this goal meant that the woman could no longer, in Cicely Hamilton's words, be viewed as 'a breeding machine'. In *Marriage as a Trade* (1912) Hamilton stated that maternity would only be worthy of reverence when it was a freely chosen state: 'Motherhood can be sacred only when it is voluntary, when a child is desired by a woman who feels herself fit to bear and rear it. . .' But such was not now the case.

As long as child-bearing was an involuntary consequence of a compulsory trade — as, to a great extent, it still is — there must

have been innumerable women who, year after year, bore children
whom they did not desire to bear; who suffered the discomforts of
pregnancy and the pangs of childbirth not that they might rejoice
when a man was born into the world, but that a fresh and unwelcome
burden might be added to their lives. And how unwelcome was that
burden in many cases is proved by the voluntary and deliberate
restriction of the modern family![28]

In response to the eugenists' protests that the feminists' defence of such
limitations of fertility posed the problem of racial degeneration Alice
Vickery noted that Galton only looked at male heredity and she asked
what the eugenists saw as the woman's contribution. Answering the
question for them she declared that the natural selection of mates could
only take place if women were economically independent; the race
could only be improved if women's condition improved. Therefore
limitation of family size and female emancipation were the conditions
of racial progress.[29] F.W. Stella Browne, a militant feminist who was to
make her name after the war as a defender of abortion, was similarly
preoccupied by the eugenist argument. In 'Some Problems of Sex'
(1916) she insisted that despite the race suicide fear the essential point
was to establish the right of the woman not to have children. Turning·
to the socialists she warned that an 'endowment of motherhood' could
be a trap in that it might be used to keep women restricted to child-
bearing: 'Under present conditions, maternity endowment would be
peculiarly liable to become an engine of exploitation and oppression.'
The opposition of some feminists to any discussion of sex she described
as too boring to contemplate and similar women's attempts to turn all
the energies of the women's movement to the political struggle she
attributed to the 'dogmatic and tyrannical suffragist bureaucracy.'[30]
Returning to the eugenists in a 1917 article, 'Women and Birth Control',
Browne protested against the pressure under which women were put to
breed by both the state and propagandists such as those of the Eugenics
Educational Society. Before such demands could be legitimately made
the government would have to address itself to the reforms in those areas
which Browne saw as having a direct impact on the family: housing, land
tenure, agricultural reform, trade, sex education, public health, divorce,
illegitimacy, and universal adult suffrage. But even if the state attended
to such needs the question of birth control remained a personal decision
for the woman. Browne argued that on the one hand women who wanted
children should not be ostracised if they had them out of wedlock; on
the other, those who did not want them had the right to take the means

necessary to avoid them — including recourse to abortion. In defending
the right of abortion Browne had adopted the most radical stance to be
assumed in the course of the population debate.[31]

Few feminists publicly defended birth control but, as Browne's
testimony suggests, this fact has to be viewed in the light of the
tremendous burden placed on women at the end of the nineteenth
century to prove themselves as mothers or at least pay lip service to
the ideal. 'Race-motherhood' and 'mothercraft' were the new deities
before which women's freedom was to be sacrificed. A child-rearing
technology emerged in the 1890s stimulated by imperialism, socialism,
the New Philanthropy, and the eugenists' concern for healthy stock.[32]
Health visitors, public nurses, and charity investigators descended on
working-class homes to see that mothers were carrying out their duties.
The first duty of the fit was to bear children and as was seen in the
earlier discussion eugenists complained that it was being shirked by those
influenced by feminism. Walter Heape described the 'awakening of
woman' in *Sex Antagonisms* (1913) as the most dangerous occurrence
of the previous half-century. This movement led by the 'mentally
deranged' threatened to deliver the nation to those female misfits who
had failed as wives or mothers. More pernicious than the demand for
the vote was their insistence that men control their sexual desires. In
thus seeking to break the 'iron fetters of nature' women were, declared
Heape, dooming the species to extinction.[33] S.H. Halford sounded the
same warning in 'Dysgenic Tendencies of Birth Control and of the
Feminist Movement.' Education and emancipation were rendering the
finest women unfit for child-bearing. 'Women exist primarily for sexual
ends,' stated Halford, and their 'sexlessness' was both a crime against
society and a threat to the physical well-being of men whose
'. . .inevitable need calls for preferential consideration over the
sentimental grievances of women'.[34]

This attack of the biological determinists on women's attempts to
limit the burden of pregnancies was supported by the churches. The
Reverend R. Ussher in *Neo-Malthusianism* (1897) attributed the 'sterility'
of women to their increased educational and employment opportunities.
Boyd Carpenter, Bishop of Ripon, and Winnington-Ingram, Bishop of
London, hit out at small families which were the result of 'fashionable
marriages'.[35] Father Bernard Vaughan lamented the fact in *The Sins of
Society* (1906) that, 'Present up-to-date parents ridicule the notion of
having big families; so that instead of being proud, Society is becoming

ashamed of owning to a nursery full of children.' Such flaunting of 'legalized prostitution' he asserted, sprang directly from women's selfish desire for leisure and luxury.[36] In 1908 the Anglican Church took an official stand on the issue when the Lambeth Conference condemned '. . .the practice of resorting to artificial means for the avoidance or prevention of child-bearing'. It was a sign of the times that Christian leaders based their censuring of birth control, not so much on biblical, as on eugenic teachings. It was the threat which it posed the race and the 'nervous enfeeblement' it caused the individual which were the reasons advanced by the bishops to explain their hostility to family limitation.[37]

Given the continued opposition of respectable society it is not surprising that few women would go as far as Stella Browne in defending artificial fertility control. Yet, as radical as her proposed solutions were, her initial concerns were shared by large numbers of feminists. Her position, at first glance so far removed from that of the purity campaigners, converged with theirs on the central issue of the woman's right to control her own fertility. Like them she found it possible to turn the eugenist argument of the primacy of motherhood, ostensibly aimed at subjecting reproductive behaviour to greater social control, to the purposes of feminism. Like them she recognised the fact that child-bearing involved, not just procreation, but every aspect of the relationship of the sexes.[38]

Notes

1. J.A. and O. Banks, *Feminism and Family Planning* (New York, 1964); Constance Rover, *Love, Morals and the Feminists* (London, 1970).
2. James Marchant, *Birth Rate and Empire* (London, 1917), p.181; on the situation in America see Linda Gordon, *Woman's Body, Woman's Right* (New York, 1976), 95 ff.
3. E. Blackwell, 'The Human Element in Sex,' *Essays in Medical Sociology* (London, 1902, 1972 reprint), I, p.47. It was traditionally believed that unresponsiveness not only inhibited the male but could prevent conception.
4. Shaw, 'The Supreme Menace,' *Penny Illustrated Newspaper* (10 September, 1910), p.329.
5. Josephine Butler, *Personal Reminiscences of a Great Crusade* (London, 1896); Ellice Hopkins, *The White Cross Army* (London, 1883).
6. C. Pankhurst, *The Great Scourge* (London, 1913).
7. T.L. Nichols and his wife Mary Grove Nichols produced a series of works on medicine and morality frequently cited by feminists; for Nichols' equation of 'free love' and birth control see *Marriage in All Ages and Nations* (London, 1886), pp.163-4 and *Human Physiology* (London, 1872); see also Effie Johnson, 'Marriage or Free Love.' *Westminster Review*, 152 (1899), pp.91-8.
8. 'Ellis Ethelmer' was the pen name of Mrs Wolstenholme Elmy and her husband Ben Elmy. Mrs Elmy was on the central committee of the Ladies National

Association and also active in the movement for higher education. *Woman Free* (London, 1893), pp.100, 12, 92. See also Ellis Ethelmer, 'Feminism,' *Westminster Review*, 149 (1898), pp.50-62.

9. Swiney, *The Bar of Isis* (London, 1912, 3rd edn.), pp.16, 32, 46; see her *The Awakening of Women, or Women's Part in Evolution* (London, 1905), and 'An Ethical Birth Rate,' *Westminster Review*, 155 (1901), pp.550-4 in which she noted that few who bewailed the decline of the birth rate showed the same concern for the high infant and maternal mortality rates.

10. Aldred, *The Religion and Economics of Sex Oppression* (London, 1906), see also Aldred to *Freewoman* (18 July, 1912), p.179; and above chapter 10, ft. 50.

11. Miller, *The Strike of Sex* (London, 1895).

12. Ellice Hopkins (ed.), *Life and Letters of James Hinton* (London, 1878), p.272; Leatham to *Freewoman* (7 December, 1911), p.52; (4 January, 1912), p.151; F.W. Newman and E. Blackwell, *The Corruption Called neo-Malthusianism* (London, 1889), pp.6, 7.

13. Tolstoy, *The Kreutzer Sonata* (Oxford, 1940 [1st edn. 1889]), p.148.

14. Pearce to *Justice* (4 October, 1902); see also the hostile review of H. Seymour's *The Physiology of Love* in *Shafts* (January 1898) in which the editor insists that the sex question has to be taken into 'higher realms.'

15. See for example the statement that a prolific mother is now viewed as 'a curse and downdraft' in Olive Schreiner, *Woman and Labour* (New York, 1911), p.58.

16. Shaw, preface to *Three Plays by Eugène Brieux* (London, 1911), xliii.

17. Butler, *Personal Reminiscences*, pp.102-3; and for one specific campaign of women against doctors see Richard D. French, *Antivivisection and Medical Science in Victorian Society* (Princeton, 1975), p.247.

18. I owe this information to Edward Bristow who is about to bring out a history of anti-vice-crusading in England. The American social purity movement has been portrayed as supporting 'conservative birth control'; David J. Pivar, *Purity Crusade, Sexual Morality and Social Control 1868-1900* (Westport, Conn., 1973), p.255.

19. Schreiner, *Woman*, p.269. Schreiner attributed the fall in family size directly to 'the regulation of the number of births after marriage.'

20. Blackwell, 'The Human Element,' p.78; 'The Moral Education of the Young in Relation to Sex,' *Essays*, p.293. The safe period was also lauded in Ellis Ethelmer, *The Human Flower: A Simple Statement of the Physiology of Birth and the Relations of the Sexes.* (Congleton, 1892), pp.44-5; Blackwell is cited by Fryer as also recommending in *Medical Address on the Benevolence of Malthus Contrasted with the Corruptions of the Neo-Malthusians* (1888) when necessary the douche and coitus interruptus. I have not been able to locate this work. See Peter Fryer, *The Birth Controllers* (New York, 1965), p.313.

21. Carpenter, *Love's Coming of Age* (London, 1948 [1st edn. 1896]), pp.23, 203, 204.

22. Stockham, *Karezza* (Chicago, 1896), pp.39, vii, 22; and see Stockham. *Tokology: A Book for Every Woman* (Toronto, 1916).

23. See for example George Dangerfield, *The Strange Death of Liberal England* (London, 1936), pp.190-1.

24. Besant worked with W.T. Stead, the best known of the moral purity journalists, in The Link Society set up to watch public morals. See Raymond L. Schults, *Crusader in Babylon: W.T. Stead and the Pall Mall Gazette* (Lincoln, Nebraska, 1972), p.232. A consistent defender of feminism Stead insisted that women had a duty to the race not to have large unhealthy families: 'Every pair who have married and have reached a sufficiently lofty

moral level' had to decide how many children they intended to have. Stead shocked the 1910 Divorce Commission by insisting that women should not only have a veto over the number of children but that they should inform their prospective spouses of their views before marriage. *Review of Reviews* (1900), pp.178-9; (1911), p.80.

25. Clapperton, *Scientific Meliorism* (London, 1885), pp. 302, 177, 304.
26. Clapperton, *Margaret Dunmore* (London, 1888), p.203.
27. E. Lynn Linton, 'The Wild Women as Social Insurgents,' *Nineteenth Century,* 30 (1891), pp.596-605; 31 (1892), pp.455-64; Caird, 'A Defense of the So-Called "Wild Women",' *Nineteenth Century,* 31 (1892), pp.811-29 and Caird, *The Morality of Marriage* (London, 1897), pp.167, 185; Snowden, *The Feminist Movement* (London, 1911), p.24; Glasier, *Socialism and the Home* (London, n.d.).
28. Hamilton, *Marriage as a Trade* (London, 1912), pp.211, 159.
29. Vickery, *Sociological Papers* 1 (1904), p.60; 2 (1905), p.21; and for other feminist attacks on eugenics see *Freewoman* (1 August, 1912), pp.204-5; Anna Martin, 'The Mother and Social Reform,' *Nineteenth Century and After,* 73 (1913), pp.1060-79.
30. Browne, 'Some Problems of Sex,' *International Journal of Ethics,* 27 (1916), p.465; in the same journal see Warne Fite, 'Birth Control and Biological Ethics, 27 (1916), pp.50-63; Elsie Clews Parsons, 'The Future of Parenthood,' 26 (1915), p.514; see also Browne on Ellen Key, *Malthusian* (September, 1914), p.70 and Margaret Sanger, *An Autobiography* (New York, 1938), p.129.
31. Browne, 'Women and Birth Control,' in Eden and Cedar Paul, (eds.), *Population and Birth Control: A Symposium* (New York, 1917), p.254.
32. Anna Davin, 'Imperialism and the Cult of Motherhood,' Paper delivered to the British Sociological Association, Aberdeen, 1974; Peter W.G. Wright, 'The Birth of Child Rearing as a Form of Social Control,' Paper delivered to the B.S.A., Manchester, 1976; Carol Dyhouse, 'Good Wives and Little Mothers: Social Anxieties and the Schoolgirl's Curriculum, 1890-1920,' *Oxford Review of Education,* 3 (1977), pp.21-35.
33. Heape, *Sex Antagonisms* (London, 1913), pp.4, 207. Heape was also the author of *The Breeding Industry* (Cambridge, 1906). For a popularisation of the view that the woman's chief duty was to breed see also Grant Allen, 'Plain Words on the Woman Question,' *Fortnightly Review,* 52 (1889), pp.448-58 and *The Woman Who Did* (London, 1895 2nd edn.).
34. Halford, 'Dysgenic Tendencies of Birth Control,' in Paul, *Population,* p.238. See also John Thorburn, MD, 'Female Education from a Physiological Point of View,' in C.J. Cullingworth *et al., Six Introductory Lectures* (Manchester, 1884), pp.81-94.
35. Ussher, *Neo-Malthusianism* (London, 1897), p.184; Carpenter to *Daily Express* (27 April, 1904); Winnington-Ingram to *Daily Chronicle* (20 October, 1905).
36. Vaughan, *The Sins of Society* (London, 1906), p.135. Vaughan was later to admit that at least with the spread of birth control 'the number of abortions, though still enormous, is relatively fewer. . .' *The Menace of the Empty Cradle* (London, 1917), p.52; and see also the statement that bridge is replacing baby in William Platt, *Love and Parentage (A Practical Ideal)* (London, 1909), p.114. Platt singled out Clapperton and Florence Dixie for attack and suggested that childless women be given the white feather: *The Perils of Birth Control* (London, 1924), p.58.
37. E.R. Norman, *Church and Society in England 1770-1970* (Oxford, 1976), p.270. See also Rev. Geo. W. Clark, *Race Suicide: England's Peril* (London, 1916). Non-conformists tended to be more liberal. See the evidence of Rev. W.F. Lofthouse in James Marchant, (ed.), *The Declining Birth Rate* (London,

1917), pp.372-76; Flann Campbell, 'Birth Control and the Christian Churches,' *Population Studies,* 14 (1960), pp.131-47.

38. To the list of women who supported the spread of birth control information could be added the names of Lady Florence Dixie, author of *Gloriana or the Revolution of 1900* (London, 1890); Teresa Billington Greig, militant suffragist and author of *Commonsense on the Population Question* (London, 1915); Mrs. Fenwick Miller, member of the London School Board and active neo-Malthusian; and Anna Martin who in 1908 with Alice Vickery began a private birth control clinic in south-west London. See M. Breed and Edith How-Martyn, *The Birth Control Movement in England* (London, 1930), p.13.

PART FOUR

THEORY AND PRACTICE

12 BIRTH CONTROL AND THE WORKING CLASSES

The enormous literature produced by Malthusians, neo-Malthusians, eugenists and socialists that dealt in one way or another with the issue of fertility control had as its central concern the reproductive habits of the working classes. Did the century-long debate have any effect on either the ideas or practices of working families? The purpose of this and the following chapter is to determine how the working classes' response to the possibility of family limitation was influenced by new and old attitudes towards procreation, economic and social pressures, and differing male and female views of child-bearing.

The bulk of the population literature was written by and for the middle classes but it is difficult to see how workers could not have been eventually influenced by this deluge of propaganda. The results were not always what the writers expected. The neo-Malthusian message, suffused as it was with an anti-labour bias, had the effect of leading many workmen, already suspicious of practices considered 'unnatural', into viewing their adoption as in some ways a betrayal of class. A Mr Hill of Lambeth stood up at a population debate in March of 1881 to testify that despite the Malthusians he had twenty-one children and wished he had twenty-two. In May of the same year a Mr Oakley of Tower Hamlets insisted, 'The aristocracy is afraid lest the people should become too numerous.' When one worker in the labour classic *The Ragged Trousered Philanthropist* ventures the opinion that 'hover population' is the cause of distress he is reproved: '"How can marriage be a cause of poverty," said Owen, contemptuously, "A man who is not married is living an unnatural life." ". . .A single man can save money if he likes," said Slyme [the villain], "I'm not speaking of a single man," replied Owen, "I'm referring to those who live natural lives." '[1] The fact that those who spoke for the working classes continued to associate family limitation with the reactionary tenets of Malthus suggests that the Malthusian League may have actually impeded the acceptance of at least the idea of birth control by the masses. In any event it was not until 1913 that the League began to provide actual contraceptive information, as distinct from tracts on population problems.

Any suspicions harboured by the lower classes that fertility control was part of a policy of conservative social engineering could only have been reinforced by a familiarity with the eugenists' arguments. Since the eugenic movement's first priority was to establish its credibility in academic circles few direct responses were made to the creed by workers. The reply they might have made, had they bothered to answer a pseudo-science which for all its jargon was but a new means by which to keep the lower orders in their place, was given by 'Kennington Cross' in a mock-Cockney poem entitled 'Darwinism'.

> My Gawd, 'ow 'ast Thou made this bloomin' wurld?
>   I cawn't find out; I've tried until I'm sick;
> Is it Thy Will thet Ruin should be 'url'd
> On 'arf the race, w'ile 'arf goes prank'd an' curl'd,
>   Becors the poppylashun is too thick?
>
> Yus, Ive bin readin' Darwin, an' I find
>   The struggle fer survival of the fit
> Explains the mystery to w'ich we're blind;
> Thet some of us to Ruin is assign'd
>   Becors we ain't all ekal in our wit.
>
> They serve their end? — My Gawd! 'ast Thou, then, made
>   A wurld o' cannibals? The strong ter live
> Upon the patient workers they degrade?
> If thet's the scheme, then, Gawd, I am afraid
>   Ye arsk a rev'rince thet I cannot give.[2]

Working men were naturally hostile to any theory which employed the concept of their 'uncontrolled breeding' as a means to belittle their intelligence and morality. What they thought of fertility control *per se* is a separate question and one extremely difficult to answer for Victorian England. Indeed it is hard to obtain information on the attitudes of nineteenth-century working men towards almost any aspect of sexuality. Those who left autobiographies or memoirs were for the most part members of the 'labour aristocracy' strongly influenced by the bourgeois ideal of respectability. Such sources are the last places in which to look for references for anything but the most acceptable forms of behaviour. The picture they present is of an austere regiment of disciplined, self-taught men striving for a life of propriety and abstinence. In some even domestic concerns are portrayed as possibly dangerous diversions from the serious task of self-improvement. 'With my home life', wrote John Bedford Leno, 'I am not desirous of dealing.

The fact is that it would fail to prove interesting to strangers, and it was with no conception that it would that I commenced this autobiography.'[3] The impression these works leave is of aspiring artisans who, in order to concentrate their efforts on intellectual advancement, repressed their sexual interests to some extent. At twenty-four Thomas Cooper met 'the dear one' but he asserted that until then he had never spoken to a woman. Marriage was viewed by Cooper and those of like mind as a burden which could crush the beginnings of a painfully acquired education: 'To share, as a true and affectionate husband ought to share, the cares of his wife, and of a young family, most fearfully cuts off prospects of great mental improvement for a working man.' Similarly to become a parent was in James Burns' words to give 'hostage to the state'.[4]

What the radical artisan culture prized most highly was 'the great work of self-culture' and this was a work that was not carried on in the home. John C. Miller in *Courtship and Marriage* (1861) advised working girls that their prospective spouses, if they were the better sort, would be at the Midland Institutes, the Mechanic Institutes, and Working Men's Associations. According to Henry Solly it was in the working men's club that the moral and intellectual tone of the artisans was raised; it permitted them to return home sober yet refreshed.[5]

Such determined and self-disciplined men when they did enter the discussion of morality did so in order to castigate the licentiousness of the aristocracy and to do battle with the 'vices of the oppressor'.[6] These were the working men who because they considered prostitution a form of sexual exploitation of the poor supported Josephine Butler's campaign against the Contagious Diseases Act and W.T. Stead's crusade against 'modern Babylon'. In their authobiographies such as W.E. Adams' *Memoirs of a Social Atom* (1903), Frederick Rodgers' *Labour, Life and Adventure* (1913), and Thomas Okey's *A Basketful of Memories: An Autobiographical Sketch* (1930) one finds few references to sexual attitudes aside from the general complaints about the immorality of the age.

The fact that these works rarely mention the birth control debate does not mean that the issue was ignored by the working class as a whole. Rather it raises the question of the extent to which the classic working man's autobiography presents an accurate reflection of home life. The stress on self-control, thrift, cleanliness, and education in such accounts appears at times almost dehumanising.[7] They have to be read in part at least as self-conscious attempts to win public recognition and approval of the virtues of labour. It must be remembered that middle-class writers continued to titillate their readers with tales of the incest, illegitimacy, prostitution, common law marriages, and 'sale of wives' purportedly endemic to working-class neighbourhoods.[8] A better balance is struck if the artisan autobiographies are contrasted with less determinedly moralistic portrayals of working life such as that offered by George Meek. 'We did everything but fall', he wrote of an early encounter with a girl, and proceeded to relate how his fickle loves preferred postmen or pastry cooks. A similarly sensual tone is found in the songs of the music hall, particularly Marie Lloyd's 'A Little Bit of What You Fancy Does You Good'. That the pursuit of sexual pleasure could be impeded by the threat of pregnancy was recognised. The *Pleasures of Matrimony,* a mid-century chapbook, in commenting on the possibility of a wife's infertility made it clear that such a prospect would be welcomed by many.

> I doubt but that it is an allay to many of one's nocturnal pleasures, to think upon the charge he is bringing upon himself, by satisfying a little amourous itch; but when he had done it and done it, and done it again, and finds there is no danger, then he falls to it without fear or wits.[9]

And, of course, it was to banish just such fears that the working-class agitator Daniel Chatterton had provided birth control information in his *Babies and Bunny Rabbits.*

From the 1870s onward there was, especially in London, a shift away from the radical artisan culture.[10] A work and club life style yielded to the attractions of home and family. Shorter working hours and increased distances between shop and home meant working men spent more time with their families. Moreover as mortality rates declined and survival became less of a game of chance, parents devoted more attention to their children. Compulsory schooling on the one hand and tighter restrictions on factory employment on the other led to children being viewed less as potential wage earners and more as dependents whose well-being was determined in part by the family's budget not being outstripped by the number of mouths to feed. There was still the possibility of having children as a form of 'insurance' against destitution — a tactic William Graham considered logical enough.

> The labouring poor are induced to marry and to have children because a large family may save them in their old age from the workhouse, instead of sending them into it sooner. A man childless,

when past his work, will go into the workhouse for certain unless he has been unusually frugal; but children *may* save him, and meantime he has lived his natural life as well.[11]

The gradual introduction of social welfare legislation at the turn of the century was to go some way in making such provisions less crucial. Thus, as a result of a complex constellation of social forces, the home was to become increasingly central in the life of the worker and the question of restricting the number of children it housed ever more important. 'And even now working-class morality is on the change,' reported Stephen Reynolds in 1911, 'Statesmen are much perturbed by what is termed race-suicide. . .The older fashioned working man will not consider voluntary limitation of the family. To his mind it is unnatural and wicked. But the younger generation is keenly interested in its possibilities and personal advantages, and its advantages to the children who are born.'[12]

The census data available in 1911 bore out Reynolds' contention. The number of births per thousand married males according to social grade gave the upper and middle class 119, skilled workmen 153, and unskilled workmen 213. Such figures have been used ever since to support the view that the practice of family limitation was an innovation, the knowledge of which 'trickled down' the social hierarchy from the upper to the lower classes. Norman Himes spoke of, '. . .this limited percolation downward of contraceptive knowledge'. 'The new fashion in smaller families clearly began "at the top", ' wrote Richard and Kathleen Titmuss, 'and the middle classes and skilled artisan groups were not slow in following the example set by their masters as subsequent years were to show. . .The example set by the rich in choosing the alternatives to children was faithfully copies as idea and practice seeped down through society.'[13] Researchers, assuming that they were dealing with a problem of the diffusion of an innovative technique, have until recently treated birth control very much as if it were a new discovery. They have focused their attention on the 'accessibility', 'distance', and diffusion of contraceptive information as it seeped, trickled or percolated from the white to the blue collar workers, from the metropolitan centres to the hinterland. This approach to the problem, which further assumed the inevitable 'embourgeoisement' of the working classes, did cast light on the attempts of the middle class to force its life-style on the workers but it ignored two points: that birth control was not a nineteenth-century discovery and that some working-class groups such as textile workers were utilising some means of family regulation as early as mid-century.[14]

For the nineteenth-century working classes the questions of fertility, infant and child mortality, and the economic utility of children would all have a bearing on whether or not methods of control would be considered. The fact that working-class families remained larger than middle-class families did not in itself prove that the worker was 'ignorant' of means of restriction. What it did indicate was that the two strata had two different goals which they sought to achieve in their own particular fashions. The high fertility norm of the working class was rational given the fact that children raised frugally and put out to work were valuable assets. Moreover, even in the large family, birth control could have been used not to restrict size *per se,* but to space births. When the working-class family declined in size it did so not simply because new means of control were available, but because a new target family size had been adopted.

Proof that the adoption of fertility control was more the consequence of adjustments made to new economic conditions than merely the result of the adoption of innovative ideas was available in the figures which revealed the fertility differentials which existed *within* the working classes. Fertility first fell in the textile areas where there was a good deal of female employment; birth rates remained high in the mining and heavy industry areas where there was little. Out of an interest both in protecting their family's economic stability and assuring themselves a degree of liberty, women who had worked outside the home revealed a greater desire than those who had not to control family size.

By the turn of the century it was clear that a sizeable proportion of the working classes was practising family planning and as the danger of war with Germany increased there were even reports of a 'birth strike'. In Huddersfield it was claimed, 'Recently a "Labour" representative at a meeting of the Town Council remarked: "Aye! The times gone by when we'll breed soldiers to be shot at for a shilling a day or workers to addle brass [earn money] for manufacturers and starve ther'sen." '[15] The Countess of Warwick in an article entitled 'Race Suicide' quoted a working woman as saying that she and her husband would, because of their political beliefs, not have children.

'The conditions of life in England are not worth perpetuating, and neither of us would willingly bring children into the world to take their chance and run their horrible risks as we did.' She stopped for a moment in order to be sure of her self-control, and then she told me that in her view, though all her heart cried out for little children, sterility was the only protest that could be made against the cruel conditions of modern life under capitalism. 'I know that my husband and I are desirables from the employer's standpoint. . .So we will not produce any more slaves for the capitalists; *and I can tell you that there is not one decently educated young married woman of my acquaintance who is not of the same mind.* You could go into a score of houses known to me in this town alone and find strong, vigorous women whose childlessness is their one possible protest against the existing wage slavery.'[16]

That some working class-couples adopted some form of fertility control as a means of dissenting against the social conditions of the nation was no doubt true but it was a gross exaggeration to ascribe the general fall of the birth rate to such motives. Such alarms were engendered by the sudden realisation that the working classes were ceasing to produce the excessively large families so long associated with them.

If a working-class couple did decide to restrict family size what tactics would they adopt? Given the temperance and self-control which was the pride of so many artisans some would simply abstain from sexual intercourse. According to Paul Thompson, '. . .there can be no doubt that both the fall in illegitimacy and the fall in the number of children born within marriage from the mid-nineteenth century was achieved by restraint. Edwardian adults, whether married or not, were having less sexual intercourse.'[17] Sidney Webb was one of the first to suggest that economic and sexual foresight were related. He used the figures on the declining numbers of births of the members of the Hearts of Oak Friendly Society to argue that it was the thrifty and intelligent in the working class who were restricting family size. Similar conclusions were based on perusals of the accounts of the Railway Benevolent Institution and the Great Western Railway Provident Society.[18] Clearly 'restraint' of some kind played a role but it is difficult to believe that it consisted simply in abstention. What evidence is there that other means were employed? The best is the upsurge of commercial literature in the 1890s which publicised sex manuals, contraceptives, and abortifacients. The particular interest of this material is that like the earlier quack productions it was provided by men simply out to make money and so was freed of the jarring didacticism of the Malthusian handbills. In turning to the commercial production of manuals and appliances one is reminded that they too responded to the forces of both supply and demand. They would not have been produced in large numbers unless a market already existed; once businessmen recognised the potential they would use advertising to further stimulate demand. There is no way of knowing the full extent of such developments but it is obvious that by the 1890s a major shift was occurring. In the previous decade new vulcanisation processes permitted the production of thinner, more comfortable sheaths and diaphragms. Cheap postal rates and advertising in the penny press gave entrepreneurs access to a national market. Surgical shops blatantly advertised their wares in window displays and their managers had leaflets distributed. By the turn of the century the channels of birth control information ranged from the local barbershop to the advertising columns of mass circulation dailies.

The commercial exploitation of the desire to limit fertility is a subject which has received surprisingly little attention. And yet it was the private sector which was going to be the most active in making, selling, and distributing contraceptives. Historians have shunned this area of the question presumably because they know how to deal with medical, moral, and economic writings on fertility but feel ill at ease when confronted by the tawdry handbills of seedy businessmen. What is ignored is the fact that such individuals frequently had a knowledge of the needs, hopes, and fears of the public not shared by doctors or economists. Those whose business it was to know if there was a market for contraceptives and to whom they could sell such products had to be amongst the best informed on birth control practices or what has been called the 'most private enterprise'.[19]

The most striking discovery that emerges from an analysis of the commercial birth control literature is that contraception continued in the 1890s to be presented as a form of self-help medicine and as such was associated with traditional cures and folk remedies on the one hand and popular pseudo-sciences such as phrenology on the other. A good example of the way in which the enterprising would turn the lingering interest in folk wisdom to their own purposes are the turn of the century editions of *Aristotle's Masterpiece* which now carried advertisements for contraceptives on their last page. In the 1894 edition published by J. Smith the traditional tales of the way in which a wife could fulfil her role as a 'fruitful vine' were followed by C.J. Welton's Catalogue of Female Preventatives including the 'Interceptor' which sold for three shillings or two for five shillings, the 'enema syringe', and 'Dr. Picot's Ladies' Safety Cones or Female Pessaries' at two shillings six pence per box of twelve or five shillings for one that could be used repeatedly. Similar durability was claimed for the five shilling 'Paragon

Sheath: One of these will (with care) last for years. This is worn by the husband.' The catalogue also listed a range of sex manuals by Allbutt, Trall, Chavasse, Foote, Cowan, and a *Handbook on Phrenology*.

The appearance of the text on phrenology in the advertisement is of interest because this pseudo-science which had by the 1890s lost all credence among the respectable, still enjoyed some popularity amongst the lower classes. Phrenology and birth control were to be curiously related if only because both represented forms of medical self-help condemned by official medicine. This link was reinforced by the phrenologists' assertion that by their analyses of one's mental 'faculties' marriage and motherhood could be improved. Lydia Folger Fowler of the Fowler family who dominated the phrenological movement in New York was the second American woman to receive a medical degree and the first to hold a medical professorship.[20] In her own works she did not defend contraception but her British followers took this step. J.B. Keswick, a phrenologist and hydropathic practitioner began *Woman: Her Physical Culture* (1895) with a discussion of the usefulness of phrenological charts in establishing good conjugal relations and then proceeded to provide a remarkably full account of the woman's right to limit her fertility. He discussed menstruation and the necessity of girls being informed of its function. The claim that many women remained ignorant of such facts of life was illustrated by the account of one's complaint: 'When I was married, I was totally in the dark respecting this part of my nature; and when my first baby was within a few minutes of the portals of existence, I positively did not know where it was coming from.'[21] The knowledgeable woman, Keswick asserted, did not, as many claimed, have low sexual desires; her restraint was occasioned by fear of pregnancy. In his discussion of contraception there was a peculiar juxtaposition of ideas; the first being that a woman had the right to control her own body, and the second, that parents had to avoid spreading their limited stock of 'vitality and life force' over too many children. On these premises Keswick criticised doctors for not informing their patients on how to limit pregnancies. It was his opinion that the use of drugs or alum after intercourse was dangerous, cold water injections ineffective, and the sponge unreliable. Withdrawal he acknowledged as the most popular method but he thought it too was injurious. 'A sheath for the male organ has been recommended. This is safe so long as it does not burst. The loss is principally a magnetic loss in using the cover for the male organ.' The author preferred female methods such as, '. . .an injection of sweet oil into the womb before sexual intercourse. To do this it is necessary to have a proper enema for the purpose, which can be supplied, under cover, post free, for four shillings, from the author. . .The female pessary is also perfectly safe, when it is not convenient for a lady to use the oil enema. This can be used without the knowledge of the husband.'[22] Ending on this conspiratorial note Keswick listed the prices for his enemas, syringes, douches, and character readings from photographs.

There were many cases of this same bizarre mix of pseudo-scientific and sexual knowledge. In 1891 Henry Loader, a phrenologist of Newcastle, was charged with selling, along with other lewd material, *The Wife's Handbook*.[23] In 1902 Ida Ellis, a self-proclaimed expert in phrenology and palmistry, produced a study of birth control entitled *Modern Views on the Population Question*. This tract was notable for the fact that it provided an account of one extreme form of contraception: 'By taking small doses of arsenic male vigour is destroyed, which renders a man incapable of begetting children, but it also shatters the strongest constitution and produces many evils.' Ellis was equally critical of extended nursing, the 'safe period,' and the taking of drugs to induce miscarriage: '"Prevention is far better than cure", as the old adage puts it and there is happily no law to prevent the use of contraceptives.'[24] In 1891 Ernest May established *The Malthusian Herald* which in turn became the *Hygienic Advertiser* to advertise both his sex tracts and health food products. In their columns jostled announcements for 'Gem Bread' pans, the 'Ida' nut grinder, Cadbury's Cocoa, Gottschling's Healtheries' 'Mouthcloser' — which assured a closed-mouthed sleep — and the sex manuals of Stockham, Foote, Nichols, and Allinson.[25] What all of this suggests is that the idea of birth control already had a place in the working classes' own scientific sub-culture and therefore the adoption of family limitation did not signify a capitulation to the teachings of neo-Malthusians or eugenists.

The Malthusian League rarely acknowledged the wide range of commercial works on procreation which were advertised in the popular press. The best selling appeared to have been Dr T.R. Allinson, *A Book for the Ladies* and Johnston Douse, *A True Remedy for Poverty! A New Treatise on the Population Question for the Married of Both Sexes* which boasted in 1895 of twenty-seven editions. They were followed by Dr D. Lalor, *Physiological View of Marriage,* Andrew White, *The Husband's Handbook,* M.A. Dumas, *A Treatise for the Ladies,* Dr J.A. Barnes, *The Female Friend and Adviser,* William Wakefield, *The Wife's Doctor,* the anonymous *To Married People, A Book of Useful Recipes,* and a variety of publications that claimed to contain 'invaluable information' by which marriage was 'made easy'. The newspapers and the manuals also carried information on contraceptive appliances. Allinson advised his readers of W.E. May's 'Domestic, Medical, Surgical and Hygienic Specialties' and Allbutt praised W.J. Rendall's soluble quinine pessaries. Because there was no legislation in England such as the American Comstock Laws which forbade the advertisement and sale of contraceptives there is little in the way of legal records by which one could establish the extent of the marketing of 'surgical and India rubber appliances'.[26] We do know at least that the demand was such that by the 1890s a number of firms had entered the market. E. Lambert and Sons of Dalston which in the twentieth century was to emerge as the leading provisioner of contraceptives was established in 1877. It had as its competitors such firms as The Surgical Rubber Company, A. Dumas' Surgical Appliances, and the Hygienic Remedy Company.[27] These companies in turn produced their own handbills, catalogues, and sex manuals. An example was the shop of W.R. Harrison on Holywell Street which distributed under the name of 'W. George' *Words of Wisdom on Courtship and Marriage.* It contained advertisements for abortifacients, the 'New Menstrual or Period Protector for Ladies', and the 'Malthusian Outfit' which consisted of four rubber sheaths, two skin sheaths, one check pessary, one sponge, and one enema.

It might be thought that if one avoided passing surgical shops, refused to pick up handbills, and ignored the suggestive advertisements of the cheap press it would have been possible to remain ignorant of the sale of contraceptives. Such was not always the case. Even dressmaking journals such as *Myra's Journal* or a religious paper such as *The Rock: A Popular Church of England Newspaper* carried information on how to avoid pregnancy. The social purity movement periodical the *Sentinel* warned that even the most respectable papers sometimes unwittingly carried 'blind' advertisements. The customer who wrote inquiring after a vaguely defined product received by return post a flood of information on 'men only' aids. Similarly those who used the press to announce a birth or marriage brought down on themselves a deluge of birth control leaflets. In 1891 a Mr H. Young was charged under the Post Office Act for using the mails to badger those whose names he found in the birth columns. He had charged a guinea for his information and used that traditional establishment for the exchange of sexual advice by men, the barbershop, as his mail drop.[28]

Even with the commercialisation of contraceptives it was still true that many would not be used by working-class couples until well into the twentieth century. Catholic families which were in the main working class would have additional religious reasons for shunning them. Others simply found them too expensive, or associated them with prostitution, or as in the case of the douche, found they required a water supply and privacy which was not always available in the working-class home.[29] Yet this additional publicity in favour of birth control did make the general public increasingly aware of the feasibility of limiting family size. And this in turn played a role in making women increasingly impatient with husbands who showed no interest in avoiding unwanted pregnancies. The investigations of the Women's Co-operative Guild provided ample evidence that working-class women were struggling to establish the right to control their own bodies. One contributor to *Working Women and Divorce* (1911) insisted that men, '. . .should learn respect for women and sexual self-restraint'. Another complained, 'No one can possibly imagine what it is unless you go through it, to feel you are simply a *convenience* to a man.'[30] In *Maternity: Letters from Working Women* (1915) the Guild offered further testimony. 'But no amount of State help can help the sufferings of mothers', wrote one woman, 'until the men are taught many things in regard to the right use of the organs of reproduction, and until he realizes that the wife's body belongs to herself. . .'[31]

Other women did more than just complain. F.W. Newman angrily declared in the 1880s that 'benevolent ladies' were spreading birth control information. In 1896 Julia Dawson recommended in the columns of the *Clarion* a birth control tract which led to it soon being sold out, no doubt because it contained information on how pessaries of cocoa butter and quinine could be made at home. Ada Slack attempted to have the subject of fertility control discussed by the Women's Co-operative Guild in Accrington and it was reported that some 'advanced women' were similarly active in Lancaster. In Elderton's analysis of the decline of fertility in the north of England there were a number of references to restlessness amongst working-class wives. In Leigh, 'One man visits the town and gives "Lectures to Women Only", when various sexual matters are discussed and information is given. This is followed by the sale of various medicines and appliances, vaginal syringes, preventive pessaries etc.' In Gorton it was reported that, 'The subject is freely talked about and openly discussed in the workshops where girls and young women work, and also during the dinner hour. . .The married women have frankly told our correspondent that they make their husbands take precautions to prevent conception, the two methods of prevention being in use the sheath and coitus interruptus.'[32]

Hannah Mitchell's autobiography *The Hard Way Up* provides a
graphic account of the way in which a working woman at the turn of
the century came to the decision of insisting on the right to protect
herself from pregnancies. She at first feared even marriage because she
had seen how it soon reduced girls to 'prematurely aged women'.

Probably I should have hesitated, even then, but for the newer ideas
which were being propounded by the Socialists. Men and women
were talking of marriage as a comradeship, rather than a state where
the woman was subservient to, and dependent on, the man. Limiting
the population as a means of reducing poverty was one of the new
ideas, new to me anyhow.

She gave up her eighteen shilling a week job, married, took in
dressmaking, and '. . .soon realized that Socialists were not necessarily
feminists in spite of the item in their programme affirming their belief
in the complete social and economic equality of women with men.'
Her husband failed to recognise her contributions to the family budget
but more importantly was indifferent to her suffering in childbirth.
'One thing emerges clearly from much bitter thinking at that time, the
fixed resolve to bring no more babies in the world. I felt it impossible
to face again either the personal suffering, or the task of bringing a
second child up in poverty.' Similar feelings of resentment were
attributed by an Edwardian daughter to her mother: 'My mother
nursed a bit of bitterness because she had a big family and would have
liked to have done different. . .' Such situations, as Cicely Hamilton had
pointed out, must have been common when women had pregnancies
forced on them. Mitchell concluded, '. . .that although birth control
may not be a perfect solution to social problems, it is the first and the
simplest way at present for the poor to help themselves, and by far the
surest way for women to obtain some measure of freedom.'[33]

What methods of contraception would women have employed? Until
at least the Second World War coitus interruptus was the most popular
form of contraception in England. This meant that women would have
to ensure that their husbands were 'careful'. For those who could
afford them there were various female appliances such as the douche,
pessary, and diaphragm. That the latter two were often used, despite
male hostility, is suggested by the fact that a common claim of
advertisers was that they could be used 'without a husband's knowledge'.
Home-made versions were produced; the sponge and the pessary made

of lard or margarine and flour. Extended nursing and attempts to establish a 'safe period' were also continued in an effort to at least space births. In their determined struggle to control their own bodies women revealed remarkable daring and ingenuity. Dr R.L. Dickinson stated that during the First World War some women actually preferred work in factories where lead was used, '. . .in the expectation, often warranted, that it would render or keep them sterile'.[34] Simple abstinence was, of course, the safest way of avoiding pregnancies but for women with unthinking husbands it called for the greatest skill of all.

> I'd sit up at night, after my husband had gone to bed. [relates Aida Hayhoe] He say, 'Aren't you coming to bed?' I say, 'I've got to mend these before I go to bed. They'll want them in the morning. You can go but these have got to be done tonight.' . . .See, I had three children. And I didn't want no more. My mother had fourteen children and I didn't want that. So if I stayed up mending, my husband would be asleep when I came to bed. That were simple, weren't it?[35]

Notes

1. *Malthusian* (March 1881), p.203; (May 1881), p.223; Robert Tressel [Robert Noonan], *The Ragged Trousered Philanthropist* (London, 1955 [1st edn 1914]), pp.24, 26, 296.
2. *New Age* (23 May, 1908), p.71.
3. Leno, *The Aftermath with Autobiography of the Author* (London, 1892), p.29.
4. Cooper, *The Life of Thomas Cooper* (London, 1872), p.93; Burns, *The Autobiography of a Beggar Boy* (London, 1855), p.116.
5. Miller, *Courtship and Marriage* (London, 1861), pp.12, 13, 23; Solly, *Working Men: A Glance at Some of Their Wants* (London, 1863), pp.13-14; and see R. Detroisier, *On the Necessity of an Extension of Moral and Political Instruction Among the Working Classes* (Manchester, 1831).
6. Thomas Cooper, *Eight Letters to Young Men of the Working Classes* (London, 1851), p.9; for attacks on abortion see James Burns, *Three Years Among the Working Classes in the United States* (London, 1865), pp.67-8, 78.
7. See Brian Harrison, 'Under the Victorians', *Victorian Studies,* 10 (1967), pp.258-61; R.Q. Gray, 'Styles of Life, the "Labour Aristocracy" and Class Relations in Later Nineteenth Century Edinburgh,' *International Review of Social History,* 18 (1973), pp.428-452; Stephen Reynolds, *A Poor Man's Home* (London, 1909).
8. See for example Anon., *Morality of the Masses: Who is Responsible?* (London, 1884); Andrew Mearns, *The Bitter Cry of Outcast London* (London, 1883).
9. George Meek, *Bath-Chair Man by Himself* (London, 1910), pp.130, 170; Author Reid, *The Pleasures of Matrimony* (Glasgow, n.d.), pp.16-7; on courting see

Joseph Lawson, *Progress in Pudsey During the Last Sixty Years* (Stannington, 1887); Ted Willis, *Whatever Happened to Tom Mix?* (London, 1970); Dereck Thompson, 'Courtship and Marriage in Preston Between the Wars, *Oral History*, 3 (1975), pp.39-44; on sexual images in work songs see Martha Vicinus, *The Industrial Muse: A Study of Nineteenth-Century British Working-Class Literature* (London, 1974), pp.30, 40-2, 290.

10. G.S. Jones, 'Working-Class Culture and Working-Class Politics in London, 1870-1900: Notes on the Remaking of a Working Class,' *Journal of Social History,* (1974), pp.460-508.

11. Graham, *The Social Problem* (London, 1886), p.440. The death rate after the 1860s fell by 15 per cent; for children 1-5 by 33 per cent, yet for infants under one it remained high. See 'Supplement to the 65th Annual Report of the Registrar General,' *Parliamentary Papers,* 18 (1905), cv.

12. Reynolds, *Seems So! A Working-Class View of Politics* (London, 1911), p.266.

13. James Marchant, (ed.), *The Declining Birth Rate: Its Cause and Effects* (London, 1917), p.9; Norman E. Himes, *Medical History of Contraception* (London, 1936), p.238; R. and K. Titmuss, *Parents' Revolt: A Study of the Declining Birth Rate in Acquisitive Societies* (London, 1942), pp.66, 73.

14. On women's work and fertility see *John Innes, Class Fertility Trends in England and Wales 1876-1934* (Princeton, 1938), p.45; Roger Smith, 'Early Victorian Household Structure: A Case Study of Nottinghamshire,' *International Review of Social History,* 15 (1970), pp.78-9; on the plight of women in areas where work outside the home was limited see Lady Florence Bell, *At the Works: A Study of a Manufacturing Town* (London, 1907); Wil Jon Edwards, *From the Valley I Came* (London, 1956), p.186; N. Dennis, F. Henriques, C. Slaughter, *Coal is Our Life: An Analysis of a Yorkshire Mining Community* (London, 1956), pp.208-9.

15. Ethel M. Elderton, *Report on the English Birth Rate* (London, 1914), p.105; on one working-class family's radical support of birth control see C. Stella Davies, *North Country Bred: A Working-Class Family Chronicle* (London, 1963), p.101.

16. 'Race Suicide,' *The Hibbert Journal,* 14 (1915-1916), p.752.

17. Thompson, *The Edwardians: The Remaking of English Society* (London, 1975), p.71.

18. Webb, *Industrial Democracy* (London, 1887), II, p.639; P.W. Kingsford, *Victorian Railwaymen: The Emergence and Growth of Railway Labour* (London, 1970), pp.179-80.

19. John U. Farley and Harold J. Leavitt, 'Population and the Private Sector,' *Journal of Social Issues,* 23 (1967), pp.135-42.

20. See Lydia F. Fowler, *Woman, Her Destiny and Maternal Relations; or Hints to the Single and Married* (London, 1964); Angus McLaren, 'Phrenology: Medium and Message,' *Journal of Modern History,* 45 (1974), pp.86-97.

21. Keswick, *Woman: Her Physical Culture* (London, 1895), I, pp.87-8.

22. Keswick, *Woman,* III, pp.107, 108, 109; and see Keswick, *Sexual Physiology* (Carlisle, 1891).

23. *Malthusian* (February 1892).

24. Ellis, *Modern Views on the Population Question* (London, 1902), p.12.

25. *Malthusian Herald* (June 1891); *Hygienic Advertiser* (1891-1892).

26. See Anthony Comstock, *Frauds Exposed* (New York, 1880) and *Traps for the Young* (New York, 1883).

27. Lamberts were tried for the sale of *The Wife's Medical Handbook* and preventive appliances; *Malthusian* (February 1899), p.12; see also John Peel, 'The Manufacture and Retailing of Contraceptives in England,' *Population Studies,* 17 (1963), pp.113-5.

28. On Young's trial see *Malthusian* (November 1891), p.81; see also the trials of James White (January 1911), p.3; T.W. Stewart (January 1914), p.2. It was reported that advertisements for syringes were even found in theatrical programmes. See Elphinstone Begbie, *A Private Letter from E.B. to J.S. [John Swiney] on the Birth Rate Question* (London, 1905); *Sentinel* (May 1900), p.81; Peter Fryer, *The Birth Controllers* (New York, 1966), p.184; and on sales of both contraceptives and abortifacients see 'Report from the Select Committee on Patent Medicines.' *Parliamentary Papers,* 9 (1914), pp.30-2, 223-9, 274 and 'Report from the Joint Select Committee on Lotteries and Indecent Advertisements,' *Parliamentary Papers,* 9 (1908), pp.400-15, 457, 475.

29. Mrs Ring, a member of the Industrial Law Committee and the Women's Industrial Council, explained why many working-class women still resorted to abortion: 'Methods of prevention are disagreeable and difficult, as well as being expensive. Alum in cold water and so on are awkward, and properly working syringes, and the sponge and rubber articles, are very often difficult to buy, and are sometimes apt to irritate.' Marchant, *Declining Birth Rate,* p.279. In Lewis-Faning's sample only sixteen per cent of the women married before 1910 who practised birth control used appliances; the rest relied on withdrawal. E. Lewis-Faning, *Report on an Enquiry into Family Limitation and Its Influence on Human Fertility During the Past Fifty Years. Papers of the Royal Commission on Population. Volume One* (London, 1949), pp.7-10.

30. *Working Women and Divorce* (London, 1911), pp.38, 70.

31. *Maternity: Letters from Working Women* (London, 1915), pp.27-8 and see pp. 48, 65, 68.

32. On Dawson see *Malthusian* (February 1896), p.14; on Slack, *Malthusian* (August, 1897) and her letter asking for 'Sex Hygiene classes for married women' to the Manchester *Cooperative News,* (15 March, 1913); Elderton, *Report,* pp.34, 61.

33. Mitchell, *The Hard Way Up: The Autobiography of Hannah Mitchell, Suffragette and Rebel* (London, 1968), pp.88-9, 99, 102; Thompson, *Edwardians,* p.58.

34. Advice on the use of the douche was carried in the medical column of the Manchester *Cooperative News;* on pessaries see Robert Roberts, *The Classic Slum: Salford Life in the First Quarter of this Century* (London, 1973), pp.51-2; for a recipe for a pessary of cocoa butter, boric acid and tannic acid found in the papers of Violet McNaughton who left England in 1909 see Linda Rasmussen *et al., A Harvest Yet to Reap. A History of Prairie Women* (Toronto, 1976), p.72; on Dickinson see Himes, *Medical History,* p.173.

35. Mary Chamberlain, *Fenwomen: A Portrait of Women in an English Village* (London, 1975), p.77.

ABORTION IN ENGLAND, 1890-1914

The idea and practice of birth control not only differed from class to class; it differed from sex to sex. Women were harder hit by a pregnancy whether it was desired or not and it followed that their attitudes towards family limitation would necessarily be distinct from those of men. This issue has been overlooked by historians and demographers who have focused on only one means of birth control — contraception. Assuming that the decline in fertility was a consequence of a diffusion of new knowledge they have concentrated on the role of mechanical contraceptives. They have in the process overlooked the importance of two traditional methods of fertility control: abstinence and abortion.[1] The lack of interest in abortion is especially surprising. At a time when coitus interruptus was the most widely used method of contraception numerous women would inevitably have discovered that a 'mistake' had been made. What then? Clearly those who were intent on limiting family size would now have to contemplate the option of abortion as a second line of defence.

Abortion has received little attention from historians because it has not been viewed as a 'respectable' subject of research. Quantifiers, moreover, are put off by the difficulty, if not impossibility, of establishing the incidence of acts which were illegal and therefore hidden from public scrutiny.[2] One suspects, however, that a third reason for the lack of discussion of even the possible importance of abortion is the fact that the practice was a female form of birth control. Historians and demographers have until recently been reluctant to accept the notion that women would play an active part in determining family size.

The importance of the study of the history of abortion is that it casts a fresh light on a number of vital questions: women's responses to their physical functions, the medical profession's view of women's health, and male and female attitudes towards sexuality. The problem is that we know very little of the extent of the practice. From 1803 onward the inducement of miscarriage was treated as a statutory crime and so references to it were restricted almost solely to reports of the trials of criminal abortionists. The number of court cases involving such people is of some interest but it of course bears no necessary relationship to the actual number of women seeking to terminate their

own pregnancies by the use of traditional folk remedies or new patent
medicines. Not surprisingly we have only allusions to abortion by
women who sought them.[3] We do have, however, a fairly full record
of the activities of one London-based medicine company which in the
1890s was selling tonics that paraded as abortifacients.[4] A short history
of this enterprise and the revelations occasioned by its collapse is
instructive. It shows how the unscrupulous could use the law against
abortion to prey on helpless women. In this chapter I intend, however,
to provide more than the story of one sensational case of fraud and
extortion. I will go on to argue that if women resorted to quack cures
it was because the medical profession was withholding from them
information necessary for the control of their own fertility. I will
suggest that the development of new methods of birth control and the
controversy over their use at the turn of the century took place in the
presence of a reality not yet fully perceived by historians — a
widespread tradition of abortion based on folk remedies. Finally, I will
advance the argument that the fact that significant numbers of women
(including working-class women) sought abortions is strong evidence
that they were not passive in relation to their own fertility: they wanted
to control it and were willing to go to considerable lengths to do so.

In April of 1896 Richard, Edward and Leonard Chrimes acquired a
London office in the Imperial Buildings, Ludgate Circus. Office is
perhaps too grand a term to use. What the Chrimes rented was a room,
the street side of which was covered by a large sign trumpeting the
benefits of Bovril. This unfurnished room, taken in the name of
'H.F.B. Montrose', was to be little more than a mail drop.

The brothers had been already involved for some time in a number
of semi-legal business ventures and now, after attempts at launching a
magazine had failed, turned to the sale of 'female remedies'. The
product they were to sell by mail from their Ludgate establishment was
a simple blood tonic that came in the form of blue and pink pills and
a mixture. It was a quite harmless medicine made up in wholesale lots
by a respectable Leicester chemist, a Mr Wand. In their sales
promotions, however, the brothers implied that their pills were in fact
abortifacients. A typical advertisement read:

Ladies Only

THE LADY MONTROSE
— MIRACULOUS —
FEMALE TABULES

> Are positively unequalled for all
> FEMALE AILMENTS. The most OBSTINATE
> obstructions, Irregularities, etc.
> of the female system are removed in
> a few doses.[5]

Such advertisements were sent out to a variety of publications and it was later reported that the Chrimes spent up to two thousand pounds on advertising. The expenses were especially heavy because the papers knew what the products were supposed to be and accordingly charged five times the usual amount for their insertion. The advertiser's task was, while remaining within the letter of the law, to come as close as possible to declaring that the product in question would precipitate a miscarriage.

Business was sufficiently brisk to warrant the Chrimes setting up a number of letter drops. In 1896 Edward rented a second office at 7 Pleydell Street in the name of 'Mr. Knowles.' In May, 1897 it was enlarged to two rooms and the police were later to state that it received a steady stream of registered letters. It was from this office that 'The Panolia Company' handled the sale of another wonder drug — 'Panolia.'

The Chrimes brothers' business operated as follows. A woman who was pregnant, or at least who thought she was, and wished for whatever reason to terminate her pregnancy would come across an ad for 'Lady Montrose' pills. Having written for information she would receive in return a printed and lithographed order form on which she was required to enter her name and address. After having sent off the order she would either receive the 'Lady Montrose' tablets or a further letter informing her that a far more effective abortifacient was available — 'Panolia'. It was part of the Chrimes' ploy to claim that the very fact that 'Panolia' was not openly advertised was proof of both its power and its superiority to competing patent medicines. Its price ranged from three shillings six pence to thirty-two shillings for 'extra strength'. If a woman complained that she had no success with one product she would be steered to another and if this in turn failed she would be offered a more powerful and more expensive dose. All the products were completely useless. One can only imagine the growing terror of the woman who, as she paid ever greater sums for medicines, found her condition increasingly difficult to conceal and the possibility of any safe termination of pregnancy increasingly remote.

The Chrimes' enterprise worked very well — so well that they opened a third office at One Bouverie Street which was connected by an internal passage with 7 Pleydell Street. The Bouverie Street room was rented by Edward for the 'Mona Company' which sold the 'Mona Specific' which like 'Panolia' was to be forced on clients who had enquired about 'Lady Montrose' tablets. The brothers also had an office at 89 Farringdon Street rented in the name of 'Bradbury Brothers' but to what particular use it was turned remains unclear.

The Chrimes' operation was almost fool-proof. In selling cheap, useless tonics at exorbitant prices to desperate women seeking abortion — a criminal act — the Chrimes ran no risks. The woman who finally realised that the products she had purchased were worthless could not complain to the authorities, would perhaps not even inform her family, for fear of implicating herself. On the other hand the woman who mistakenly believed she was pregnant, took the pills and found that she was no longer would become a believer in such quack remedies and might very well pass on her ill-founded information to friends.

The only apparent risk the brothers ran was that of being exposed by the press. Indeed the *Star* did run a story on Richard Chrimes organising a fraudulent competition involving a hair soap he was selling from the Farringdon Street office. Presumably the paper was put onto the case by a dissatisfied customer. It was a grim irony that the selling of reputed abortifacients — the use of which was a criminal offence — was a less hazardous proposition than the hawking of hair soaps. And there was the further irony that all the Chrimes' activities were taking place within a few blocks of the Central Criminal Courts at the Old Bailey.

The Chrimes brothers' business might have profitably continued for years and escaped the notice of both the authorities and the historian had they not decided in the fall of 1898 to blackmail the women they had already swindled. It will be recalled that clients had been required to send their names and addresses to the Montrose company. Over the course of two years these have been carefully saved by the brothers and pasted into ledgers. By 1898 they had more than 10,000 on file. Whether or not the idea of extortion had been part of their plan from the very beginning, though it seems likely, is not terribly important. The point is that now the Chrimes were in a position, thanks to the law against abortion, to attempt to extort a few pounds from each of their past victims with the threat of revealing to the world her purchase of an abortifacient.

The first thing needed for the venture was a new letter drop which would not compromise the brothers' other schemes. On 10 September, 1898 Leonard took an office in the name of 'Mr Charles J. Mitchell' at the Trafalgar Buildings on Northumberland Avenue. This office was not located in the City as were the Chrimes' earlier establishments; it was presumably chosen because its proximity to Trafalgar Square provided it with a solid, respectable-sounding address.

Two days later on 12 September the brothers purchased twenty-five reams of paper and a cyclostyle for four pounds sixteen shillings. At the same time they ordered printers to prepare 12,000 letter-heads and an equal number of addressed envelopes. The names and addresses for the latter were delivered to the printers in the forms of slips of paper pasted into forty-two ledgers.

The actual blackmail letter had to be prepared by the brothers themselves. To cover their tracks they took a typewriter on trial offer — typed and then cyclostyled the threatening letter — and returned the machine to the dealer on 6 October. The letter read as follows:

Trafalgar Buildings
Northumberland Avenue
October, 1898

Madame

I am in possession of letters of yours by which I can positively prove that you did on or about___commit, or attempt to commit, the fearful crime of abortion by preventing or attempting to prevent yourself giving birth to a child. Either of these constitute a criminal act punishable by penal survitude, and legal proceedings have already been commenced against you and your immediate arrest will be effected unless you send me, on or before Tuesday morning next, the sum of £2 2s, being costs already incurred by me, and your solemn promise on oath as before God that never again, by whatever means, will you prevent, or attempt to prevent yourself giving birth to a child. No notice whatever will be taken of your letter unless postal orders (cheques, stamps, &c will not be accepted) for the above amount and enclosed therein and received by me on the aforesaid day. Failing to comply with these two requests, you will be immediately arrested without further warning. All legal proceedings will be stopped on receipt of the £2 2s, &c, and the incriminating documents, letters &c., which I hold of yours will be returned, and you will hear nothing further of the matter.

I am, Madame, yours &c
(Signed) Chas. J. Mitchell
Public Official

N.B. — Communications must only be sent through the post.[6]

There was still the danger that the police might catch wind of the affair and have the Trafalgar Building watched. Therefore the next problem was to recruit a go-between who, unaware of the crime in which he was innocently involved, would pick up the letters and deliver them to the brothers far from London. On 22 September Norman John Gibson answered an advertisement for a post as junior clerk at the Trafalgar Building. His employers — the Chrimes — told him he would start work on 26 September at the salary of eighteen shillings a week. Young Gibson had almost no work to do but the brothers did tell him, that he was to be entrusted with an important task in a week or two's time — the transporting of a large number of letters from London to Brighton. In the meantime the Chrimes finished up the last of their preparations which included the closing of one of their offices taken for 'R. Randall and Company' at 73 Ludgate Hill.

By the first week of October all was in readiness. On the sixth Richard withdrew one hundred and fifty pounds from his banking account and purchased the necessary stamps. On the seventh the letters — 8,100 in all — were sent off. Every precaution was taken to prevent anyone from accidentally stumbling upon the plot. The letters were sent in three envelopes — an outer one, one for the returned funds, and a safety envelope which requested the post office, should the letter open accidentally, to return to sender.

Once the letters were in the post the Chrimes left London, Gibson having been instructed to pick up all mail delivered to the Northumberland Avenue office on 8 October and bring it to them in Brighton in three large canvas bags on the 10.55 a.m. train. Here the brothers committed their first serious blunder. They had miscalculated the efficiency of the postal service — Gibson found no letters awaiting him. The Chrimes had also apparently forgotten that the eighth was a Saturday which meant that when Gibson was sent back to London he had to be told to wait until Monday, the tenth, before making the trip again.

But what of the women who had received the blackmail letter? The Chrimes were counting on their victims being terror stricken at the thought of a husband, a parent, an employer, a policeman hearing of their attempts to precipitate a miscarriage. The brothers' belief that even those women who had realised the ineffectiveness of the exorbitantly-priced pills feared public disclosure and prosecution sufficiently to pay was borne out by the pitiful pleas that began to arrive at the Trafalgar Building. One woman who had given birth to her child wrote in confusion and consternation,

Dear Sir,
I am very sorry I have done wrong. I did not know I had done wrong
to myself or anyone else. . .But if I have done wrong I ask you to
forgive me, as I did not know I was doing wrong. I will promise that
I will never do wrong any more, for Christ's sake. Amen.[7]

The letter contained the demanded two pounds two shillings as did one
from a servant girl who, though protesting the fact that she had not
been pregnant, feared dismissal if her employer was informed of her
situation.

Dear Sir — I write in answer to your letter and also enclosing two
guineas. I want you to return the paper which you hold against me,
and I promise not to repeat what I have done as long as I live. . .I
should not like my missus to know, else I shall lose my situation.
Hoping you will send the paper by return of post and stick to your
promise not to bother me any more about it. Send a receipt back for
the £2 I have sent you. The reason I have not sent £2 2s was I could
not get a postal order on Saturday.[8]

Other letters begged for time to collect the necessary amount.
When Gibson arrived at the Trafalgar Building on the morning of
the tenth there were four hundred and seventy-five letters containing
two hundred and forty pounds awaiting him. So were the police. A
Mrs. Kate Clifford, wife of a warehouseman and caretaker in the City,
had been a purchaser of 'Lady Montrose' pills. They had no effect and
she had her baby. When the letter from 'Charles J. Mitchell' arrived it
was opened by Mr. Clifford who went through all three envelopes with
Victorian indifference to the privacy of his wife's correspondence. The
letter read, he went straight to the police. Constables were thus lying
in wait and arrested Gibson upon his arrival. The police, having
established that his role was that of go-between accompanied him to
Brighton but the Chrimes failed to appear at the appointed place. It is
likely that they too had been observing the Trafalgar Building and
witnessed their man's capture. They immediately went to ground. On
the twelfth Richard sold his house at Brixton and moved to Penge.
It was here that he and Edward were arrested a month later; Leonard
was apprehended 20 November at St. Austell in Cornwall.
Meanwhile each post brought additional letters containing their
pittance or plea for mercy to the Northumberland Avenue office.
Between 14 October and 17 October 1,785 arrived, 413 letters bearing

£819. The response rate achieved by the Chrimes — given the fact that some women undoubtedly gave false names when ordering the drugs, that some had changed addresses, that some could not at such short notice lay their hands on the money demanded, that some were about to reply when the press reported the affair — was remarkable.[9] Eight thousand one hundred letters had been sent out and in the space of a few days close to 3,000 replies were received. And hapless would-be victims continued to write to the brothers' other offices for abortifacients. Eight hundred and seventy-seven orders were pushed through the mail slot of the 'Lady Montrose' establishment at Ludgate Circus between 28 October and 23 November. The Chrimes were not there to receive them. Their trial took place in mid-December, Richard pleading not guilty while his brothers threw themselves on the mercy of the court. All were found guilty; Richard and Edward were sentenced to twelve years imprisonment for 'intent to extort'; Leonard, because of his youth, to seven years.

At first glance it might be assumed that the Chrimes' affair was simply an isolated though sensational case, the work of three ingenious criminals foisting their wares on the unsuspecting. The real importance of their trial, however, was that it revealed the fact that in late Victorian society thousands of women were seeking to terminate their pregnancies by a variety of means. To put the activities of the Chrimes in perspective it is necessary: first, to note that there was a multitude of charlatans selling the same sorts of medications; secondly, to examine the opposition of the medical profession to the induction of miscarriage and the effect this had in driving women to quacks; and thirdly to establish the attitude of both middle and working-class women towards the control of their own fertility.

A perusal of the literature of the turn of the century indicates that, except for the blackmail attempt, the activities of the Chrimes were in no way unique. Indeed their trial prompted several observers to speak openly for the first time about a question which had been heretofore a taboo subject. A contributor to the *Westminster Review* declared, 'That such practices [abortion] have been common in all classes of society there is great reason to believe, quite apart from the pathetic and startling evidence to that effect furnished by a recent trial for blackmailing.'[10] In the medical journal the *Lancet* appeared a long series of articles on various medications that paraded as abortifacients complete with the list of newspapers that regularly advertised them. According to the *Lancet*'s reporter the charlatans appeared to prefer the Sunday and weekly press.[11] Their advertisements filled the columns of such small London papers as the *Barnet Press*, the *Edmonton Weekly Guardian*, the *Hampstead Express*, the *North London Echo*, the *North Middlesex Echo*, the *East London Advertiser*, the *Middlesex Gazette*, *Hackney Express*, the *Hackney Mercury*, the *South London Mail*, the *Bethnal Green News*, dozens of provincial papers and even a religious publication, the *Rock*. As an example of what could be found one might peruse the pages of *Illustrated Bits* for the year 1899. Ads for 'Ottey's Strong Pills' and 'Towle's Pennyroyal and Steel Pills for Females' ran beside notices for both the classic sex manual *Aristotle's Masterpiece* and Dr. T.R. Allinson's new *A Book for Ladies*. In its report of the Chrimes' trial for 27 November, 1898 *Reynold's Newspaper* declared it surprising that any respectable paper should advertise such wares; in the same issue were a dozen ads for surgical appliances and five for abortifacients. Indeed ads for abortifacients appeared in a wide variety of publications including both Hardie's *Labour Leader* and the feminist journal, the *Freewoman*. In the provinces one could turn to a publication such as *Waddington's List of Fairs* for 1895 which contained the advertisements of 'H.J. Davies, Consulting Chemist, Leeds and Headingley'.

Davies' Emmenagogue Mixture
Is the best Medicine ever discovered for all Irregularities and Obstructions, however obstinate or long standing. Thousands have been relieved by this miraculous remedy and thereby saved illness, trouble and expense. Perfectly harmless, never fails to bring about the desired result, as testified by thousands of married and single females. Price 2/6, 3/6 and 5/- per Bottle.

The same Davies also advertised the sale of 'Malthusian Appliances and Specialties.'

The Chrimes were not unique; indeed their undertaking was to appear a modest venture when compared to the activities of those selling 'Madame Frain's' medications. The trial of its distributors, charged with inciting women to attempt to procure miscarriage, took place less than twelve months after the Chrimes'.[12] In the course of proceedings it came out that William Brown and associates had operated 'Madame Frain's Herbal or Medical Institute' on Hackney Road over the space of several years. From this base they had launched an extravagant advertising campaign that included the sending out of large numbers of women dressed as nurses to the suburbs of London and Manchester to distribute handbills vaunting the efficacy of their product. It, like the pills, was quite useless, sold at prices ranging from seven shillings six pence to twenty-two shillings per bottle and enjoyed a sale which more than compensated for the costs of promotion which were in excess of twenty-eight hundred pounds.[13]

The Chrimes' notoriety was due to their clumsy attempt at blackmailing their victims. There were less risky ways for charlatans to gouge clients. 'Madame Frain' on occasion simply did not send the product which had been paid for and defied the customer to complain to the authorities. The *Lancet* referred to a 'Professor Leslie' who used the shakedown method of forcing his patients to buy ever larger bottles of his concoction — a mixture of senna and rue. And having fallen victim to one quack there remained the possibility of the woman being preyed on by others; quacks were known to sell their lists of customers to fellow practitioners. Thus the cautious firms such as 'E.T. Towle's' and 'Blanchard's', though they were amongst the largest purveyors of abortifacients, if one judged by volume of advertising, were never to be prosecuted.[14]

What was the medical profession's attitude toward abortion? The reader of the leading professional publications of the 1890s such as the *Lancet* and the *British Medical Journal* is struck by the reluctance of physicians to discuss even the issues. The fact that abortion was illegal was taken as reason enough for the profession to continue to support the notion that it was both medically and morally wrong; it would only condone the termination of a pregnancy by a surgeon if a mother's life was in danger and full medical consultation took place. Yet many women had to rely on self-induced abortions as a form of fertility control because doctors, though they might advise the restriction of family size, failed to provide the information on contraception which would make this safely possible. Earlier in the century doctors might have opposed abortion because of the dangers it posed to the mother but by 1900 hospital abortions could be performed with relative safety. They were to be refused to all but a few. Doctors thus forced women to look for aid elsewhere.

The concern that charlatans were not alone in providing such women with real or reputed abortifacients found frequent expression in the medical press of the 1890s. The medical profession held up for special scrutiny the work of midwives, chemists, and herbalists. In 1892 the Select Committee on Midwives Registration heard testimony from doctors that unsupervised midwives would '. . .increase criminal abortion and the criminal still-birth business'.[15] Doctors had always been suspicious of midwives and following the Chrimes' trial they again asked for more stringent controls of this calling. Chemists had also been harshly criticised before the Select Committee referred to above: 'The registration of chemists has not prevented them from selling oceans and tons of medicine each year for the purpose of causing abortion.' After Chrimes the attack was kept up: 'Independently of the advertised nostrums there is nothing commoner than the sale over the counters of prescribing chemists of pills for the purpose of bringing on a delayed menstruation.'[16] Similarly when a herbalist, Nancy Bedford of Wigan, was convicted of selling abortifacients the *Lancet* pontificated, 'It shows what things go on and what crime is practised in the name of herbalism.'[17] But when a physician, Dr James Ady, was tried for abortion the *Lancet* did not call for closer government supervision of *his* profession.[18] Doctors were, in short, falling victim to the irresistible urge of turning the public concern over abortion to their own purposes in order to eliminate the competition of semi-professional medical personnel.

The physicians proved to be as much concerned by the fact that some abortifacients did work as by the fact that quacks sold some that did not. Doctors acknowledged that there were three types that could, by sufficient irritation of the lower bowel, induce expulsion. First, compounds of aloes and iron, secondly compounds of iron and purgative extracts, and thirdly traditional herbal remedies such as savin, ergot of rye, penny-royal, slippery elm, rue, squills, and *hiera picra.*[19]

The effectiveness of the home remedies is difficult to determine. There are reasons to suppose that the dangers posed by such drugs might well have been exaggerated. The general public usually became aware of a woman's attempt at abortion only when something went seriously wrong. A successful inducement of miscarriage would pass unreported. Moreover it is likely that doctors, in their opposition to women's attempt at such 'medical self-help,' would seek to frighten them in portraying the risks run. It is true, that savin, ergot of rye, slippery elm, diachylon, penny-royal and quinine crystals were all potentially poisonous and had to be used with great care. Yet several of these 'home remedies' were to be eventually taken over by professional obstetricians. Ergot is a substance that causes smooth muscle — such as that found in the uterus — to contract and today in the form of ergotmetrine is used both to induce labour and help with the expulsion of the placenta. Slippery elm was used to cause dilation of the cervix, a similar technique was employed until recently in English hospitals using a form of seaweed.[20]

Doctors further recognised that women did not always rely on quacks or chemists but could discover for themselves the sorts of medications they needed. The best example of such medical 'self-help' in the 1890s was the discovery and expanded use of a lead compound, diachylon as an abortifacient. Its employment came to light when the *Lancet* reported in 1898 on the lead poisoning of a twenty-three year old married woman in Sheffield who admitted to 'taking "stuff" to bring on a miscarriage.'[21] A few years earlier there had been an outbreak of lead poisoning in the city due to contamination of the town's water supply. The local women were quick to note that those who had been pregnant had aborted and so they struck on the idea that a small degree of lead could be used to induce miscarriage. Diachylon was readily at hand in every working-class home for use on cuts and sores, as a plaster and for drawing milk away after parturition. Now it was put to a new use. In the words of one doctor, 'I have reason to suspect that in this district the practice of taking diachylon in the form of pills to bring on miscarriage is far more prevalent among the working-class than is generally supposed.' From Sheffield the use of diachylon spread to Leicester, Nottingham, Birmingham and later to Barnsley and Doncaster.[22] What impressed physicians in the increased use of this abortifacient was that it was not a patent medicine or quack cure popularised by handbills or newspaper advertisements but a home remedy passed on by word of mouth.

Hence its slow progress, for the women of this class do not travel farther than to and from their nearest market town or centre. The direction of the spread along the northern part of thickly populated manufacturing populations, subject to bad trade or overcrowding, rather than from the east or west or south, where the country is more sparsely inhabited, can be readily understood.[23]

In 1906 diachylon was still restricted to the area of South Yorkshire, Bedfordshire, Leicestershire, Warwickshire, Notts and East Derbyshire. By the time of the 1914 Parliamentary Report on Infant Mortality its appearance was being reported in Lancashire. An investigator in the Burnley and Nelson region stated that diachylon was retailed in penny-worths and made up into pills. One chemist had admitted to selling fourteen pounds — that is five hundred pennyworths — in one year.[24]

Who were the women seeking abortion and what was their view of their right to do so? The evidence cited above seems to suggest that they were predominantly from the working and lower-middle classes but one has to be cautious in making such a generalisation. As contemporary commentators noted, the middle-class woman because she could afford more skilled methods would less frequently have her abortion brought to the attention of authorities.

Among women of the proletariat it will be readily understood that abortion is carried out less skillfully than in the case of women belonging to the well-to-do class, for the proletarian women are unable to pay for such highly-skilled assistance. It is for this reason that a much larger proportion of criminal abortions are discovered in the case of proletarian women than in the case of the well-to-do.[25]

Indeed the law punished not so much the act of abortion as the poverty of the woman unable to afford a discreet physician.[26] 'I have been told that these abortionists will make from £2000 to £3000 a year in Manchester and other large towns. . .' stated Dr R. Reid Rentoul, 'I know cases in Liverpool, and already eight to ten ladies come to one asking you to perform a criminal abortion.'[27] Rentoul's claim that middle-class women were asking their doctors to provide them with abortions was substantiated by an exasperated contributor to the *Lancet.*

There is apparently a good deal of ignorance on the part of some women about the right and wrong of the matter. Not very rarely a woman will say that when she and her husband married they agreed that there should be no family, that they formed plans of life which the presence of a family would seriously interfere with or completely alter, and she will, after the occurrence of two months' amenorrhoea has suggested pregnancy, come to her medical man asking him, as she may euphemistically term it, to help her and impressing it upon him *more feminarum* that he really *must* help her.[28]

Such a woman, continued the writer, believed that despite the law there was no crime as long as the child was not alive and to argue with her was 'futile'. In his autobiography, *My Father and Myself,* J.R. Ackerley, late editor of the *Listener,* left a candid account of one woman's attempt — his mother's — to obtain an abortion in 1895.

. . .my brother was neither intended nor wanted and efforts, probably of an amateur kind, were made to prevent his arrival. . .

Doctors were confidentially consulted, various homely remedies
prescribed, and all manner of purges, nostrums, and bodily exercises
employed to bring about a miscarriage. But my brother was not to
be quenched.[29]

By 1906 the idea that a middle-class woman might seek abortion was
sufficiently 'thinkable' for Granville-Barker to make it a central issue
in his play, *Waste*. After the death of the heroine as a result of an
unsuccessful attempt at abortion Wedgecroft, a physician, states that
he knows several doctors who could have carried out the operation
quite easily.

I could give you four addresses. . .but of course I wasn't going to
give her one. Though there again. . .if she'd told me the whole
truth. . .My God, women are such fools! And they prefer
quackery. . .look at the decent doctors they simply turn into
charlatans.[30]

In these few lines Granville-Barker summed up what appears to have
been the feelings of many physicians who saw themselves as being
somehow 'victimised' by women demanding their assistance in an
operation that the profession refused to countenance. Following the
Chrimes trial the medical press carried numerous reports of doctors
who were caught in this quandary. They presented themselves as the
sorry recipients of stories told to them by middle-class women who
were either seeking abortion — at times threatening suicide if their
wishes were not complied with — or who had already succeeded in
inducing their own miscarriage. One physician wrote that he knew a
woman who had used a knitting needle to abort herself on thirty-five
separate occasions with no apparent ill effects.[31] The ability of
determined women to attain their goal even in the face of the medical
profession's hostility was greeted by doctors, at least in their public
pronouncements, with expressions of both horror and amazement.

Middle-class women were thus not uninterested in abortion but the
evidence suggests that because of both their ability to call on
professional help and their husbands' greater willingness to employ
contraceptive measures it would not be they but working-class women
who would provide the main clientele for home remedies and quack
cures.[32] Abortion was for a number of reasons a logical form of birth
control for the working-class woman to adopt. Though dangerous it
provided her with some control of her own body. It meant that she

was not completely helpless if her spouse was opposed to contraception.[33]

That some working men were opposed, that they viewed the imposition of fertility control as in some way an attack on their manhood was suggested in the previous chapter. Even at a much later date Richard Hoggart could still report:

> He [the working-class husband] wants food and his own bout of relaxation when he comes home. I suppose this explains why, as it seems to me, the wife is often expected to be responsible for contraceptive practice. . .The husband's shyness and an assumption that this is really her affair often assure that he expects her to take care of it, that he 'can't be bothered with it'.

An unexpected child would often be the result '. . .unless a miscarriage is procured.'[34] In 'Attitudes to Conception' in *Samples from English Culture* Josephine Klein agreed that in working-class homes,

> . . .children are considered altogether the woman's domain. This begins with the regulation of their conception, sometimes to the extent that the woman is blamed for an unwanted pregnancy and fears to tell her husband about it. Husbands are not expected to abstain from sexual intercourse, or to use their own methods of contraception, though a 'good' husband is often commended for being 'careful'.[35]

Thus for the working classes abortion could be both a supplement and an alternative to contraception. In 1910 Havelock Ellis expressed his belief that it was '. . .perhaps specially marked among the poor and hard-working classes'.[36] Referring to what he took to be working women's stoical acceptance of the necessity of abortion, a contributor to the *Malthusian* of March 1890 stated: 'When they are "in for it", they are ready to resort to even criminal means of escaping evils which they would not guard against when they had the power.'

A second reason why working women might view abortion as a 'thinkable' option was that though it posed a serious threat to a mother's health, it could involve the least human cost.[37] In allowing the working-class couple to postpone the decision of controlling pregnancy to a later date in the reproductive cycle abortion gave the family living at a subsistence level time to assess whether they could support an additional child.[38]

Finally it is important to note that women who sought abortion did not consider what they were doing to be wrong. This was brought out in the letters of the Chrimes' victims and evidence of such attitudes were to be found every time serious observers questioned working women. Havelock Ellis stated that women felt no regret and could not understand the legal and medical opposition to abortion. The Birkett Committee on abortion was later to report, 'Many mothers seem not to understand that self-induced abortion was illegal. They assumed it was legal before the third month, and only outside the law when procured by another person.' Working-class women clung to the traditional view that life was not present until the foetus 'quickened'. They did not perceive themselves as pregnant but as 'irregular'. They took pills, not to abort, but to 'bring on their period'. Such attitudes were to be retained well into the twentieth century. An investigator of a Liverpool slum reported:

> For example, [the resident of] Ship Street regards birth control as a sin but abortion before the age of three months a perfectly legitimate measure. . .though so few of the Mums use contraceptives the majority have at some time or other tried to bring on an abortion. Pills, jumping down stairs, etc. are perfectly legitimate up to the end of the third month, after which the woman stops in case she hurts the baby.[39]

Thanks to the recent appearance of autobiographies providing accounts of working-class life at the turn of the century we now have some appreciation of the extent of abortion. In Salford, according to Robert Roberts, the poor relied on quack remedies, penny-royal syrup, hot soapy water, and vet's abortifacients. The older women of the neighbourhoods, the 'Old Queens', continued to favour aloes and turpentine and the 'controlled fall downstairs'. If all else failed the professional was called in.

> The skilled abortionist, though, valued herself by no means cheaply. Our local practitioner, my mother told us long afterwards, was never crude enough to mention fees for kindly services rendered. 'Any trinket will do dear', she used to say — 'in gold'! This meant rock bottom price — half a soveriegn![40]

Walter Greenwood, in *There Was a Time,* reports the words of Mrs Boarder speaking of a neighbour's plight.

'Well, I've had my fill of bringing up a family — not that I've a
complaint against any of 'em, but I want no more. There's Alice
Radcliffe I've just left. Like a bear with a sore head 'cause there's
another on the way. Bottle after bottle 'o pennyroyal she's supped
but it hasn't worked. My God! I thought things were bad enough
for me, but her. . .Eleven of 'em, and now another, and him only
bringing home eighteen shillings a week when he can get it. If he
was mine I'd've told him to blow on it long ago.'[41]

Ted Willis, son of a Tottenham barrow boy, was to learn in later life
that he was the consequence of just such unsuccessful attempts.

It is no wonder then that the thought of an additional child drove
my mother to desperation. She tried everything possible to get rid
of me. She bought gin she could ill afford and drank it neat. She
carried the tin bath in from the back yard, filled it to near-boiling
water and then lowered herself into it, scalding her flesh so painfully
that she was in agony for days. She ran up and down stairs until
she was exhausted. And when all this failed to check my progress,
she procured some gunpowder — enough to cover a six pence —
mixed it with a pat of margarine, and swallowed it. This was
reckoned in those days to be almost infallible, but it succeeded
only in making her violently ill. In the end she reconciled herself to
the inevitable, and I emerged, none the worse for those adventures,
to add another dimension to her problems. She bore me no ill-will
for my perverse behavior: once I was there I was there, to be
accepted and fed and loved along with the others.[42]

Similar practices were uncovered by government inquiries. In Selly
Oak near Birmingham, the local women were able, in the words of a
midwife testifying before the Birth Rate Commission, to hit on a
number of solutions:

Q. You say that preventive measures seem to be known by the
   better class of working people, but the knowledge has not yet
   penetrated down to the labouring classes?
A. In our neighbourhood they make pessaries with cocoa butter and
   quinine. But that is not so much done among the women I meet,
   as by the wives of the well-to-do men in the factories.
Q. Are other preventive means employed?
A. That is the only one I know of. The labouring women among

whom I work do it by bringing on miscarriage.

Q. What are the methods used in producing abortion – diachylon pills?

A. Yes, they get the diachylon from a diachylon plaster and swallow it; that is one thing. Also they boil down copper coins and swallow the liquor; and this has brought on some very bad cases of illness. Then they take quinine crystals to a very great extent; that is the present fashion. And some take quantities of salts.[43]

Midwives estimated that in the Burnley and Nelson area five to forty per cent of the working women drugged themselves at one time or another.

It is difficult to determine if working-class women were seeking recourse to abortion at the turn of the century more frequently than in the past but the increased reportage of such practices was forcing the British public to acknowledge that, given the burdens of working-class motherhood, such measures were to be expected.[44] Commenting on living conditions in Middlesborough Lady Florence Bell declared: 'Nor perhaps can one wonder at the deplorably increasing number of women who take measures to prevent the child from coming into the world at all, a practice which is no doubt spreading in this community.' She went on to quote the words of a woman who had barely survived four pregnancies in four years: ' "It is not right", she said desperately, "It is wicked that a woman should be killed by having children at this rate".'[45] The testimony of such working women concerning the whole issue of child-bearing was collected by the Women's Cooperative Guild. One spoke of those who took drugs because they, '. . .felt they could not carry children, some perhaps because of bad husbands, others because they could not properly feed and clothe those they had.' The same respondent stated that she knew of three women who had lost their lives in such attempts. Another wrote that women were turning to whatever means were necessary to control their fertility: 'Race suicide if you will, is the policy of the workers of the future. Who shall blame us.'[46]

The abortion issue was instrumental in directing social observers finally to give some serious consideration to working women's attitudes towards maternity. It was a sign of the times that the focus of the first novel of Somerset Maugham, a young medical intern completing his obstetrical training in Lambeth, should be the child-bearing experiences of the working women of south London. The novel, which ends with the death of the heroine during miscarriage, begins with a discussion of birth.

> 'You'll be 'avin' your little trouble soon, eh, Polly?' asked one good
> lady of another.
> 'She said she wasn't goin' to 'ave no more, when the last one come.'
> This remark came from Polly's husband.
> 'Ah,' said the stout old lady, who was in the business, and boasted
> vast experience. 'That's wot they all says; but, Lo' bless yer, they
> don't mean it.'
> 'Well. I've got three, and I'm not goin' to 'ave no more, bli'me if I
> will; 'tain't good enough — that's wot I says.'
> 'You're abaht right there, ole gal,' said Polly. 'My word, 'Arry, if
> you 'ave any more I'll git a divorce, that I will.'[47]

The importance of the abortion issue was that it revealed — despite the
assumption of women's passivity in relation to their own fertility — the
extraordinary risks they would run to control it. That they had to
continue to resort to old-fashioned and frequently dangerous remedies
was a consequence of the medical profession's refusal to provide them
with information on contraception. Indeed even the Malthusian
League — the supposed mouthpiece of the birth control movement —
was slow in fulfilling this task. Only from 1913 onwards did it begin to
interest itself in public meetings and fully appreciate the extent to
which working-class women relied on abortion. One of the movement's
leaders, Bessie Drysdale, spoke of a young girl in Sussex who '. . .told
me that she had never heard of preservatives, only of people taking
drugs. . .' (*Malthusian* [Jan., 1911] p.23.) Another wrote to the
Malthusian, 'We know no preservatives though I have taken pills given
me when two months but have always been afraid.' (October 1915
p.76). A husband, asking for information, stated, 'The wife has been
taking a 5s box of capsules to bring on her courses, but it is no good.'
(June 1914, p.44). A 'Mrs. S.' of Middlesborough reported that the
'respectable' had little idea of the extent of illegal operations. 'Any
working man or woman knows that there is any amount of this
business going on, sometimes with terrible results.' (April 1916, p.33).
A 'Mrs. B' of Leeds confessed that her last pregnancy almost drove
her to suicide. 'I did not do so but I did something almost as bad and
which almost cost me my life, leaving me very weak. We are now living
apart, because I would rather lose my husband than live thro' that time
again.' (October 1916, p.76). It was on the basis of this sort of eloquent
testimony that, following the Great War, Marie Stopes was to campaign

for the necessity of the mass diffusion of birth control information.[48]

Little has been written of the practice of abortion at the turn of the century and given the fact that it was a criminal offence it is unlikely that much hard information on its incidence will ever come to light. It has been the purpose of this chapter to serve simply as a reminder that any discussion of birth control is incomplete if the option of inducement of miscarriage is not included. Even when methods of contraception were more widely employed abortion would remain necessary as a second line of defence against undesired pregnancies. This point was to be made by Stella Browne in one of the earliest defences of women's right to abortion. 'The right to prevent the conception of life must logically and justly include the right to remove the life-seed which has been fertilised against the mother's will, either through accident or intention.'[49]

Despite the pronouncements of the legal and medical professions large numbers of Victorian and Edwardian women were to seek abortion. If the activities of the Chrimes and the 'Madame Frains' teach us anything it is that there was then — as there is today — a demand for abortion and if that demand is not met by the medical profession it will be met by others. In an article which appeared in 1907 Irene MacFadyen spelled out the alternatives.

> I need hardly say that I am fully aware that the withholding of recognition by the medical profession and society in general that the mother's claim [to regulate her fertility] is right within proper limits is producing great evils. If the doctor passes by on the other side, the quack is always at hand.[50]

Notes

1. On the role of abstinence see Paul Thompson, *The Edwardians* (London, 1975), p.72.
2. See L.A. Parry, *Criminal Abortion* (London, 1931); Alice Jenkins, *Conscript Parenthood? The Problem of Secret Abortions* (London, 1940); Ministry of Health, Home Office, *Report of the Interdepartmental Committee on Abortion* (London, 1939). On America see the forthcoming book of James Mohr, *Abortion in America: The Origins and Evolution of National Policy, 1800-1900.*
3. See for example the extraordinary letters of Henrietta Stanley to her husband in which she wrote, 'A hot bath, a tremendous walk & a great dose have succeeded. . .' Nancy Mitford, *The Ladies of Alderley* (London, 1938), pp.169-71. Balfour's mistress, Lady Elcho, claimed she had induced her own miscarriage by strenuous bicycling. Kenneth Young, *Arthur James Balfour*

(London, 1963), pp.138-9.
4. The account of the Chrimes affair which follows is based on reports carried in
the *Lancet*, 2 (1898), p.1807; *British Medical Journal*, 2 (1898), p.1270; 1
(1899), pp.110-11; *The Times* (17, 19, 20, 21 December, 1898), London *Star*
(28 September, 14 October, 21 November, 16, 21 December, 1898).
5. Advertisement reproduced in the *Lancet*, 2 (1898), p.1807.
6. Letter reproduced in *The Times* (17 December, 1898).
7. Letter reproduced in *The Times* (20 December, 1898).
8. Letter reproduced in the London *Star* (21 December, 1898).
9. George Ives, *A History of Penal Methods: Criminals, Witches, Lunatics*
(London, 1914), pp.356-7.
10. 'A Crime and its Causes,' *Westminster Review*, p.151 (1899), pp.131-9.
11. 'Quacks and Abortion: A Critical and Analytical Inquiry,' *Lancet*, 2 (1898),
pp.1570-71, 1651-53, 1723-25, 1807-08; 1 (1899), p.174. On indecent
advertisements see also W.A. Coote (ed.), *A Romance of Philanthropy* (London,
1916), pp.158-9; British Medical Association, *Secret Remedies: What They
Cost and What They Contain* (London, 1909) and *More Secret Remedies*
(London, 1912).
12. On the Frain trial see *The Times* (21 November, 1899).
13. *Lancet*, 2 (1899), pp. 111, 1540; *British Medical Journal*, 2 (1899), pp.1583-4.
Quacks recognised that women preferred discussing their medical problems
with other women. In addition to 'Madame Frain' and 'Lady Montrose,'
abortifacients were advertised by 'Widow Welch,' 'Nurse Grey,' 'Nurse Powell,'
'Madame Hypolite,' 'Madame L.,' 'Mrs. C.,' and 'A Lady, the Daughter of a
Late Eminent Physician.' The *Bethnal Green News* advertised, 'Madame
Phoebe's Herbal and Botanical Ladies' College of Health' as '. . .the only
establishment in London where Ladies have the opportunity of consulting
one of their own sex on all Female Ailments and Irregularities.' (1 June, 1895).
14. Even respectable medical companies were to take advantage of the demand
for abortifacients. The 1914 Select Committee on Patent Medicines was told,
'. . .in the instructions headed "Advice for Females" accompanying "Beecham's
Pills" women suffering from "any unusual delay" are recommended to take
five pills a day. The proprietor admitted in evidence that the most common
cause of such delay is pregnancy.' *Lancet*, 2 (1914), p.704; and on Professor
Leslie see *Lancet*, 2 (1898), pp.1651-3.
15. 'Report from the Select Committee of the Midwives' Registration Bill,'
Parliamentary Papers, 14 (1892), p.25; and see Jean Donnison, *Midwives and
Medical Men: A History of Inter-Professional Rivalries and Women's Rights*
(London, 1977).
16. *Lancet*, 1 (1899), p.468; *Parliamentary Papers*, p.31; *British Medical Journal*,
1 (1899), p.110.
17. *Lancet*, 1 (1898), p.238.
18. *Lancet*, 1 (1898), p.242.
19. *Lancet*, 2 (1899), pp.1844-5.
20. For their help in assisting me in gaining an understanding of the possible
efficacy of abortifacients I would like to thank Professor D.J. Gee of the
University of Leeds and the Historians' Medical Information Bureau of
Wadham College Oxford. See also C.J. Polson and R.N. Tattersall, *Clinical
Toxicology* (London, 1959), pp.545-9; C.J. Polson, *The Essentials of
Forensic Medicine* (London, 1963), pp.430-7.
21. George F. Crooke, 'Fatal Case of Acute Poisoning by Lead Combined in
Diachylon,' *Lancet*, 2 (1898), pp.255-6.
22. Crooke, 'Fatal Case,' p.256. J.W. Scott stated that a Dr. Pope reported
plumbism as early as 1893 in Leicester. 'Notes on a Case of Lead Poisoning

from Diachylon as an Abortifacient,' *Quarterly Medical Journal*, 10 (1901-1902), pp.148-52.

23. Arthur Hall and W.B. Ransom, 'Plumbism from the Ingestion of Diachylon as an Abortifacient,' *Lancet*, 1 (1906), p.511.

24. 'Infant Mortality in Lancashire,' *Parliamentary Papers*, 39 (1914), p.70. Diachylon was finally placed on the poison list in 1917.

25. Sigmund Engel, *The Elements of Child Protection* (London, 1912), p.257.

26. Dr William Hitchman reported that the price of a professional abortion ranged from three to thirty pounds. 'Popular Abortion and Infanticide,' *Malthusian* (September, 1883), p.441.

27. 'Select Committee on the Midwives Registration Bill,' p.30.

28. *Lancet*, 1 (1898), p.235. Perhaps the best known case of the 1890s involving a respectable medical man was the trial of W. Maunsell Collins, former surgeon to the Royal Horse Guards, whose patient, Mrs. Uzielli, the wife of a stockbroker, died of septic peritonitis. Collins was tried for murder and sentenced to seven years imprisonment. L.A. Parry, *Some Famous Medical Trials* (London, 1927), pp.40-54. On professional care available to the middle class see also J.A. and O. Banks, *Feminism and Family Planning* (New York, 1964), pp.86-7.

29. *My Father and Myself* (London, 1968), p.49.

30. H.G. Granville-Barker, *Three Plays* (New York, 1909), pp.283-4. *Waste* was to have been put on at the Savoy. As the Examiner of Plays refused it a licence it had its premiere on 24 November 1907 before a select audience at the Imperial Theatre, Westminster. Other plays in which the abortion theme was dealt with at the turn of the century included Frank Wedekind's *Spring Awakening* and Eugène Brieux' *Maternity* which was translated into English by Mrs. Bernard Shaw. See Brieux, *Three Plays* (New York, 1911).

31. *British Medical Journal*, 2 (1898), pp.749, 841-2, 1013-4.

32. On social differences in attitudes toward birth control measures see Earl Lomon Koos, 'Class Differences in the Employment of Contraceptive Measures,' *Human Fertility*, 12 (1947), pp.97-101; Lee Rainwater, *And the Poor Get Children* (Chicago, 1960), pp.54-6.

33. On working-class women and the difficulties of controlling births see M.S. Pember Reeves, *Round About a Pound a Week* (London, 1913), p.102; Margery Spring Rice, *Working Class Wives: Their Health and Conditions* (London, 1939), p.44.

34. *The Uses of Literacy* (London, 1971), p.45.

35. *Samples from English Culture* (London, 1965), II, p.439 and see also M. Young and P. Wilmott, *Family and Kinship in East London* (London, 1957), p.6.

36. *Studies in the Psychology of Sex* (Philadelphia, 1910), VI, p.603.

37. Kingsley Davis and Judith Blake, 'Social Structure and Fertility: An Analytical Framework,' *Economic Development and Cultural Change*, 4 (1955), p.235.

38. Recourse to abortion was attributed in particular to two groups of working women: domestic servants whose employ depended on them having no family and textile factory workers whose family income could be seriously jeopardised by an unexpected pregnancy. See *Lancet*, 2 (1898), pp.1651-3; 'Physical Deterioration Committee,' *Parliamentary Papers*, 32 (1904), p.127.

39. Madeleine Kerr, *The People of Ship Street* (London, 1958), pp.137, 174. See also Moya Woodside, 'Attitude of Women Abortionists,' *The Howard Journal*, 11 (1963), pp.93-112; Madeleine Simms, 'Midwives and Abortion in the 1930s,' *Midwife and Health Visitor*, 10 (1974), pp.114-6; Ellis, *Studies*, VI, pp.601-10.

40. *The Classic Slum: Salford Life in the First Quarter of the Century* (London, 1973), pp.127-8.
41. *There Was a Time* (London, 1967), p.62.
42. *Whatever Happened to Tom Mix* (London, 1970), p.8.
43. James Marchant, (ed.), *The Declining Birth Rate: Its Causes and Effects* (London, 1917), p.274.
44. *Malthusian* (June 1914), 42 estimated that one hundred thousand women a year took drugs to induce miscarriage. One of the first histories of the birth control clinics included the statement: 'The figures obtained at the birth control clinics indicate that there are few mothers of large families who have not at some time attempted abortion.' M. Breed and Edith How-Martyn, *The Birth Control Movement in England* (London, 1930), p.18.
45. *At the Works: A Study of Manufacturing Town* (London, 1915), pp.168-9, 196.
46. Women's Cooperative Guild, *Maternity: Letters from Working Women* (London, 1915), p.46.
47. *Liza of Lambeth* (London, 1951, 1st edn. 1897), p.3. For a reference to abortion in a feminist novel see Lady Florence Dixie, *Gloriana; or The Revolution of 1900* (London, 1890), p.137.
48. Stopes spoke of, '. . .the prevalence and horror of the poor and ignorant woman's attempts at early abortion. . .' *Wise Parenthood* (London, 1926), p.10. See also Annie Besant, *The Law of Population* (London, 1877), p.24 and Dr. H.A. Allbutt, *Artificial Checks to Population* (London, 1918, 14th edn.), p.15.
49. F.W. Stella Browne, 'Women and Birth Control,' in Eden and Cedar Paul (eds.), *Population and Birth Control: A Symposium* (New York, 1917), p.254.
50. 'The Birth Rate and the Mother,' *Nineteenth Century*, 1 (1907), pp.429-35.

CONCLUSION

The First World War swept away many of the ideological preconceptions and the economic conditions which had favoured the large families of the nineteenth century. But its effects should not be exaggerated. The late Victorian sexual iconoclasts so frequently held responsible for popularising a new spirit of scepticism and hedonism in which birth control would be 'thinkable' turn out to be Havelock Ellis, Grant Allen, George Bernard Shaw, and H.G. Wells – the old eugenically-minded social theorists.[1] Even Marie Stopes who in the 1920s freed birth control from the grip of the neo-Malthusians could not, as the name of her organisation testifies – 'The Society for Constructive Birth Control and Racial Progress' – escape the eugenists.[2] Similarly many of the social and economic changes which led to a reappraisal of family limitation were not created, but spurred on by the war. The decline of heavy industry, the rise of the service sector with the dramatic entry of women into white collar work, the continuing reduction in infant mortality, the growth of state interest in the welfare and education of children and the resulting extension of their years of dependence upon parents all contributed to the change. Because it was necessary, birth control would become respectable.

There was no reason why birth control should have been an issue hotly debated by economists, physicians, and politicians. It did, of course, attract the freethinkers as a means of attacking the teachings of the churches, but the religious debate was to be of little importance. The churches' refusal to be drawn into the argument was a demonstration of their abdication to physicians and social scientists of the role of moral censor.

Birth control was really a neutral instrument with the potential of being used to permit either greater freedom or greater social control. It was for this reason that it raised hopes in some, and fears in others. Their combined reactions to it provide an image of the nineteenth century. Pessimistic Malthusians opposed it because it seemed to violate the self-control and discipline which they were seeking to enforce on a nascent industrial work force. Utilitarians and radical artisans saw it as a potential means of individual self-improvement. It was this individualism and the association of fertility control with Malthus' name that in turn led the Owenites and Chartists to permit their attacks on

254

Malthusianism to spill over into a rejection of a couple's right to limit family size. The birth control ideology did have its progressive dimensions which reflected the artisan's interest in medical self-help and the woman's in freedom from undesired pregnancies but these were largely stifled by the establishment of the Malthusian League.

In the latter half of the nineteenth century the response of socialists to birth control demonstrated continuities from earlier decades but also revealed new splits. The issue neatly divided the radical libertarians who saw in contraception a new freedom, from the SDF hostile to all palliatives, from the Fabians who turned to eugenics. Indeed the reaction of the eugenists was a classic example of the way in which the shift occurred from an individualist to a collectivist biologism by those who sought to turn to their own purposes of social control the 'population problem'.

The issue of birth control split the left but, we have suggested, the woman's 'right of self defence' against unwanted pregnancies was a rallying cry which could attract the support of most sections of the women's movement. No less interested in protecting their kind were the members of the British medical profession. Their response to the question was but one indication of the extent to which the profession's concern for power and status could override the interest of the health of its patients.

There was never any pure ideology in favour of birth control; it was always entangled with Malthusian economics or freethought philosophy or eugenic considerations. Similarly there was never any pure opposition; it too carried its burden of social, sexual or political preconceptions. But when all was said and done neither side was going to have that great an effect on the reproductive behaviour of the masses. The employment of means of fertility control by the working class is explained, not by reference to the intellectual debates, but by an examination, first, of its economic and social situation and secondly, of its traditional attitudes towards procreation. And within the working class one would find the crucial differences between the sexes in their attitudes towards the prevention of pregnancies. The employment of birth control would demonstrate, not the diffusion of some new, middle-class, male ideal, but the tenacity of class, cultural, and sexual divisions.

Notes

1. For accounts which attribute to the eugenists the role of sexual rebels see Peter T. Cominos, 'Sexual Respectability and the Social System,' *International Review of Social History,* 8 (1963), pp.18-48, 216-50; and Eric Trudgill, *Madonnas and Magdalens: The Origins and Development of Victorian Sexual Ideas* (London, 1976).
2. Marie Stopes, *Married Love* (London, 1918) and *Wise Parenthood* (London, 1918); and see Keith Briant, *Marie Stopes: A Biography* (London, 1972).

INDEX

Abortion: and abortionists 33-4, 243, 246; eighteenth-century 31-5; inducement by drugs 31, 32-4, 81, 123, 224, 241-8; inducement by mechanical means 244; and middle class 243-44; nineteenth-century 53, 117, 123-5, 126, 130, 135, 147, 181, 207, 210, 231-50; 243-44; therapeutic 240; and working-class 244-50
Abstinence: 127-9, 198-9, 203, 221, 228, 231
Ackerley, J.R. 243
Acton, William 100, 127-8, 131
Adams, W.E. 217
Advertising: of abortifacients 232-3. 238-9, of contraceptives 77, 221-2, 225
Agnodice 31
Aldred, Guy 161, 169, 173, 200-201
Alison, Archibald 62, 66
Allbutt, Henry 112, 132-3, 152, 186, 223, 225
Allen, Grant 210, 254
Allinson, T.R. 181, 224, 239
Amberley, John Russell Viscount, 93, 100, 116, 129-30
Amery, L.S. 188
Anarchism 159, 185-86
Anti-Malthusians 61-75 *passim*, 158-62
'Anti-Marcus' 91
Anti-semitism 152, 166, 189, 190
Aristotle's Works, 28-9, 79, 84, 222, 239
Armstrong, John 29
Asquith, Margot 119
Astruc, Jean 23
Atkins, J.B. 188
Aveling, Edward 110, 177, 178
Ayres, Mary Ann 100

Bagehot, Walter 68
Balfour, Artbur James 154, 250
Banks, J.A. and O. 94, 100, 119
Barker, Joseph 108
Barmby, Goodwyn 73, 74
Barnes, J.A. 224

Barnett, Canon S.A. and Henrietta 189
Barr, James 112
Barry, Martin 125
Base, Benjamin 72
Bax, E. Belfort 162, 165, 172, 179
Baxter, G.R. Wythen 90
Bebel, August 162, 170
Bell, Lady Florence 248
Bentham, Jeremy 51
Bergeret, L.F.E. 130
Besant, Annie 108, 120, 159, 176, 177-9, 185, 186, 189, 204
Bickersteth, Henry 80
Billington-Greig, Teresa 211
Birkett Committee 246
Birth rate: decline of 11, 107, 116, 143, 197, 219
Blackmail 234-7
Blackstone, William 31
Blackwell, Elizabeth 128-9, 131-2, 198, 201, 202, 203
Blanchard's 240
Blatchford, Robert 153, 181, 182
Blundell, James 81, 121
Boer war 133, 141, 148, 184-5, 188, 193
Booth, Charles 141, 142, 145
Booth, William 109
Boswell, James 19-20, 21, 23-4
Bradlaugh, Charles 92-3, 108, 159, 177, 178
Bray, Charles 65
Bray, J.F. 65, 66
Brodum, William 26
Brody, R. and J. 79
Brougham, Lord Henry, 45
Brown, George 131
Browne, F.W. Stella 206-8, 250
Buchan, William 21, 35, 80
Bull, Thomas 123
Bulwer, W.H. 45
Bunting, Mary 202
Burns, James 217
Burns, John 185
Burrows, Herbert 110, 171, 172
Burrows, J. 21
Butler, Josephine 198, 199, 202, 217

Caird, Mona 205

Cam, Joseph 22
Carlile, Richard 50, 52-7 *passim*, 64
    69, 84-5, 90, 92, 93, 95-6, 97
Carlyle, Thomas 62, 90, 92, 166
Carpenter, Boyd 207
Carpenter, Edward 172, 203
Carr, George Shoobridge 183
Cazeaux, Pierre 125
Chadwick, Edwin 90
Champion, H.H. 172
Champneys, Francis 134
Chant, Mrs Ormiston 202
Chapple, W.A. 150, 188
Chartism 44, 66, 69, 73, 92, 107,
    254
Chatterton, Daniel 174-6, 193, 218
Chavasse, P.H. 122, 124, 127, 223
Chemists 241
Chrimes, Richard, Edward and
    Leonard 232-8
Clapperton, Jane Hume 194, 204-5,
    210
Cleave, John 57, 175
Clifford, Kate 237
Coates, Marion 170
Cobbe, Frances Power 202
Cobbett, William 66, 69, 158
Collins, W. Maunsell 252
Combe, Andrew 80
Condorcet, M.J., marquis de 49
Conolly, John 87
Contraception: commercialisation
    of 221-5; methods of: coitus
    interruptus 25-8, 51-2, 95, 119-20,
    122, 130-31, 133, 223, 226-7;
    coitus reservatus 203-4; condom
    21-5, 52, 120-21, 136, 223, 225,
    226; diaphragm 52, 132, 135, 222;
    douche 52, 122-3, 131, 133, 135,
    138, 222, 223-4, 225, 226;
    pessary 121-2, 222, 224, 225, 226,
    227-8, 247; prolonged nursing 67,
    125, 130, 203, 224, 228; 'safe
    period' 125-7, 130-31, 139, 203,
    224, 228; vaginal sponge 51,
    121-2, 131, 223, 225, 227
Conway, Moncure 177
Cookson, Montague 99-100, 156
Cooper, Thomas 217
Corn laws 48-9
Corry, John 21
Cottage Physician 81
Cowan, John 122, 125, 223
Crackenthorpe, Montague: see
    Cookson

Crouch, Thomas 26
Culpepper, Nicholas 34
Curtis, J.L. 79

Darwin, Charles 141, 155, 182
Darwinists 143, 183, 184
Davies, H.J. 239
Dawson, Julia 181-2, 226
Defoe, Daniel 32, 33, 34-5
Dialectical Society 93, 100, 116,
    129, 177
Dickens, Charles 62
Dickinson, G. Lowes 150
Dickinson, R.L. 228
Dilke, Charles 164, 175
Divorce 74, 97, 99
Dixie, Lady Florence 210, 211
Doherty, John 61
Doubleday, Thomas 67, 74, 76, 90,
    92, 127, 195
Douse, Johnston 224
Drysdale, Bessie 249
Drysdale, Charles R. 108, 110, 116,
    129, 132, 144, 148
Drysdale, Charles V. 111, 135, 148
Drysdale, George 92, 93, 96, 98-9,
    108, 114, 120
Duffey, E.B. 117
Dumas, M.A. 224
Dunglinson, Robley 120

Economic change 36, 43, 65, 159,
    218-19, 220, 254
Elcho, Lady Mary Wyndham 250
Elderton, Ethel M. 226
Elliotson, John 125
Ellis, Havelock 147, 245, 246, 254
Ellis, Ida 224
Emigration 48, 159, 174
'Endowment of Motherhood' 146
    148, 189, 192, 206
Engel, Sigmund 151
Engels, Friedrich 159, 170
Eronia 27
Ethelmer, Ellis (Elizabeth
    Wolstenholme Elmy) 172, 200,
    208-9
Eugenics 112, 141-54, 215-16, 254;
    opposition to 153-4, 156, 194,
    206; and socialism 143-4,
    152-3; and women, 145-7
Euthanasia 150, 151, 192
Eversley, D.E.C. 72

Fabianism 153, 177, 186-93, 255

Fallopio, Gabriello 21
Family limitation: and attitudes
    towards children 36, 53, 191-2,
    207-8, 218-20; and education 93,
    147, 188, 218; and health 53,
    83-4, 125
Farrer, W. 26
Fawcett, Henry 47-8, 188
Fawcett, Millicent 47-8, 202
Feminism: and birth control 48,
    94-101, 111, 146-7, 197-208, 255;
    and doctors 202; and eugenics
    199-200, 204, 206, 208
Ferri, Enrico 163
Fisher, Marie C. 176
Foote, Edward B. 123, 223, 224
Foote, G.W. 178-9
Fowler, Lydia F. 123, 223
Frain, Madam 239-40
France 44, 55, 66, 74, 84, 127, 130,
    135
France, Hector 120
Freethought 56-7, 69, 93, 107, 176,
    177
Fryer, Peter 90
Fullham, Stephen W. 90

Galton, Francis 141-2, 144, 146-7,
    148, 150, 187, 206
Gardiner, S. 170
Gaskell, G.A. 184
Gay, Joseph (Francis Chute) 24
Gedge, Johnson 90
George, Henry 159, 175, 177, 180
George, W. (W.R. Harrison) 225
Gibson, N.J. 236-7
Glasier, Katherine Bruce 196, 205
Gleason, R.B. 124
Glover, George 45
Godwin, William 43, 49, 70
Goldman, Emma 169
Graham, James 26
Graham, William 218
Grant, Brewin 97
Granville-Barker, H.G. 244
Gray, John 65
Green, Mary 31
Greenwood, Walter 246
Greg, W.R. 68, 81
Grose, John 22-3, 33
Gross and company 79
Grote, Harriet 48

Halford, S.H. 207
Hall, Charles 75
Hamilton, Alexander 32

Hamilton, Cicely 205, 227
Hancock, Edward 97
Hardie, Keir 109, 196, 239
Harrison, J.F.C. 72
Harte, Richard 99
Haycraft, John Berry 149
Hayhoe, Aida 228
Hayward, Abraham 93
Headlam, Stewart 177-8, 186
Heape, Walter 207
Hennell, Mary 66
Herbalists 34, 241
Hethertington, Henry 57
Hickey, William 20
Hickson, W.E. 65, 67
Himes, Norman 219
Hinton, James 201
Hobhouse, L.T. 156
Hobson, J.A. 153, 183, 184
Hodgkin, Thomas 65
Hodson, John 20
Hoggart, Richard 245
Hollick, Frederick 139
Holmes, J.P. 123
Holyoake, Austin 57, 93
Holyoake, George Jacob 97, 107,
    108, 116
Hood, Thomas 62
Hopkins, Thomas 65
Hunter, Dr 82
Hyndman, H.M. 159, 165

Independent Labour Party 196
Infanticide 39, 51, 53, 88, 90, 91,
    130, 176, 181
Isted, J. 26

Jones, Ernest 66, 92
Jones, Richard 51
Jordan, J. 79
Joynes, J.L. 110, 160-61, 169
'Justitia' 159

'Karezza' 203-4
Kautsky, Karl 169
Kay, J.P. 45, 48, 49
Kempner, N. 159
Kennett, White 25
Keswick, J.B. 223
Key, Ellen 147
Kick Him Jenny 30
Kidd, Benjamin 155, 183
Kingsley, Charles 76
Klein, Josephine 245
Knowlton, Charles 52-7
    passim, 82, 84, 85, 108

Laing jr. Samuel 66
Laing sr., Samuel 66, 74
Lalor, D. 224
Lambert, E., and sons 225
Land reform 66, 159, 174, 177
Lane, Joseph 159
Laurie, James 129
Laverenst, Ann 31
Law: and abortion 31, 231, 234,
    239; and Aldred-Witcop trial,
    173; and birth control 56, 108,
    224, 225, 229-30; and Bradlaugh-
    Besant trial 108
Leake, John 20
Leatham, Isabel 201
Lee, Robert 125
Leno, John Bedford 216
Lewis-Faning, E. 11
Lidgett, Elizabeth 202
Linton, E. Lynn 205
Linton, James 91, 92, 97
Livesy, J. 65
Lloyd, Marie 218
Loader, Henry 224
Longson, William 55
Loudon, Charles 57, 67
Lovett, William 92
Low Life 30
Ludlow, J.M. 62, 65
Ludmerer, K.M. 143
Lyttleton, A. 177

MacFayden, Irene 250
Malthus, T.R. 43-4, 45, 47, 49, 52-3,
    61-6 *passim* 70, 71, 73, 81, 109,
    157, 158, 159, 175, 192
*Malthus: Re-examined in the Light
    of Physiology* 68
Malthusian 109-11, 132, 148, 249
Malthusian League 107-13, 132, 148,
    157, 174, 177, 215, 249
Malthusians 11, 43-51, 62-6 *passim,*
    143; opposition to birth control
    49-51, 254
Mann, Tom 159
Marcet, Jane 46, 62
Marchant, James 134, 198
'Marcus' 90
Marriott, Joseph 63
Marten, John 21-2
Martin, Anna 210, 211
Martin, David 72
Martin, Emma 97, 98
Martin, Victoria C.W. 149
Martineau, Harriet 47, 62, 96

Marx, Eleanor 114, 170
Marx, Karl 110, 158, 159, 161-2,
    163, 170, 191
Mason, S. 125
Masterman, C.F.G. 153, 171
Masturbation 25-7, 79-80, 96, 120,
    133
Matras, J. 11
Maugham, Somerset, 248
May, W.E. 224, 225
Mayhew, Henry 65
McArthur, Mary 196
McClintock, Dr 131
McCulloch, J.R. 50, 63
Mearns, Andrew 175
Medical profession: and abortion
    240-42, 244; and birth control
    11, 14, 81-3, 111-13, 116-136
    passim, 255; and venereal
    disease 22, 80, 136
Meek, George 218
Mendel, Gregor 142
'M.G.H.' 93
Midwifery 118, 240-41
Miles, George 91, 92
Mill, James 51
Mill, John Stewart 66, 74, 75, 91, 92,
    93, 94, 97-8, 101, 116, 145, 160,
    167, 187
Miller, Florence Fenwick 157, 211
Miller, George Noyes 201, 204
Miller, John C. 217
Mitchell, Hannah 227
Montefiore, Dora 164, 170
Morality 91
Morris, William 161, 167-8
Morrison, Arthur 151
Morrison, Charles 48, 49
Morrison, James 73
Mortality rates 209, 218, 229
Mosley, Oswald 119
Mummery, A.F. 184

Napheys, George H. 117, 120, 124,
    125, 126
National Birth Rate Commission 134,
    247
National Vigilance Association 202
Neo-Malthusians 94, 107-113,
    passim, 114, 145
Newman, Francis 128, 131-2, 201,
    226
Nichols, T.L. 127, 130, 186, 200,
    208, 224
Nicoll, S.W. 47, 49
Nitti, F.S. 162, 168

Noyes, J.H. 143

Oastler, Richard 61
O'Brien, J. Bronterre 63, 66
O'Connor, Fergus 66
Ogilvie, William 66
Okey, Thomas 217
Oldham, Henry 117
Oliver, Thomas 135
Onania 26
Osterwald, J.F. 26
Owen, Robert 49, 52, 55, 66, 72, 73
 74, 144
Owen, Robert Dale 52-57 *passim*,
 72, 74, 84-5, 91, 95-6, 97, 174
Owenism 43, 46, 48, 49, 63, 69,
 72-4, 92, 254

Parker, Jno. Hy. 93
Pankhurst, Christabel 199-200
Pankhurst, Emmeline 196
Paris, Dr. 79
Paul, Eden 151
Pearce, I.D. 201
Pearson, Karl 142, 144, 145-6, 148,
 187, 189
Peel, John 119
Perkins, Mrs 24
Perry, R. and L. 79
Philips, Mrs 24
Philpotts, Eden 195
Phrenology 78, 222, 223, 224
Place, Francis 50, 51-56 *passim*, 63
 69, 72, 75, 84-5, 91, 92, 95, 96, 119
Pleasures of Matrimony, The 218
Poor Law 45, 154
Pouchet, F.A. 125
Press: medical: *Boston Medical
 Journal* 82; *British and Foreign
 Medical Review* 82, *British
 Medical Journal* 100, 129, 130,
 240, *Lancet* 100, 130, 238, 240,
 242, 243, *Medical Times and
 Gazette* 79, 100, 129, *Medical
 Press and Circular* 100; popular:
 Black Dwarf 64, 70, *Bulldog* 70,
 Brighton *Cooperator* 63, London
 Examiner 70, *Freewoman* 201, 239,
 Justice 160, 163, 164, 165, 166,
 168, 170, *Labour Leader* 239,
 *Labourer's Friend and Handicraft's
 Journal* 63, London *Dispatch* 64,
 London *Mercury* 69, *Myra's
 Journal* 225, *National
 Cooperative Leader* 61, 75,

Newgate Monthly Magazine 53, 55,
 Northern Star 64, *Paul Pry* 96,
 Reynold's Newspaper 239, the
 Rock 225, 239, *Sentinel* 225,
 Social Democrat 160, *Tatler* 22,
 Trades Newspaper 63, 70,
 Westminster Review 238
Prostitution 19-20, 23-4, 32, 53, 55, 69,
 98, 128, 132, 150, 165-6, 198, 199,
 217
Proudhon, P.J. 159, 185

Quacks 19-36 *passim*, 79-84 *passim*,
 122, 251
Quelch, Henry 164, 172
'Quickening' 31, 34-5, 124, 246

Raciborski, Adam 125
Rae, John 158
Ravenstone, Piercy 64
Read, Carveth 150
Religion and birth control 15, 207-8,
 210-11, 226, 254
Rendall, W.J. 225
Rentoul, Robert Reid 150, 243
Reynolds, Stephen 219
Ricardo, David 72, 188
Rickards, G.K. 65, 66, 74
Ricord, Dr 79
Ritchie, David G. 182-3
Roberts, Robert 246
Robertson, John 81
Robertson, John M. 109, 158, 178-81,
 183-5, 193, 194
Robin, Paul 169
Rodgers, Frederick 217
Roebuck, J.A. 93
Roosevelt, Theodore 182
Routh, Armand 134, 135
Routh, C.H. 122, 130-32
Rowntree, Seebohm 141
Ruddock, Edward 122, 123, 125,
 127
Ruskin, John 166-7
Ryan, Michael 58, 82

Sadler, Michael 61
Saint-Simonians 74
Saleeby, C.W. 147, 150
Sanger, Margaret, 15, 158
Scharlieb, Mary 135
Schofield, Dr 134
Schreiner, Olive, 203
Scrope, G.P. 61, 62, 66
Self-help, medical, 78-87 *passim*

Senate, E., 26
Senior, N.W. 51
Sex: and artisans 217-18; doctors' attitudes towards 127-8; and Fabians, 193; feminists' attitudes towards, 198-201
Seymour, Henry 185-6, 194-5
Seymour, T. 21
Sharples, Eliza 60, 97, 98
Shaw, Charles N.L. 199
Shaw, George Bernard 186, 190, 202, 254
Short, Thomas 32, 35
Simmons, G. 73
Simpson, J.Y. 121
Sims, J. Marion 126, 131
Slack, Ada 226
Smith, Henry 149
Smith, J. 222
Smyth, A. Watt 188
Snowden, Ethel 205
Social Democratic Federation 159-70 *passim*, 185, 255; and prostitution, 164-5; and suffragettes 165; and women's work, 163-4
Socialism: and birth control 159-93 *passim*, 255; and eugenics, 144, 145; and Malthusians 109-110
Socialist League 161
Society for Constructive Birth Control and Racial Progress 113, 254
Solly, Henry 217
Solomon, Samuel 26
Southcott, Joanna 33
Southwell, Charles 74
Spence, Thomas 66
Spencer, Herbert 67-8, 74, 92, 127, 142-3, 162, 169, 182, 190
Spinke, J 21, 22
Stacey, Enid 196
Standring, George 109, 110, 113, 115
Stanley, Henrietta 250
Stead, W.T. 122, 209-210, 217
Stephens, J.R. 90
Sterilisation 112-3, 141, 148, 150
Stockham, Alice B. 203, 224
Stopes, Marie 113, 249, 254
Suthers, R.B. 182
Swanson, Isaac 20
Swiney, Frances 200
Symons, J.C. 49

Tate, George 123
Taylor, Harriet 98

Taylor, John W. 11, 133-4
Temperance 78, 118, 148, 165
Thomson, A.M. 182
Thompson, Paul 221
Thompson, William 60, 65, 74, 85-6, 94, 95
Thornton, W.T. 66
Thoughts on the Means of Alleviating the Miseries Attendant Upon Common Prostitution 32
Tilt, E.J. 83, 121, 122, 123, 125
Titmuss, Richard and Kathleen 219
Tolstoy, Leo 201
To Married People 224
Towle, E.T. 240
Trall, R.T. 126, 223
Trigg, Dr 21
Trowser, Hutches 72
Truelove, Edward 57, 108, 173
Turner, Daniel 23
Tytler, H.W. 35

Underwood, Michael 36
Ure, Andrew 80
Ussher, R. 207
Utilitarians 43, 51, 254

Vaughan, Bernard 207, 210
Venables, Robert 81
Venereal disease 20-25, 31, 120, 136, 148, 199
Venette, Nicolas 29
Vickery (Drysdale), Alice 110, 111, 182, 206, 211
Vincent, G.G. 65
Vincent, Henry 101

Wade John 46, 48, 49, 50
Wakefield, William 224
Ward, Mary Augusta (Mrs Humphrey Ward) 189
Wardlaw, Ralph 73
Warwick, France Evelyn countess of, 220
Watson, James 57, 107
Watts, Charles 107
Weatherly, Lionel A. 123, 125
Webb, Beatrice 157, 162, 186, 189-90
Webb, Sydney 162, 186-9, 221
Welden, W.F.R. 142
Wells, H.G. 151, 154, 186, 190-93 254
Welton, C.J. 222
Wesley, John 80

Weyland, John 67
Whatley, Richard 46
Wheeler, Anna 95, 98
Whetham, C.D. 150, 152
Whetham, W.C.D. 147, 150, 152
White Andrew 224
White, Arnold 149, 152
White Cross Army 199
Wickstead, T.H. 175
Wilde, Oscar 177
Willis, Ted 247
Winnington-Ingram, A.F. 207
Witcop, Rose 173
Wollstonecraft, Mary 32-3
Women: and employment 47, 163, 188,
        207, 220; and fertility control 14,
        24-5, 30, 47, 95, 135, 179, 226;
        working-class 45, 162, 181-2
Women's Cooperative Guild 226, 248
Wooler, T.J. 75
Working class: birth control 12-14,
        27-8, 35-6, 53, 72, 215-228 *passim*;
        hostility to Malthusians 61-75
        passim
Wright, Frances 60, 85, 97

Young, H. 225